DALLAS PRATT

A Patchwork Biography

Dick Chapman

Designed and published by Mark Argent
57a St Philip's Rd, Cambridge CB1 3DA
www.silverfen.com and www.markargent.com

First published 2004

ISBN 0-9547488-0-8

Set in 11.8pt Bembo

Printed by the Lavenham Press, Lavenham, Suffolk

Distributed by The American Museum in Britain, Claverton Manor, Bath BA2 7BD
www.americanmuseum.org

DALLAS PRATT

A Patchwork Biography

Pieced together, from his journal

and other writings, by Dick Chapman

Mark Argent
Cambridge

Introduction

Please imagine you and a friend are dining in the restaurant of the National Theatre in London. It is Tuesday 21 August 1984. At a nearby table an elderly man is eating on his own: avocado, salmon trout.

You and your companion play the game of trying to guess who he is. The fun of it is that he is so self-effacing you have almost nothing to go on. He speaks to the waiter too quietly for you to gauge his accent. But the cut of his dark grey suit seems to say American, east coast, Ivy League. A retired doctor? A psychiatrist? His scholar's stoop suggests an academic. Or a writer, maybe a poet. Or perhaps a collector of rare manuscripts or ancient maps. His dessert arrives, chocolate roulade. His face lights up like a child's. Unmistakably, he has a sweet tooth.

In fact, all your guesses are right. But what you did not deduce is that this solitary meal, followed by *Antigone* at the Cottesloe, and a long walk across London, is his way of celebrating his seventieth birthday, the whole day spent by choice alone.

Yet he is no recluse. He has recently returned from his home in the South of France where he entertained fourteen house guests, is staying at one of his three London clubs, before a few weeks at his manor house in the West of England, with a succession of weekend guests, and then returning to his two homes in America, which he shares with about ten colleagues and friends.

Nor would anything reveal that he was born, during the Gilded Age, into one of America's wealthiest families; that, as a small child, he performed acrobatics with Douglas Fairbanks, watched by Mary Pickford. No hint that at the age of twenty-two he shot a leopard in India, and a few weeks later met a young Englishman with whom he formed a life-long union. Nor that, during World War II, he worked at the Valley Forge army hospital caring for psychiatric casualties from the war zones. Nothing to indicate that, in their forties, he and the Englishman founded a highly original museum together. Nor that in his fifties he danced on the stage of an opera house in Brooklyn in the role of a black mammy and, in his seventies, adopted a calf.

All of these things are features of the life of Dallas Pratt. Yet none of them is the reason for writing (or reading) his biography. What is significant about him, it seems to me, is not what he did but what he was, and how he became that person. Far more than most people, he made considered decisions at every step, balancing his inclinations against his thinking and against his extensive reading of philosophy and psychology. From the start, he made all the important choices himself: on his nationality, his education, his career and his beliefs; about what to read, where to travel, what to collect and, above all, whom to live with. He defied the expectations of other people and resisted the traditions of his family. Starting with a mixture of extraordinary advantages and disadvantages, he took the unusual circumstances of his birth, upbringing and talents as his raw material and, bit by bit, put together a personality and a way of living. His whole life can be seen as a continuing act of self-creation.

As he lived his life, he wrote about it. He recorded his experiences, his impressions and his opinions almost every day, starting at an early age. He was writing letters and poems before the age of ten, essays and magazine articles starting in his early teens, lectures from his twenties on, two full-length books and, most of all, his journal which he began aged seventeen and continued, on and off, to within a few weeks of his death.

All his writings put together make a full-length self-portrait, or rather more than full-length. At a rough word count, they amount to about the same as the complete works of Shakespeare. The bulk of the material is in the thirty volumes of his journal, which contains a lot else besides an account of his doings: notes on his reading and collecting, philosophical ruminations, clippings from newspapers and magazines, lists of people sent Christmas presents, even recipes. It is not a continuous narrative, still less a diary. It jumps about in time, and the older he grew the more he wrote about the past. At seventeen, he wrote about himself aged four. When sixty, he wrote about himself aged four, seventeen, thirty, forty and sixty.

I hoped, when I started on this project, to be able to present the story of his life entirely in his own words, simply putting the events described in the journal into the order in which they happened, omitting irrelevances, and adding a word or two of my own here and there to link the extracts together. I found, though, that the journal, despite its length, is far from complete. Sometimes it lapses for months, or even years. Major happenings in Dallas's life go unmentioned. Important aspects of his personality and development are scarcely hinted at.

As a result, I soon found that I was writing a biography. Wherever possible I used his words but it was just as often necessary to use my own. To fill in the sections of Dallas's life not covered in the journal, I used his other writings, especially his letters, as well as his mother's press-cuttings books and letters. I consulted members of his family and many of his friends and colleagues, used works of reference, archives of old newspapers and magazines, other memoirs, my own diaries, and my recollections of more than thirty years friendship with him and his circle.

My researches led to some fascinating conversations and correspondences with people Dallas had known, in the many different worlds he had inhabited. I was extremely fortunate to find a few people who had known him even longer than I had. Several times I was glad to be working when I was: any later would have been too late. As it is, I spent months trying to locate a woman who remembered Dallas as a child. She was hard to find because in her eighties she had decided to revert to her maiden name. She died a few days before I had hoped to speak to her.

Squeezing eighty years of living between the covers of a book can only be done by leaving a lot out, in this case mostly people. Dallas had numberless colleagues, friends, acquaintances and many relatives whom he kept in touch with either by seeing or corresponding with them. To include more than a few of them would turn this volume into a catalogue of names. Dallas did not seek out the rich, the titled and the famous, nor were they the people he mostly spent his time with, but, for one reason or another, again and again they came his way. When they did, he liked to write about them. They are easier to include than other people if only because they need no introduction. As a result, they are rather over-represented.

The question arises: would Dallas Pratt have wanted his life revealed in this way? In February 1936, aged twenty-one, he wrote in his journal: "I write for myself alone. This, after all, is not for publication!" But in 1985, aged seventy-one, as he goes into detail about a past event, he adds the phrase: "in case anyone is interested". This can only mean that by then he did have other readers in mind. By then he had made a start on organising and indexing what he had written and ensured its survival. If he had lived longer, he might have produced this book himself, or something more or less like it.

My own connection with him is that we were close friends for nearly half his life. He was in his mid-forties when we met, I in my late twenties. Each of us was a partner in what a historian friend called an "Atlantic alliance": Dallas Pratt, American, lived with an Englishman, John Judkyn; I, English, with an American, Ben Duncan. The four of us, as we got to know each other, discovered an extraordinary rapport. In the later years of Dallas Pratt's long life we were amongst each other's closest, longest-known friends, visiting each other's houses whenever we were on the same side of the ocean, exchanging long letters when we were not, and travelling together to many parts of the world. As for my capability for the work of editing and writing, whenever I suffered from self-doubt I turned for reassurance to one of Dallas's rare instances of gross exaggeration. In volume twenty of the journal he wrote: "Dick, when he applies his mind to any problem, invariably succeeds".

MY THANKS

Many people have helped me with this book, in all sorts of different ways: I am extremely grateful to every one of them. Most of all it is a pleasure to thank Dallas Pratt's niece Linda Hackett; Bill McNaught and his colleagues at the American Museum; the Bell-Knight family, and David Finkbeiner.

EDITORIAL NOTE

Dallas Pratt was unselfconscious about his spelling. Feeling at home on either side of the Atlantic, he mixed American and English freely. I have preserved his inconsistencies, as they seem to be a part of him. I have not used ... to indicate words omitted, nor [ ] for words or names added to make the meaning clear. My aim has been to be accurate but not pedantic. The one thing I have expurgated is any mention of specific sums of money. Attempts to convert them into current figures are quickly superseded by further inflation, rendering them not just meaningless but positively misleading.

Dick Chapman
Cambridge 2004

Oct. 14th, 1923

Dear Mamma
                    I thank you
very much for the nice letter
you sent me. We went
to the Kountzes this week
-end and the country
is lovely. We are staying
at Daddys Apartment and
like it very much. Cynthia
is a Fox at Foxcroft I am
in the Jr. II A div class and am
very glad. Cynthia is
very happy at her school.
Grandma B. is opening
the 84th St. house and
we think that we are going
to live with Daddy. Lots of
love to you and Cartty.
        from Dallas.

O O O O O ✗ + + + + + + + + =

P.S. Hope you have a nice
winter.

Chapter One

1914–1924

Nought to ten

Oct, 14th 1923

Dear Mamma,

Thank you very much for the nice letter you sent me. We went to the Kountzes this weekend and the country is lovely. We are staying at Daddys Apartment and like it very much. Cynthia is a Fox at Foxcroft I am in the Jr II A div class and am very glad. Cynthia is very happy at her school. Grandma B is opening the 87th St house and we think that we are going to live with Daddy. Lots of love to you and Carty.

    from Dallas.

P.S. Hope you have a nice winter.

A boy of nine, Dallas Pratt, sends his mother a letter telling her where he thinks he is going to spend the winter!

Mother and son are writing rather than seeing each other because he is in New York and she is in Europe. She had divorced Dallas's father, Daddy, when Dallas was four years old. She then married and divorced a second husband. Carty was husband number three.

Courteously, Dallas writes to Mamma mostly about other people. His sister Cynthia, three years older than himself, is at her boarding school in Virginia. Mamma's parents, the Benjamins, are returning from their summer residence at Ardsley-on-Hudson, a big Elizabethan-style house a little way up the river from New York City, to their house on East 87th Street, described later by Dallas as "a very large and gloomy mansion just off Fifth Avenue".

The "we" of the letter includes not only Dallas and his sister but also their governess and at least one nursemaid. While Mamma was living in Europe, six days away by ocean liner, Cynthia and Dallas were in America, either at school or, during school holidays, with relatives or family friends. Pastel miniatures of Dallas and Cynthia as infants, and their childhood photographs, show them as fine featured, beautifully dressed, and well groomed. The little group of children and servants went from one household to another in a human form of pass the parcel, from their Daddy, to their Benjamin grandparents, to their cousins, the Coes, on Long Island, and so on. At least the Coes had children. They were older than Dallas, and never became major figures in his life but were not two generations older like his grandparents.

Time at Ardsley-on-Hudson must have passed slowly. Writing much later of his grandmother, he described her as "conservative" and "lacking in sparkle". "I remember her as a stately, rather imperious figure, going for drives in an open car holding a parasol."

Dallas writes about his progress at the Buckley School. This was, and still is, a traditional all-boys school on East 73rd Street, conveniently close to the Benjamins' mansion and Daddy's apartment. Daddy had himself been a pupil there in the 1890s. In 1923 Dallas was starting his last year there.

The letter ends with a childish drawing of his mother about to board a train. She is surrounded and, indeed, dwarfed by no fewer than twenty-six pieces of luggage: hatboxes, suitcases, trunks. This is the first of his pictures of his mother that he was to continue making for the rest of his life though, after this, in words.

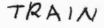

His mother, in effect, had deserted him. Most wealthy parents in those days delegated the care of their children to governesses and nursery maids, but she went much further than that, living on a different continent, seldom seeing her children, and showing not much interest in them even when she was with them.

Yet, however little Dallas meant to her, she clearly meant a great deal to him. Far from turning away from her, he seems to have been glamourised, even awed by her. If he occasionally stood up to her, he did so hesitantly. He never went so far as to denounce her either to her face or behind her back. In many ways she remained the most important person in his life, even long after she was dead.

Remembering her thirty years after her death, he wrote:

Although not without much capacity for affection, her
relations with relatives, friends and those who served her
were often troubled by extreme emotionalism, resulting in
explosions of temper, and "scenes" sometimes ending in
what she called "nervous prostration".

Perhaps as a consequence of the way his mother treated him,
Dallas developed a curious trait in his own personality. Her con-
trariness and her tantrums seem to have left him with a need for
people whom he both loved and feared, and to whom he related
with a mixture of submission and defiance. The lopsided relationship that he had with her seems to have set a pattern that was
repeated several times in the most significant relationships that he
had with other people during the whole of the rest of his life. As
an adult it appeared sometimes as if he sought out people who
stirred those conflicting responses, whether as patients in his years
as a psychiatrist, as colleagues in his work in various organisations,
as friends, or as lovers.

The letter written when he was nine can only have survived
because his mother kept it. Perhaps she was proud of the neat
handwriting and polite style, and charmed by the little drawing.
She was certainly not embarrassed by the light it cast on her as a
sample of American motherhood.

Dallas, on the other hand, must have known just what he was
doing when, sixty years later, after finding the letter amongst the
papers of his recently deceased sister, he gave it and another letter,
written seven months later, pride of place as the first two items in
the first volume of his collected writings, which he called his
journal. With these two letters he introduced the whole story of
his life. The second one completes the vignette of Dallas aged
nine.

May 8th 1924

Dear Mamma

The K.G.'s are over and the last drill was Fine! How are you? I hope you are well. Where are we going this summer? Can we go to Wyoming? Please let me know. Cynthia is getting along very well and won TWO BLUE RIBBONS for good riding. Isn't it fine! We went to spend the week-end at Short Hills, N.J. with Mrs Kaufman had a fine time. This afternoon I joined a society to prevent cruelty to animals and got a badge. Daddy took me to see *America* a very good movie. I am on the Honour Roll with an average of 94 and 1st in the class.

Love and x x x x x x x x x put them on top of each other
DBP this is my signature

Thank you very much for the cunning little dog my god-father brought over and Dear thanks you for the pin.

The K.G.'s were the Knickerbocker Greys, a military drill unit for boys attending independent schools in New York City. Dallas was photographed in its Confederate-style uniform in 1923, as his father had been in 1892 (see page 183). It owes its contradictory north-south name to its origins in the 1860s, when it was founded by women from the South, married to New York husbands, who wanted their sons to have something of the South's traditional military school training. It continues to this day, and still trains a number of Buckley School boys.

"Where are we going to this summer? Can we go to Wyoming?" He does not even suggest that they join their mother in Europe. He is referring to the summer home of his cousins, the Coes. As well as their home on Long Island, the Coes had a ranch, formerly owned by Buffalo Bill, set in beautiful country at Cody, Wyoming. More important to Dallas and Cynthia, there was the company of their cousins, three boys well into their teens but also a girl the same age as Cynthia, only four years older than Dallas. That is, indeed, where they spent their summer, crossing the American continent in style, in the Coes' private railway car.

"Daddy took me to see *America*, a very good movie." Daddy's choice of film shows spirit. Nine-year-old Dallas was about to have to make perhaps the most important decision of his life, whether to remain American like his father, or become English like his new step-father. This 1924 silent film about the American Revolutionary War showed the English as appalling villains, so much so that it was, for a time, banned in Britain.

"We went to spend the weekend at Short Hills, N.J., with Mrs Kaufman had a fine time." Louis G. Kaufman was a highly successful businessman, president of many banks and director of several corporations including General Motors. He had married his wife Daisy in 1900. In 1923 she became Daddy's mistress.

Daddy had remarried in 1919, two years after being divorced by Mamma. His second wife was Mrs Katherine Barrymore, also recently divorced. Her first marriage, which had lasted seven years, was to the actor John Barrymore and was characterised by, on his part, neglect, abuse, absence, infidelity and alcohol. He described it later as "the first of my three-and-a-half marriages, all of them bus accidents." Her marriage to Daddy lasted half as long, not quite three years.

The relationship of Daddy and Daisy Kaufman was completely different from any other in the lives of either of Dallas's parents. It lasted. Nearly twenty years later, when Louis G. Kaufman died in 1942, Daisy and Daddy, this devoted, elderly couple, at last married. She was the mother of eight children, two of whom attended the wedding, with their spouses. Dallas was best man. It was the seventh, and last, of the marriages of Dallas's father and mother. How he felt about it is not recorded. The information

14

about Daddy and Daisy given here comes from other sources. Dallas avoided speaking or writing about his father, perhaps because the subject did not interest him, or because it was too painful. If questioned he would say "He was a New York club man", or "He drank" and, as soon as he could, speak of something else. After fighting in France in World War I, Dallas's father worked as a Wall Street stockbroker, belonged to half a dozen New York clubs, and died in 1947.

Much more central to Dallas's life was Dear. In the 1924 letter, Dallas writes: "Dear thanks you for the pin." Dear was the name Cynthia and Dallas gave to their English governess Maud Duke. Dear, who never married, was motherly by nature and lavished affection on her charges, kissing and cuddling them. When they ate with their parents, so did she, unlike any other staff, even Mamma's secretary. As governess her position in the family was a step above the domestic servants. They, not she, did all the cooking, cleaning, bed-making and laundry.

Dallas loved his mother in a different way, regarding her with adoration and awe. Her world was of the nightclub rather than the nursery. Her photographs in *Vogue* and *Town and Country* at that time emphasise her well-cut clothes and superior manner. What she wore was too chic to be touched by baby hands.

Dear was the most important person in Dallas's childhood, perhaps in his whole life. Born in Lincolnshire in 1888, she was twenty-seven when she came in 1915 to look after baby Dallas and four-year-old Cynthia. She had previously been employed as governess for eleven years by several families in Europe, including some aristocratic Italians. Dallas recalled, many years later:

> As soon as we were old enough to appreciate such things, Dear would regale my sister and myself with intriguing tales of her time in Italy. Dear's stories included many references

to Robert Browning who had died in 1889. Dear recited Browning's verses:

> Open my heart and you will see
> Graved inside of it, "Italy".

This may suggest that Dear was an intellectual but, writing about her when he was twenty-two, his head filled with Hinduism, Hume, Freud, D. H. Lawrence and Spinoza, Dallas described her as "certainly the finest character among the people who have figured most prominently in my life but of the type which, for all its virtues, is, after all, completely unintellectual."

Through all the comings and goings, the marriages and divorces, Dear was the one constant element in the children's early years. Her devotion enabled Cynthia and Dallas to grow up capable of living their lives as successfully as they did. Dallas went on talking and writing about her to the end of his days. In his seventies he wrote:

> "Dear" as we affectionately named Miss Duke, was engaged for a trial period of three weeks. Outlasting several changes of stepfathers and stepmothers, she stayed for fifty years, long enough to bring up my niece and nephew and then to give me the satisfaction of taking care of her in her declining years.

The two letters quoted, and commented on at such length, belong at the beginning of this story, if only because that is where Dallas chose to position them in his collected writings. They give a picture of some of the circumstances of his childhood, but he was nearly ten when he wrote them.

Dallas's parents, Alexander Dallas Bache Pratt and Beatrice Mai Benjamin, married in 1909 when he was twenty-six and she was twenty. The magazines of the day admired their New York house

for its "daring". Its light, airy rooms were a break from the heavy
style of the previous generation. For the summer months, they
had another house, at Islip on Long Island. They had their first
child, Cynthia, in 1910. Dallas was born at Islip on 21 August
1914. In 1917 they moved their out-of-town residence from Long
Island to Newport, Rhode Island.

Recollections of his earlier years come throughout his lifetime
of writing. Aged seventeen, soon after starting what he called his
journal, he re-visited Newport, and wrote:

> The last time I had visited this old port was at the age of
> four, when we had lived in yellow Reed Cottage. I was
> determined to drive to the old site, to see what remained of
> a place that had impressed itself strongly on my mind. An
> old negro came in a taxi to take me, and we started the long
> drive down Bellevue Avenue and around by the ocean drive.
> Sure enough, there was Reed Cottage, painted white, but in
> other respects as I remembered it. Opposite was Mrs
> Belmont's "Marble Palace", through whose gates Cynthia
> and I had hoped to see the fairies come. A friend had told us
> they *would* come, and we had stayed up late waiting for
> them, until the mystic hour of …eight! Alas — no fairies
> came, only Nanny pushing a baby-carriage down the drive
> gave us an instant's hope (to be quickly shattered). Why she
> was pushing a baby-carriage down the drive at such an hour
> I have never discovered.
>
> Other things came into my mind: Bailey's Beach with its
> slide; the bluffs along which you walked to the Cushings'
> house; Mrs Oelrichs in her electric car, giving us a ride one
> day from the beach; my buying an accordion in the town of
> Newport at a very early age; picking mushrooms in a high
> meadow looking over the sea; gathering the scattered
> spangles Mamma's best dress had scattered on the stairs the
> night before; my doll Beebee; our Alice in Wonderland

pants and particularly my ears (I was the White Rabbit) which refused to stand up; the picnics with the Van Allens in their old Model T Ford. These and other recollections flashed across my mind.

A footnote to this, which Dallas added decades later, reveals who tricked him and Cynthia into waiting by the gate to see the fairies: "The friend was Doris Duke; how we hated her for deceiving us!" She was a neighbour in New York as well as Newport, midway in age between Cynthia and Dallas, an only child, whose father died when she was twelve, leaving her his tobacco fortune. She then became widely known as the "richest girl in the world". She was a friend of Cynthia and Dallas from babyhood and throughout their teens.

At twenty-two, Dallas wrote another recollection of that summer in Newport:

> When I was four years old, and my sister was seven and a half, we created the character of "Lady Messenger". This personage was a supernatural being whose function consisted in descending to earth from her heavenly abode and rescuing earthly creatures from their perilous planet, and transporting them bodily, to the skies.
>
> The Lady Messenger sequence was acted out many times on the bed in the nursery of Reed Cottage, Newport. Sister (so I called her at that time, though not later, when "C" came more easily) was Lady Messenger, and almost daily she arrived from heaven, dressed in a spotless white sheet, and flapping her voluminous linen wings. After circling once or twice around the bed, she descended upon me, enfolded me in her sheet, and whisked me off with her to the regions of the blest.
>
> In this game sister had the starring role, and it was a matter of some vexation to me that I was so obviously second fiddle. The best I could do was also to wrap myself in a

sheet, and to let it be known that I was a "king" — albeit earthly, and only four years of age but none the less of surpassing majesty. Only thus could I dare to associate with the awful Lady Messenger, and seem to deserve the pains which she took to save me from my enemies, and to exalt me to her own celestial habitation.

Another memory of that time, recorded by Dallas in his late seventies, was a visit to his cousin Dorothy Caruso. She was the daughter of Dallas's great uncle Park Benjamin III. In 1916 she had eloped with the world-famous tenor Enrico Caruso. Her father, although himself a writer of popular scientific books, strongly resisted her marrying a "public singer" and, according to Dallas, after the marriage never spoke to her again. It was her first marriage, of three. It was his only marriage, but he had by then had four children. Enrico and Dorothy Caruso had a daughter, Gloria, and were only separated by his death, aged forty-eight, in 1921.

> It must have been sometime in 1920, that our cousin Dorothy invited us to the Carusos' apartment in a New York City hotel. Their daughter Gloria had been born in December, 1919, and no doubt we were shown our new little cousin. I remember nothing of that, but I recall very clearly that my sister and I had been told that Enrico was a famous singer, and that we eagerly looked forward to hearing him sing. The shy little children were duly introduced to the great man, but oh dear, did he sing to us? Not at all; he merely put on a gramophone record of one of his arias, and that was all we heard. When we returned home, we loudly complained of having been deprived of the anticipated thrill.

In 1990, Dallas learned from a memoir by one of Caruso's sons, Enrico Caruso, Jr., that the great singer treated everybody as he had treated them. He always escaped the tiresome requests for a song from relatives or friends by putting on a record.

In his seventies, Dallas recorded a final memory of those days:

> On the west side of Park Avenue, in the Eighties, there's a large Gothic church, St Ignatius Loyola. Whenever I pass it I see myself, aged three or four, riding on the sidewalk a wooden push bike painted to look like a battleship. Just there, doing that, the thought occurred to me: "Men are fighting in a war". That is my sole memory of World War I.

One of those men was Dallas's father. He was in the first fighting unit of drafted soldiers to sail for Europe in the spring of 1918. There he trained as an officer and in June 1918 he took part in battle, where he was shelled, shot at and gassed. In a letter to his own mother, dated 3 July 1918, he wrote: "Some poor chaps were killed in the other Companies in our Regiment and also some in Snowden Fahnestock's Company. I was in command of the Company for four days and made my headquarters in a field and slept there with the men. My veteran Sergeant Tod, who was with me through the whole show, told me that the men said they would follow me any time into battle. That was nice, wasn't it? I ordered Tod to the hospital, by the way, but he would not go and stuck with me.

"It was a tough experience all through. I had very little sleep, and did not have my clothes off for ten days!"

Following her husband's departure for France, Dallas's mother showed herself no better as a wife than in her maternal role. The newspapers described her not only as "one of the best-dressed women in society, a dashing automobilist, and one of the best swimmers at Bailey's Beach" but also as "among the most conspicuous flirts of New York and Newport. Dame Gossip is wondering what her plans for the winter may be. Her summer was not a brilliant success. She carried one or two flirtations to a dangerous point, simply because Newport bored her to extinction."

Her immediate response to the war was to ask advice on the safest place to be. She settled in Newport when she was told there was "no safer place in the country from any German offensive" and that it was also "unquestionably the safest city in the United States from having absolutely no foreign population". There she threw herself into war work such as charity dances to raise money for ambulances. She joined a group of society women calling themselves "The First Fifty". A booklet setting out their aims stated "only by the conservation of food here shall we be able to feed those fighting abroad, our own flesh and blood, those who are keeping the HUN from your fireside and mine. These ladies shall be known as The First Fifty, who have agreed to cut their mid-day meal to two courses and their evening meal to three courses or vice versa". The chairman (male) of The First Fifty was a handsome New York socialite called Preston Gibson. The *New York American* described him at the time as "one of the most dashing figures in New York local society". He was, wrote Dallas, "so proud of his father the general and his uncle Edward Douglas White, the Supreme Court Justice".

Preston Gibson was trying to establish himself as a playwright and several of his plays had been staged, though without much success. One of them, *The Turning Point*, was found to contain lines almost identical with some of the dialogue of Oscar Wilde's *An Ideal Husband* and *A Woman of No Importance*. Preston Gibson claimed that he had not wilfully adopted the epigrams of Wilde, and attributed the resemblance to "unconscious absorption". This announcement caused wide discussion among college professors and dramatists regarding the extent to which playwrights and novelists were victims of such "absorption". The controversy proved to be good publicity and the play had a longer run than any of his other productions.

Towards the end of 1918, when the war was nearly over, Dallas's mother sued her husband for divorce, on the grounds of desertion. One newspaper commented: "The grounds on which the suit is based are viewed by the layman as peculiar, in view of the fact that the alleged deserting husband is in the army and has been for some time." She married Preston Gibson less than a month after her divorce was finalised. Understandably, her parents were determinedly opposed to the marriage. Preston Gibson had by then been divorced by two heiresses, one of whom named twenty co-respondents. A relative of Dallas's recently described Preston Gibson as "the first of a series of rascals who married her for her money". He excluded Dallas's father from this charge.

Rascal he may have been, but the young Dallas liked him. Of all the husbands of Dallas's mother, including his own father, Preston Gibson is the only one for whom Dallas, anywhere in his writings, expressed anything approaching affection, referring to him by his nickname, Winks. In his seventies Dallas wrote, "Mamma hardened her heart against him, but for me, remembering him as I pass East 63rd Street, Winks is a genial spirit". Number 159 East 63rd Street was the house where Mamma, now Mrs Preston Gibson, and her new husband and children lived in 1920. Dallas wrote in the 1980s:

> it is still there, as are the neighbouring houses. It was near Third Avenue, to the east of which were tenements. Rough Irish kids, two of them belonging to our Irish-American janitor and his wife, sometimes spilled over into our block. This was the sheltered Pratt children's first encounter with the "poor". The next exposure, for me at any rate, occurred

when I was first taken to the theatre, to see the musical *Irene*. It had the hit song "Alice Blue Gown", the words of which are graven on my memory. But there were also some scenes in a tenement house in which the heroine was abused by a brutal father. This graphic revelation of what went on "on the other side of the tracks" horrified me. The tracks, in our lives — and very visible from where we lived — were the elevated lines which ran along Third Avenue.

As well as marrying heiresses and writing stage plays, Preston Gibson had ambitions as a screen writer. In order to be close to the film community of Hollywood, he and his new family rented what Dallas describes as "an attractive house" near Santa Barbara, in Montecito, California. While living there, Dallas's mother started a lifelong friendship with another bride, seven years younger than herself, Wallis Warfield, who in 1916 had married Earl Winfield Spencer. He was the first husband of three (the next was an Englishman, Ernest Simpson; the third, the King of England, Edward VIII, who gave up his throne to marry her). The dissolute and unstable Earl Winfield Spencer was an army aviator. He had been put in charge of a training unit near San Diego in 1917. By the time she met Dallas's mother, this marriage was breaking down.

> Somehow Mamma and our stepfather made the acquaintance of Douglas Fairbanks and our family including our governess Maud Duke, called "Dear", were invited over to see his studio. Cynthia was nine and I was five. It seems unlikely that I had seen him in a film, but in the studio I remember being shown structures which, aided by trick photography, were used to create the illusion of some of the gymnastic feats for which he was becoming famous.
>
> While Dear watched from the sidelines, Mamma cried "hurrah!" as Doug and I achieved a precarious balance.

The great romantic Spectaculars, *Robin Hood*, *The Three Musketeers* etc. were not yet produced, but he was working on *The Mark of Zorro* which appeared in the year of our visit.

Also on May 28 of 1920 he married Mary Pickford. We met "America's sweetheart", and she gave me her photograph. It shows her in a girl's short dress, her golden curls falling over her shoulders, holding two kittens. She inscribed it appropriately: "To my little sweetheart Dallas — Mary Pickford".

The Preston Gibson family's time in California came to an abrupt end:

My grandparents' intense disapproval of "Winks" took the tangible form of cutting off her allowance. The "Standard Oil Heiress", whom the scandal sheets quite erroneously credited with an immense annual income, supposedly from a trust left her by her grandfather, Henry Huttleston Rogers, was reduced to whatever she could raise by selling her jewellery. The months we had spent at Montecito, California, were cut short by creditors.

The servants left and Mamma fled with Winks, leaving Miss Duke, "Dear", to look after Cynthia and me. Dear knew nothing about cooking. She managed "Jello" dessert, the awful red one, but after a week or two of that we were happy to be on the train heading back to New York. Dear had to pay for the tickets.

The family hid from the New York creditors in New Jersey for a few weeks. We were on an upper floor of a hotel in Newark. I learned to make folded paper aeroplanes and amused myself launching them out the window. Then back to 159 East 63rd Street. Still no money. Mamma finally capitulated to the inexorable grandparents, and agreed to take us to Paris and seek a French divorce. Afraid of being detained because of her debts, she crept out of the house heavily veiled. Dear was determined to save something from the clutches of the creditors, so, just as we were leaving, she gathered up a silver tea service. The four of us spent the night in the house of great-uncle George Benjamin, and the following day sailed for Europe on RMS Celtic in April or early May, 1921. On board, Mamma wrote tearfully and still lovingly to Winks. Cynthia and I decorated the letter with a drawing of a cocktail shaker (cocktails in 1921 were a new and dashing drink) to show what a *mondaine* life we were leading. But the sea got rough and I got seasick, and *stayed* seasick almost until we landed at Liverpool.

Preston Gibson must have resented being divorced by my mother. He was always improvident. Unsuccessful as a playwright, he soon faded out of the New York–Newport–Washington social set.

When Dallas's mother heard in 1926 that he had married yet another heiress her brief comment, at the end of a letter to a friend, was "P.S. I wonder how long Mrs P.G. 4th will stand it?" The answer was, not long. Dallas records that he "died in a veterans' hospital, penniless and forlorn, of tuberculosis."

From Liverpool, the four of them travelled to France. In June 1991, exactly seventy years later, Dallas described:

> my first visit to Paris, when we arrived *en famille*, I, aged 6 turning 7, to stay at the Hotel Campbell. I was put to bed early when it was still light. Mamma gave me a mask, but still I lay awake, bothered by the incessant tooting of car horns. Mamma was establishing a French residence in order to divorce her second husband, Preston Gibson. For several months we escaped from the cacophony of Paris to St. Briac, Britanny, where we had rented a villa on the sea called Les Roches Aigues. There I was taught to read by Dear, and when we returned to Paris, now in a quieter apartment in Avenue Montaigne, I discovered the value of

reading. Required to take an afternoon nap, but still unable
to sleep, reading proved to be an alternative — and an
increasingly enjoyable one. I must have progressed fairly
soon from Stevenson's *Child's Garden of Verses*, which Dear
had shrewdly started me on, to historical novels such as
Henty's.

Some memories of Paris: Punch and Judy shows on the
Rond-Point of the Champs Elysées; tubercular victims spit-
ting blood in their handkerchiefs; the delicious horror of
The Cabinet of Dr Caligari, a film to which our governesses,
unaware of its weirdness, innocently took my sister and me
and the Vanderbilt brothers Alfred and George;
accompanying my grandmother Benjamin to fittings at
couturiers, like Worth, and helping to propel her upstairs by
pushing in the small of her back; sailing my little sailboat on
the pond in the Tuileries Gardens; rolling a hoop — *conduire
un cerceau*, as the French say, with a stick to guide it;
Bagatelle gardens; Pré Catalan for tea; or the zoo at the
Jardin des Plantes.

Also in his seventies, Dallas remembered how he shared with
Dear a fondness for animals. When the family began their transatlantic travels, quarantine restrictions meant that:

> the only animal companions which could be taken along
> were stuffed ones. My best-beloved was a monkey named
> Chimpy. At the age of six, I was much preoccupied with
> what my dying words should be. My growing passion for
> the new toy soon eliminated other contenders for the
> honour, and I announced to everyone that my last word
> would be "Chimpy." But after we had been together for
> only two months, I lost him in Paris, in the Parc de
> Bagatelle. We went back several times to search, but in vain.
> I was inconsolable.
>
> Then, a few months later, in London, passing the win-
> dow of an Oxford Street toy shop, I noticed a stuffed eleph-

ant dressed in pink-striped pyjamas. I at once fell in love
with this character, and we bought him on the spot.
Predictably, I named him Jumbo. Unlike Chimpy, Jumbo has
survived. Just the other day, when I was rummaging in a
chest, there suddenly was Jumbo, with his flap ears, red
flannel mouth, and the lopsided grin which comforted my
childhood.

At the same time he recalled:

the brief companionship my sister and I had with several
dogs which stayed for a summer but for whom "a good
home in the country" had to be found when our travels
began again.

Her father's intransigence, even after her divorce from Preston
Gibson, kept Mamma out of America for three-and-a-half years.
Dallas recorded how his grandfather "relished the power over
their dependants that his wife's fortune secured for him."
Mamma's inherited wealth was in fact controlled by him. All he
would send her was a monthly allowance, which often arrived
late, and which he sometimes found excuses to reduce. Worse, for
several years he refused to pay off the debts accrued during her
marriage to Preston Gibson even after she married again, this
time a husband he found acceptable. She feared that if she
returned to New York, "rabid creditors would be waiting at the
dock to serve her." Oppressive to his daughter, William Evarts
Benjamin played the role of heavy father to his grandson Dallas
too. There was far more of a father-son relationship between the
two of them than between Dallas and his actual father, or any of
his step-fathers. On the positive side, they shared many interests,
including a love of literature. In old age, Dallas wrote:

My grandfather — Grandpa B., as he was known to his grand-children — was an expansive not to say explosive character who peppered one with anecdotes from a mind richly stocked with Victorian/Edwardian memories. He had been an autograph dealer and publisher in his youth, and an art collector in his later years, so literary matters and collecting were favorite topics. To keep the peace, however, it was necessary to be a docile and attentive listener, so willy-nilly I received a liberal education in these subjects at an impressionable age. The walls of his New York apartment were hung with 18th century portraits by Reynolds, Gainsborough and their school; in his dressing-room he kept a few literary treasures — and on all these objects he loved to expatiate.

Dallas wrote similarly about his grandfather's house in upstate New York:

I can recall some of the impressive folios on lecterns and antique Florentine tables in the Renaissance-style library of my grandparents' country house at Ardsley-on-Hudson. At eight or nine years of age, this was actually my first introduction to a fine library and to rare books. More interesting than the folios to my sister Cynthia and myself were the books on the balcony, reached by a dark little stair — particularly a set of Dickens in somber 19th century cloth bindings with gilt insets of *Mr. Pickwick*, *Oliver Twist* and the rest.

We would visit this balcony, then flee to the verandah, my sister with *The Old Curiosity Shop*, I with *Dombey and Son*, sharing between us bottles of Cantrell and Cochran ginger ale, a box of Lorna Doones, and much ice to counteract the languors of a Hudson Valley summer afternoon. On this verandah, overlooking a lawn gently sloping towards the river, we would read until the shadows of the big trees lengthened on the grass, and the voice of our governess called us back to the mundane ritual of tea with grandma:

"Children! Come in; you're reading your eyes out.
Grandma's in the drawing room."

Forced by her father into divorce and exile, Dallas's mother
remarried in Paris in December 1922. Her new husband, Charles
Aubrey Cartwright, was a British naval officer in command of a
ship in the Mediterranean. Dallas was eight years old at the time.

> My Benjamin grandmother's letter describing the marriage
> said that it was "most satisfactory to us, but naturally we
> would have preferred an American." The letter describes the
> uncertainties in the life of a Commander in the Royal Navy.
> Carty was persuaded to retire in a year or so, and was pro-
> moted to Captain, on the retired list.

Charles Cartwright was born in 1883 into the English landed
gentry. Difficult as it is to believe now, at that time these people
felt they owned not just England but the whole world. When he
became a naval cadet in his early teens, Britannia still policed the
seas. He was given his first command of a ship in the early years
of World War I. By the time he met Dallas's mother, soon after
the war ended, he was used to being in command. They married
in 1922. Dallas, who seems never to have taken to him, in later
years described Carty driving powerful cars at great speed along
country lanes, often colliding with other vehicles, and cursing
them for being in his way.

A record of this period of Mamma's life survives in letters she
wrote to her mother and to her younger brother, Henry Rogers
Benjamin, whom she called Roger. He worked with their father
in the Takair Corporation, established to take care of their Rogers
inheritance by maximising capital and minimising taxes. Their
greatest achievement was to sell out shortly before the 1929 Stock
Market crash and buy back at the bottom of the slump. During
the years that followed, they saw their fortune grow and grow.

Mamma's letters reveal that she hated life in Malta with her husband away at sea: "this place does not particularly interest or attract me. I am horribly bored. I would not mind the primitiveness of the house or the unattractive aspect of various things if Charles were here. Charles is so considerate and capable and devoted, such a comfort and joy, so handsome and distinguished in his full dress uniform with decorations and ribbons, very sweet and sympathetic and gentle."

As soon as he was released from the navy her letters, always saying she is short of money, come from the Hyde Park Hotel in London, the Excelsior Hotel in Rome, the Carlton Hotel in Biarritz and the Crillon in Paris. She seldom mentions her children; her letters are about her other preoccupations. First, her society friends, whose names range from Princesse de Faucigny-Lucinge to the Countess Frankenstein. Second, her clothes. From Biarritz, October 1923, "I live in the summer O'Rossen suit, the Callot pleated crepe black dress, and that brown Reville sport suit is exactly right for here. The Spaniards are smart and more fond of sport even than the French and the women are wearing the chicest sport clothes possible. All wear 'cloche' hats." Third, her apartment in Great Stanhope Street (now Stanhope Gate) off Park Lane in London, which she bought in 1923, and was filling with "furniture, silver etc." shipped over from her previous homes in America: "Living room to be red brocade, morning room mulberry and blue green, Charles's bedroom Greenwich blue, my room citron yellow, dining room blue" and so on for many pages. They stayed at the Connaught Hotel while the work was done and moved into the flat in June 1924. It was much admired but soon proved too small. Fourth, and finally, her ailments: "intestines which are the curse of all Benjamins, indigestion daily, bacilli colic, headaches, blood-shot eyes, anaemia, constipation, catarrh, today I had the upper wisdom tooth out, I have three teeth besides to be filled, corns on little toes, I take oxygen from a battery in the leg till I have had twenty injections, I have had three chiropractic treatments from this strong powerful Swedish woman." She wanted to have another child: "Poor Charles I am sure feels sorry we have no such expectations for in spite of what two doctors have told me there being no hindrance to preclude an increase in family, I am commencing to think there never will be for us." Worst was a large tumour beneath one of her breasts. "I have seen four doctors in Paris and they all agree I should get rid of this lump now". It was removed in January 1924, "it is horrible to feel one is so mutilated". Mercifully, it was not malignant.

Once Carty was out of the navy and they were able to spend more time together, their relationship began to deteriorate. In some of her letters she mistakenly refers to him by the name of her first husband Alex, not a good sign. In one letter she compares her husbands: "The English are so reserved they are sometimes baffling and it is hard to follow their thought processes, one feels like a child learning a new alphabet, P.G. was too intuitive, Alex never bothered to notice or comment about anything."

Recalling these times many years later, Dallas wrote:

> Early in 1924, Mamma having become a British resident, it was suggested that I might be educated at Eton and Cambridge (Carty adamantly opposed Oxford which, he declared, was known at this time for its "perverts").

Carty's knowledge of Cambridge seems to have stopped some way short of A. E. Housman, E. M. Forster, Lytton Strachey and Maynard Keynes.

But I equally adamantly — at the age of nine — insisted on continuing my schooling in America. So it was decided that I should become a boarder, after graduating in the spring of 1924 from Buckley School in New York, at Aiken Preparatory School.

Between leaving Buckley and starting at Aiken, Dallas reached the age of ten.

Chapter Two

Ancestry

A century and a half after Darwin, and fifty years after the discovery of DNA, it is hard to take seriously such concepts as inherited titles or blue blood. Dallas, a trained scientist and with some knowledge of history, knew that the ability to govern cannot be expected to run from one generation to the next, and that a genius can be the son of a dunce and the father of a dunce. Yet, for all his scepticism, he was fascinated by family trees. He had an extensive knowledge of several British and European dynasties. In his later years he devised an elaborate card game that depended on the players remembering the names, titles and spouses of Queen Victoria's children and grandchildren. He was also interested in his own ancestry, but not to any extreme, simply preserving the records he inherited rather than doing any further research.

When some of his ancestors became immensely rich in the second half of the nineteenth century, one of the methods they used to translate their wealth into social advancement was to trace their lineage as far into the past as possible. Some of them employed professional genealogists to draw up family trees that extended to the early settlers and beyond, including, in one case, to Charlemagne! It is impossible to say how accurate they are but they do raise some doubts. They represent every child as born within wedlock, and as the son or daughter of its mother's husband, which may have been true or not. To a modern eye, they appear to have an agenda. Every name is English: Foster, Stevens, Bradley, Moore, Baldwin, Bright, Hubbard, Horton and so on. It is also striking how many of the ancestral lines include somebody who arrived in America on the *Mayflower*. It is almost as if the family trees have more to do with propaganda than propagation. The message is that this is an elite group who were established in New England long before the tens of millions of later immigrants of many races and religions, who arrived in America after 1800.

Whether or not the genealogical record is accurate, it is relevant here because the people Dallas grew up amongst set great store by it. It represents his family as they saw themselves, and must have had an effect on Dallas's own self-perception. What follows is based on this record as Dallas would have absorbed it.

About ten generations run between the first New England settlers and Dallas's birth, amounting to more than two thousand ancestors. To keep the numbers manageable, in those pre-feminist days, family trees were usually pruned, emphasising the male line at the expense of the female. That perhaps made sense at the time when women, on marrying, gave up not just their names and their property but also their opportunities to do anything much except mothering. Here just three ancestral lines are summarised, those that Dallas thought of as the most important part of his heritage: the Pratts, the Benjamins and the Rogers. Their family trees appear on pages 281 to 285.

Thomas Pratt, who died in Baldock, Hertfordshire in 1539 had a grandson William Pratt who became rector of Stevenage, about ten miles from Baldock, and died there in 1629. William Pratt's tomb in Stevenage church lists all six of his children, even though some of them were not buried there. One daughter and two sons emigrated to America. The youngest of them, William Pratt (1622–1678), was only about ten years old when they crossed to New England around 1633, soon after their father's death. William Pratt prospered there, became a large landholder in Saybrook and Hebron, Connecticut, and served as Deputy to the General Court at Hartford. For the next two hundred years, the fortunes of the Pratts rose and fell. Remaining in New England, they became army officers, farmers, clergymen, a blacksmith and a dentist. They married people of English descent and had large families. In 1813 Linus Pratt married Temperance Pratt, both of whom were fifth generation descendants of William Pratt, the boy who arrived from England in 1633. Of their five double-Pratt children, their son Horace (born 1823) became a clergyman, the Rector of St. Peter's Church at Perth Amboy, New Jersey. Breaking from the tradition of this fecund family, he and his wife had a mere three children, all of them boys. To the eldest of these, born in 1849, they gave the name Dallas.

This was the first Dallas Pratt. The name Dallas was already distinguished in both Scottish and American history. His mother, born Sarah Martin, was a direct descendent of George Dallas (1630–1702) who had been Deputy Keeper of the Great Seal of Scotland. Furthermore, an aunt (his mother's sister) had married Alexander Dallas Bache (1806–1867), also distantly descended from the same George Dallas. Pride in this distinguished name not only led the Reverend Horace Pratt and his wife to name their eldest son Dallas Pratt (born 1849); he in turn named his son Alexander Dallas Bache Pratt (1883–1947), and he his Dallas Bache Pratt (1914–1994), the subject of this book.

Collateral relatives of the Pratts include other distinguished people. One of these was Alexander James Dallas (1759–1817), Secretary of the US Treasury under President Madison, after whom Dallas, Texas was named. Another was his son, George Mifflin Dallas (1792–1864), Vice President of the U.S.A., 1845–1849. Alexander Dallas Bache, mentioned above, was a great-grandson of Benjamin Franklin and was an eminent scientist and educator. He superintended the first complete coastal survey of the United States; he founded Girard College to provide an education for orphans; and he became the first president of the American Academy of Science. He resembled Dallas in many ways: his intellectual energy, his scientific interests, he even kept a journal. But Dallas did not inherit any of his qualities by direct descent. Resembling Dallas in one more way, he died unmarried and childless. Before leaving the Pratts, it may help to avoid confusion about them to mention two Pratts who were not part of Dallas's family. The Charles Pratt (1830–1891) who founded the Pratt Institute in Brooklyn, which he endowed on a grand scale, was a business partner of Dallas's Rogers grandfather. He may well have had ancestors in common with Dallas but he was not a close relative. Nor was the Francis Pratt (1827–1902) whose name survives in the great engineering company Pratt and Whitney.

Dallas showed little interest in his Pratt forebears. Asked about them, he tended to say "They came to New England in the seventeenth century and just stayed there". He took rather more interest in the Benjamins and resembled them more.

Dallas's mother was a Benjamin by birth. In its early stages the story of the Benjamins is like that of the Pratts. John Benjamin (1580?–1645), who came from Heathfield, Sussex to Boston, Massachusetts in 1632, about the same time as William Pratt arrived in Connecticut, was an early settler. Like his son Joseph

(1633–1704), and Joseph's son John (1682?–1716) he was a prosperous New England farmer. John's son, again named John (1714–1791) is recorded as a dealer in "cordwain" (cordovan leather). In the next generation the family's fortunes turned. David Benjamin (1743–1785) married Lucy Parke, daughter of Zebulon and Anna Parke of Preston, Connecticut. This introduced the name Parke or Park into the family. It was much used in future generations as a forename. David Benjamin fought in the Revolutionary War in 1775 and 1776 as a "patriot", that is to say on the side of George III. He died insolvent, and his wife died seven days later, leaving seven destitute children of whom the eldest, Park, was only fifteen years old.

He, the first Park Benjamin (1769–1824) responded to this challenge with immense energy, becoming a sea captain, a merchant, and the owner of plantations in British Guiana, and restoring the family's prosperity. In 1801 he married Mary Judith Gall of Barbados.

Their fourth child, Park Benjamin, Jr. (1809–1864), born in Demarera, British Guiana, had an affluent but sickly childhood. One of his legs was atrophied and he used crutches all his life. His parents, who stayed in the Caribbean, sent him to be educated in New England, where he lived with his aunts. His father was lost at sea in 1824 when he was fifteen, the age his father had become an orphan. But the younger Park Benjamin was neither destitute nor a man of action like his father. Park Benjamin, Jr. had a good education at Harvard and at Washington College (now Trinity College) in Hartford, Connecticut, where he shone as a debater and made lifelong friends who included the writers Henry Wadsworth Longfellow and Oliver Wendell Holmes. Literature was to be his life. He went on to publish poems, to edit and write for literary journals, to act as a literary agent and to make lecture tours. Thus many of his interests and talents foreshadow those of Dallas, his great-grandson.

Sometimes Park Benjamin prospered, sometimes he was quite hard up. His wife, Mary Bower Western, of Dosoris, Long Island, was descended from an old Dutch New York family, the Romeyns. Despite his disability, they had eight children. Several of them, in their different ways, seem to anticipate Dallas. The eldest son, Park Benjamin III (1849–1922), wrote popular books on scientific subjects. The third son, George Hillard Benjamin (1852–1927) practised as a doctor in Albany, New York. The fourth son, Walter Romeyn Benjamin (1854–1943) worked as a journalist and collected manuscripts. He edited *The Collector* which at the time was the leading trade journal in this field. The sixth son, William Evarts Benjamin (1859–1940), was Dallas's grandfather. He worked in the publishing house Dodd Mead and then joined his brother Walter in a rare books and autograph business. He also published books, including the Stedman & Hutchinson *Library of American Literature*. In 1886 he married Anne Engle Rogers (1865–1924), who was the eldest daughter of Henry Huttleston Rogers (1840–1909), one of the richest men in the world.

It was Henry Huttleston Rogers who claimed direct descent from Thomas Rogers, the ship's carpenter of the *Mayflower*, who had crossed with his son Joseph and landed at Plymouth, Massachusetts, in 1620. Their descendant, Rowland Rogers, born in 1809 in Mattapoisett, Massachusetts, worked on a whaling ship before employment as a clerk in a shipping house. In 1833 he married Mary Eldredge Huttleston of Fairhaven, Massachusetts. They lived first in Mattapoisett and their first son, Henry Huttleston Rogers, was born there in 1840. When he was still a small child they moved to the town of his mother's birth,

Fairhaven, ten miles away. Her family, once prosperous, was no longer so. The couple's little house in Fairhaven is preserved as the childhood home of Henry Huttleston Rogers. It is strikingly modest.

The life of Henry Huttleston Rogers has become something of a legend. His financial success is an extreme example of rags-to-riches and small-town-boy-makes-good. Similarly, the duality of his personality is presented in simple and extreme terms. People who suffered at his hands nicknamed him "the Hell-hound of Wall Street", "the Mephistopheles of Standard Oil", "a pirate", "a ruthless shark" and, of course, "a robber baron". His friends and family remembered him, in the words of Mark Twain, who was one of his closest friends, as "the sweetest man who ever lived". There must have been light and shade between these extremes, a man behind the myth, but perhaps the evidence to analyse him more subtly no longer exists. In any case, as far as he relates to his great-grandson Dallas, born five years after his death, it should be sufficient to summarise the story as it is generally told.

Fairhaven, where he spent his boyhood, is a small and genteel community across the Acushnet estuary from the great whaling centre of New Bedford. In the eighteen-fifties the whaling industry was at its height. His ambition, when he left school at sixteen was to go to sea as a cabin boy on a whaling ship. His parents, fearful of the dangers, dissuaded him. Instead, he worked in a grocery store, then on the local railway, living at home and saving what little he was paid.

His five years in these lowly jobs coincided with the discovery of oil in Pennsylvania. As soon as petroleum started replacing whale oil as fuel, the whaling industry and the local economy in Massachusetts that was based on it, went into rapid decline. Thousands of young men flocked to Pennsylvania in pursuit of wealth, including the twenty-one year old Rogers and a school friend, Charles P. Ellis, who had similar ambitions and a similar modest nest egg. Borrowing what they could, an amount matching their savings, they soon had their own oil refinery in Titusville, Pennsylvania. The money Rogers had saved during his five years working in Fairhaven was the capital sum that he built into one of the greatest fortunes of his time.

Still in his early twenties, Rogers went back to Fairhaven a rich man, and married his childhood sweetheart Abbie Gifford. They returned to Titusville, where they set up house and started to raise a family, remaining there for several years.

Rogers had all that was needed to succeed in that tough and ruthless environment. He relished competition and conflict, and he had technological flair. He developed and patented a process for converting crude oil into naphtha, an important development for the industry. He is also credited with the invention of the pipeline as a means of conveying oil over long distances, and he solved many of the technical problems it entailed. He had a supreme ability to choose outstanding colleagues and subordinates. Again and again, he found gifted associates from backgrounds at least as simple as his own. First, Charles Ellis, then Charles Pratt, both already mentioned. Pratt as a young man had, like Rogers, worked in a grocery store. The business these two founded together merged with John D. Rockefeller's Standard Oil, in which they became leading figures. John D. and William Rockefeller were the sons of an itinerant peddlar. Rogers worked with both of them for many years in several enterprises. Perhaps Rogers's most important characteristic of all was a willingness to take great risks, or what seemed to other people to be risks. He perhaps had the foresight to know he was betting on certainties.

By his fifties, Rogers with his wife and children, had left Titusville and moved back and forth between New York and Fairhaven. In New York they lived in a great town house, complete with stables and garages, at 62 East 85th Street. In Fairhaven, Rogers built an 85-room mansion. They travelled from one to the other on their steam yacht the *Kanawha*. By then Rogers had transformed the little town of Fairhaven, endowing it with paved streets, a water and drainage system, and a series of public buildings. His town hall, grammar and high schools, public library, Masonic lodge, Unitarian church and parsonage still dwarf everything around them. This was the start of a tradition in his family of large public benefactions which, a century later, include several charitable foundations, country houses and parks, and no less than four museums.

Tall, handsome and, when he chose to be, immensely charming and generous, Rogers was, in many of his business dealings devious, secretive and completely ruthless. Although most of what has been written about him either demonises or sanctifies him, the *Dictionary of American Biography* presumably aims at a balanced view. His entry in it contains the information about his business dealings that forms the rest of this paragraph. He was, it reports, involved in countless financial scandals and government investigations. He generally emerged from those triumphant and unscathed, though when the State of Missouri brought a suit against Standard Oil in 1905 he, at first defiant, had to admit the Standard's secret ownership of some subsidiary oil companies. One of his main occupations in his later years was resisting the dismemberment of the Standard Oil monopoly. Only after his death was the Trust broken up. He was a director of the US Steel Corporation, and a trustee of the Mutual Life Insurance Company. In 1899 he formed another gigantic trust,

Amalgamated Copper, which was responsible for some of the harshest strokes in business at that time: the "watering" of its stock, guerrilla warfare against certain private interests, and the wrecking of the Globe Bank of Boston.

His last and greatest financial triumph was a venture he undertook using only his own resources and what he could borrow on them, so that he could secure the entire proceeds for himself and his family. He saw that the great coal reserves of West Virginia would produce a fortune for the person controlling the transport link from the mines to the coast. After acquiring the necessary land and rights by stealth, he built the Virginian Railway, two hundred miles of track that were to bring his descendants enormous wealth for generations to come.

To the end of his days, Rogers gave himself no airs. He did not court high society. Nor was he an intellectual. He claimed to enjoy visits to the opera because they afforded him the opportunity of a good nap. He loved minstrel shows, stage comedies and farces, old Protestant hymns and anthems. He was, however, fond of reading. He numbered several writers amongst his friends. These, as already mentioned, included Mark Twain, who referred to Rogers as "the best friend I have". Their relationship may seem surprising as Mark Twain was a natural enemy of privilege and a champion of the downtrodden. It is said that he coined the derogatory phrase Gilded Age, in response to hearing it called a Golden Age. But he was himself entrepreneurial and might have liked to emulate Rogers. He brushed criticisms of Rogers aside. The story is told that a woman stopped him in the street in New Bedford and said "How can you be so friendly with Mr Rogers, a man whose money is tainted?" Mark Twain: "Right, Madame! 'Tain't yours and 'tain't mine!" During the last years of their lives Mark Twain and Rogers were together as much as their busy schedules allowed. Mark Twain spent many afternoons in Rogers's New York office exchanging banter with the plutocrat. In 1893, when Mark Twain's ill-fated business enterprises were facing disaster, Rogers helped him reorganise his finances, and relieved him of money worries for the rest of his life.

Rogers's first wife, Abbie, died in 1894. Two years later, and aged nearly sixty, he married Emilie Augusta Hart, who was the daughter of a wealthy diamond merchant and the divorced wife of Lucius R. Hart, the owner of a metals company in New York. Rogers died in 1909, she in 1912.

Henry Huttleston Rogers and his first wife Abbie had six children. One son was born and died in 1870, living only seven days. One daughter, Millicent, born in 1873, died aged seventeen. Her name was given to the public library in Fairhaven, which Rogers endowed, and also to a granddaughter. Of the four who survived into maturity, the eldest was a daughter, Anne Mai. As a result, perhaps, of Rogers's literary connections, she met and married the sixth child of Park Benjamin, Jr., William Evarts Benjamin. They in turn had a daughter, Beatrice Mai. Dallas was her son.

Unlike Rogers himself, all of his offspring grew up rich. His immediate heirs, his children and grandchildren, lived like royalty in the years before World War I. Towards the end of his life, Dallas recorded his recollections of some of them in an essay "Six American 'Princesses'", which was published in *America in Britain*, the magazine of The American Museum in Britain, in the year 2000. Their way of life could hardly have been more different from those of the farmers, blacksmiths, clergymen and so on who were their ancestors. In the generations after Rogers, some saw their riches to some extent dwindle. Others, including

Dallas's Benjamin grandfather, managed to make their fortunes grow.

Beatrice was the eldest of the ten grandchildren, and a special favourite of both Rogers and Mark Twain. When the two men first met, she was five years old and from then on was often with them in New York, on the yacht *Kanawha*, and at Fairhaven. Her marriage in 1909 came a few months before Mark Twain's death. He was too ill to attend the wedding. Instead he wrote to her: "I have been trying to realise that it is *you* that are going to be married; but I don't succeed. To me there are three of you. I see you clearest and know you best as a little chap; later I got acquainted with a girl of fourteen at Fairhaven bearing your name; and five or six years later still I got acquainted with this other one: this tall one, this slender one, that has inherited the quite sufficient beauty of the others and added to it. I know that it is you that is going to be married, but I don't know which one. Well, anyway, I hope you will be happy forever, dear, all four of you. This includes Mr Pratt, that abnormally fortunate man."

He was spared seeing yet more transformations as she emerged from the elaborate long dresses of the first years of the twentieth century into the short skirts and fast living that followed.

Chapter Three

1924 – 1934

Ten to twenty

Ten years old, a graduate of the Buckley School, and back from his visit to Wyoming, Dallas started his first term at Aiken Preparatory School in South Carolina in September 1924:

> It was in fact run very much on the model of a British preparatory school. The headmaster, Mr Taber was British, and so were all the masters: Mr Pritchard, the Messrs Turner, called "Senior" and "Junior", and the formidable Mr Gifford, who kept order in his class by gingering up inattentive pupils by banging them on the back of the head with a geography book, or by a frontal attack with a well-aimed piece of chalk.
>
> This, added to obligatory cold showers every morning, and above all, to a separation for the first time from my beloved governess, Maud Duke, was too much for ten-year old Dallas, and for the first term I was desperately home-sick. Maud received heart-rending letters from her "Poula", asking to be rescued. Gradually the home-sickness subsided, and a letter written at the beginning of my second year at Aiken begins: "I am having a simply lovely time and love this school. It is very nice. I like it a-lot." Everyone must

have been relieved. All the subsequent letters describe the fun and fine times I and my bosom friends (especially Augie Heckscher and Hugh Chisholm) are having. "I am in a secret club with them" I confide to Dear.

In the November 1 letter I announce with excitement that I am in the school play. "Last year I was in it but only in the chorus but this year I am a principal character in it. It is called the *Jester* and I am 2nd. Prince. We have just finished the rehearsal and I know all my part. I love acting in plays." The play in which I was only in the chorus was an adaptation of Tennyson's romantic, knightly drama, *The Princess*. Hugh Chisholm was the heroine, Melissa.

In February or March I wrote to Dear: "I am scared to death Dear, because the play is fast approaching. Gosh, I shiver. I wrote to Daddy and I hope he comes down."

On the back of this letter are Dear's comments: "I saw the rehearsal when at Aiken and Dallas was very good in it and spoke out well. He is doing very well at the piano and played a trio with great gusto."

Daddy did come down, but Mamma, whom I also hoped might come, did not. Nor, as I suggested in another letter, did she rent a cottage in Aiken ("a lot of people whom you know are here.")

In 1981 Dallas remembered that his lifelong book collecting had started at this time:

When I was about ten and living during vacations in the New York apartment of my grandfather, William Evarts Benjamin, I occupied a guest room — one not very suitable for a young boy since it was entirely furnished with original Louis XVI pieces. These I was told were very valuable and must be treated with great respect. However, I was encouraged to introduce something of my own into this period setting: books! notably a set of Edgar Allan Poe in blue half calf and one of Kipling's works bound in brilliant green calf, both purchased out of my Christmas savings, and both found, oddly enough, at Macy's. To these my grandfather added an 18th century five-volume set of Pope's *Homer*, bound in contemporary blind-tooled calf faded to a beautiful shade of old rose. When the term started at my boarding school in South Carolina the books were packed up in a closet, but when I returned for vacations I got them out and "furnished" my room with them.

During Dallas's three years at Aiken his mother continued to spend her time in England and France. In 1924 her own mother died, the oldest of Henry Huttleston Rogers's daughters. Another of these daughters died a few months later, Mai Coe, whose Wyoming house Cynthia and Dallas had visited the previous summer. Deeply distressed by these bereavements, the one surviving Rogers daughter, Aunt Cara, suffered a heart attack on board her yacht *Sapphire* at Cannes in 1925, but recovered and lived another fourteen years.

Writing regularly to her brother Roger, Dallas's mother became more and more impatient with their father who, she knew, was sitting on a fortune yet kept her short of money, and even delayed sending her all her mother's jewellery. In one letter she makes a rare reference to Dallas: "They say at Aiken he is the cleverest head in the school."

Each summer during these years, Cynthia and Dallas, accompanied by Dear, spent some time in Europe, part of it with their mother, but even when they were all in the same town, Mamma and Carty would stay at the most fashionable hotel, Dear and the children somewhere more modest nearby.

A June 1926 letter, from the Hotel de la Digue, Le Touquet, is addressed to Mamma who was on the yacht *Sapphire*, belonging to Aunt Cara and Uncle Broughton (later Fairhaven). In the casino at Le Touquet we had been to see a play, *Primrose*. "Not very good," was my comment, "but in between the acts we danced." Evening dancing in a casino! — the schoolboy, aged 11, has become pretty sophisticated.

The same letter enthuses over a trip to Dieppe. "We went all around an old chateau where some of the most beautiful ivory carvings in the world are." Then "we went in a church where there was the most beautiful carving in stone I have ever seen."

And thus, on the day trip to Dieppe, I began a lifetime of visits to historic shrines and museums.

One of the most memorable events of my three years in Aiken is announced in the January 30th 1927 letter.

"Yesterday I had a wonderful time; because I jumped the three biggest brush jumps in Aiken. They are 5 feet tall and great fun. I am going on the drags here as Daddy gave his permission."

Later in the letter I write, "Next summer at London I want to ride in Rotten Row — as Hugh Chisholm is coming to London we can ride together — and in Le Touquet." I never rode in Rotten Row, but I did ride in Le Touquet. The poor horses there, probably after the abusive life of a livery stable animal, had "hard mouths". Often I couldn't hold them back, and I would be perilously towed at speed over sand dunes and through the scrubby woods as my horse headed for home.

In June 1927, aged twelve, Dallas graduated from Aiken. That summer:

> saw us visiting the French battlefields of World War I, and in the same year we went to Bruges and Ghent, climbing the belfry at Bruges and reverently viewing the Van Eycks' masterpiece, *The Adoration of the Lamb*, in Ghent Cathedral.

In September 1927, now thirteen, Dallas arrived at St Paul's School, Concord, New Hampshire. Many of his classmates there became lifelong friends. Some, such as Hugh Chisholm and August Heckscher had been with him at Aiken. In 1980, Heckscher, after twenty-five years as a trustee of the school, published a history of it, describing how, founded in 1855, it was one of the first of New England's boarding schools for the education of the newly wealthy urban class. In its first phase its traditions were austere and strongly religious. A second era for the school had started by the 1890s, when young Mellons, Morgans and Vanderbilts were arriving there in their private rail cars. When Dallas began there, generous endowments from some of these former students meant that the school was not only well staffed and equipped but had impressive buildings and beautiful grounds covering several hundred acres along the banks of the Merrimack River. Later, St Paul's School went through further changes, transforming it into the modern co-educational school it is today. In Dallas's time it was for boys only, and modelled itself on the English public schools, though with the addition of a degree of American comfort, grace and warmth.

As in its English counterparts, its main subjects were classics, history and modern languages, followed closely by mathematics and science. Dallas excelled at all of these but, in his teens, his greatest enthusiasms were literary. He soon became a contributor of prose and verse to the school's literary magazine *Horæ Scholasticæ* which had begun publication soon after the school was founded. In 1993, he wrote this about his five years at St Paul's:

> *Horæ Scholasticæ* was the literary magazine of the school. I was Assistant Editor from 1930 to 1932, August Heckscher and Roger Wolcott Drury were Head Editors. The Alumni Editor was Willard Scudder, a Johnsonian figure who deserved, but never had, a Boswell. We were invited after Sunday chapel to coffee in his rooms in the Middle dormi-

tory. "Chappie" (as all the boys called him but not to his face!) dispensed refreshment and wit. He was a gentleman of the old school, his portly form attired in conservative, well-tailored clothes, his accent late nineteenth century Ivy League, his tastes epicurean. Augie Heckscher and his younger brother, Maury, who had started their Ashlar Press when we were still at St. Paul's, printed a number of "slim volumes" as supplements to the *Horæ*, and Chappie's *Lyrica Paulinensia*, modestly described as verses, was the first to appear — in December 1931.

Another slim volume from the Ashlar Press, also printed in 1931 and titled *In the Darkened Glass*, contains nine poems — or should I say verses? — which I wrote, mostly in my 'teens, from 1925 to 1931.

The volume is dedicated to Dear. It includes a poem Dallas wrote when he was ten:

> The sun is sinking into the West,
> Over the hills sinks he,
> And all the great wide world
> Is bathed in Tranquillity.

In November 1931, a poem Dallas wrote for *Horæ Scholasticæ* was printed in newspapers across America:

Threescore Years and Ten

> Quick, sir, help me up — and bring my cane!
> 'Tis cold tonight, but then I like it so.
> I heard a sudden tapping on the pane;
> Gray Winter's here again, and so I go
> To meet him by some gaunt and leafless tree
> Where we can whisper underneath our breath,
> And once more jest at that pale enemy
> Whom you may know by sight — I speak of death.
> Tonight the jaded year grows old with me;

I hear the fierce hounds of the wind give tongue —
Not as in Spring when zephyr's melody
Recalls those far-off days when I was young —
But loud and wrathful, harbingers of snow,
And though 'tis cold tonight — I like it so.

This was seen in the Birmingham, Alabama *Age Herald* by the twenty-seven year old Virginia Foster Durr who, in the 1960s, was an important figure in the Civil Rights Movement. Out of the blue, she wrote to Dallas at St Paul's School "This is really very splendid, keep it up!"

Another poem of this time reveals that, even at this early age, Dallas was already interested in psychiatry:

Counter of Straws

Well — I forget his name, but that's no matter;
He lost it long ago with other things
More precious. Call him Number Fifty-seven.
Inmate, like many others, of this building
With iron doors and rows of padded cells
Which men who were, of course, both wise and sane
Designed for the reception of the mad.
Well — I've been told that Number Fifty-seven,
Before he lost his senses and his name,
Was clever. People said he might go far,
Dreaming of things much better left undreamt.
Slowly the windows of his brain grew dark,
Until the sickly rays of thought quite failed
To light the crazy attic of his mind.
All the dim pigeon-holes of memory filled
With dross, — poor stuff, that scattered on the floor
If touched by some cold blast of common-sense.

So here he sits in Bedlam, counting straws —
Don't ask him what his name is, he's forgotten.

His number? Well — he's not had time to hear it —
You see, he's been so busy counting straws.

During Dallas's time at school his mother, despite her protestations of poverty, acquired a town house in Curzon Street, Mayfair, a country house, Sludge Hall, in Leicestershire, a large and elegant Paris flat at 3 Rue de Constantine and a house on Cap d'Antibes in the South of France. The London house was small compared with her Aunt Cara's great mansion nearby in Park Street, but large enough to hold parties for a hundred guests, and to house her family plus twelve living-in servants. In the late 1980s Dallas recalled this well-staffed household:

> At the highest rank were two "ladies", the secretary and the governess. When the children ate with the family, the governess did too; the secretary never. The comparatively high rank of the butler, cook and first chauffeur was indicated by the fact that they were known by their last names, but without the prefix "Mr". Cooks usually were "Mrs" in my time, whereas my grandmother Benjamin's superb Scottish cook was simply Bain. All the other servants were known by their first names. While the cook, butler and parlourmaid were responsible for certain levels (kitchen, dining-room and reception room respectively), the "Tweenie" looked after everything "between" (staircases, bathrooms, bed-making, etc.).
>
> The butler, assisted by the first footman, answered the front door, presided over service at table, polished the silver, dispensed the liquor, and valeted the gentlemen. The second footman helped with the washing up. They also packed and unpacked for my stepfather and male guests. My mother's personal maids, first Gwenneth (Maltese) and later, for many years until Mamma's death, Jeanne Lemaire, packed, looked after her dog, and did many other things for her, including

getting up no matter how late she came in at night in order to "undress" her.

At a designated hour in the morning the cook would appear in my mother's bedroom with her menus. The cook had a tremendous job, having to provide meals for all the inside staff (which included everybody except the secretary and the chauffeurs), the family and frequent guests. This meant three meals a day (although breakfast was probably delegated to the kitchen maid and footmen) plus a substantial tea with sandwiches, bread and butter, buttered toast and cake. Finally, if we went to the theatre, sandwiches would always be waiting on our return in case we were "peckish".

In London, as a teenager, the second footman looked after my clothes and shined my shoes. This young man was partly chosen for his good looks, and I remember one Adonis especially whom I worshiped from afar. Our first footman, John, was an exemplary person who by his very proper demeanor was known as "The Parson". A crisis occurred, however, when it became necessary for him to wear glasses. A bespectacled footman was not at all *comme il faut*. But he was such a treasure it was finally decided that he must stay in spite of the glasses.

The butler was garbed in sober black with a tail coat, but the footmen were gorgeous in striped waistcoats and tail coats adorned with silver buttons bearing the Cartwright crest.

The chauffeurs were of course in uniform, also with silver buttons on dress occasions. They looked very smart when we went to the theatre in the Rolls with two men "on the box". The second man had to open the doors, and watch for us coming out of the theatre so that he could immediately alert the chauffeur wherever he was parked. The Rolls had a well-modeled rooster as radiator cap, a highly polished aluminum bonnet, and a black cabriolet body covered at the rear with yellow basketwork. Our clothes matched this splendid equipage: the women in dresses from Paquin, Molyneux and other French couturiers; the men invariably in white tie and tails. The shows we saw were Cochran's Revues with Jessie Matthews and Tillie Losch; Noel Coward's *Cavalcade*; and stars like Beatrice Lillie, Gertrude Lawrence, Sybil Thorndike, Cicely Court-neidge, Ben Travers and Harry Lauder.

Sludge Hall was a place for Charles Cartwright to ride and hunt. Dallas's mother disliked English country life but sometimes entertained her friends there, including Wallis Spencer, by then Mrs Simpson (who later married King Edward VIII). The Paris apartment was a useful staging post between London and the South of France: "I need at least a fortnight in Paris for shopping and fittings." She no longer visited Le Touquet after 1930: "I am so bored with that community."

The Casa Estella on Cap d'Antibes was the most spectacular of her houses. It is cut off from the outside world down a long drive, shaded by umbrella pines, and has terraces and steps cut into the rocks leading down to the sea. Indoors, the metal stair rail is in the form of the opening notes of Debussy's *La Mer*. The long, all-white drawing room, designed for her by her friend Syrie Maugham, with a display of rare Blanc de Chine porcelain, is said to have been the setting that inspired Noel Coward's song "I've been to a marvellous party".

During the 1920s and 1930s, Dallas's mother was a glamourous presence in the fashionable word of London, Paris, St Moritz and the South of France. She loved parties and showing off her fashionable clothes, or exotic garments if the occasion was "fancy dress". Her "Queen of the Night" costume, probably worn only once, is still, after three quarters of a century, an astonishingly impressive piece of workmanship (now in the American

Museum's collection). After hearing about it, her father called her "Queen of the Nightclubs". She was not one of the famous beauties of the time, like Lady Diana Cooper, but she more than made up for it by the style and sumptuousness of what she wore. Her most admired attributes, apart from her clothes, were her emeralds and her tapering fingers, which artists portrayed as coming to a sharp point.

On 20 July 1930, she and Carty at last had the baby they had long wanted. The birth of Aubrey Cartwright is marked by only two sentences in her surviving letters to her brother in America. First, "My figure is getting back to normal". Secondly, the news that the top floor of 28 Curzon Street was being converted into a nursery. From then on, she often complained that the house was now too small.

In the summer of 1931 in Paris, Dallas, now sixteen, started a lifetime of collecting early maps. Writing in his mid-sixties, he recalled:

> That began with two mid-16th century maps by Sebastian Munster: one of the world and the other of the western hemisphere. I bought them at a bookstall on the embankment of the Seine. In contemporary colour, which is rare, they testify to the good eye of that teenager who launched me on the map hunt which I still pursue.

This comes from his summary of his map collecting, in an article, "New World, Old Maps — The Adventures of a Collector", in *America in Britain*, June 1989.

Before starting his last year at St Paul's School, Dallas and his mother had a summer vacation together, crossing Europe with a group of family and friends. Dallas and Cynthia were accompanied by Dear; their mother by Carty and her French maid Jeanne Lemaire; Doris Duke by her French governess Mlle

Reynard. Two chauffeurs drove the Cartwrights' Rolls Royce and De Lage and a third drove Doris Duke's Dusenburg. Baby Aubrey was presumably in the care of a nanny in Curzon Street. In heavy rain they visited Delft, Rotterdam, Leyden, the Hague and Rotterdam. Reports of riots in Cologne, "reflecting Hitler's stormy rise to power", diverted them from that part of Germany to Belgium, Luxembourg and France. Dallas wrote an account of the trip at the time, of which the following passages are extracts. He added the sentences printed in italics in his seventies.

> At Strasbourg we spent a hectic and, as it turned out, entirely unnecessary four hours trying to buy marks. The world was deep in the depression, an important Austrian bank had failed in May, and some rumours made one or two banks we entered unwilling to honour our letters of credit, even those of Doris known as the "richest girl in the world". We were referred back and forth between banks.
>
> Eventually we gave up — and of course had no difficulty in changing money when we arrived at the Hotel Stephanie in Baden-Baden. *We arrived rather shaken by a near accident. Carty, driving the car which was heading the procession, missed a turn and braked abruptly. The next car, with the governesses, would have crashed if the driver hadn't been able to by-pass Carty's car by shooting off the road into a field. We were furious with Carty. He considered himself an excellent driver, but he had crashed two of our cars in England.*

Their arrival in Baden-Baden was reported in the Paris edition of the *Daily Mail* with many inaccuracies: Carty was described as "Major" Cartwright, an army, not a navy, rank; Maud Duke as Doris Duke's mother; Cynthia and Dallas as Mrs Cartwright's daughters. Dallas found the clipping amongst Dear's possessions after her death.

Carty then took one of the cars and chauffeurs and set off for England. *Carty by this time was fed up with "abroad". He covered the Rhine, in spite of our desire to linger, at high speed. He either wouldn't or couldn't be bothered, to speak French. He shared the belief of other insular Britishers that all foreigners could understand English if one spoke loudly enough to them.*

The rest of us set off for Bayreuth. We stayed a week hearing the four *Ring* operas of Wagner. This to me was the most interesting part of the whole trip. *In retrospect, I am impressed by my teen-age stamina, particularly being able to take* Die Walküre *and* Das Rheingold, *neither of which I can now sit through. Of course we were very keyed up by the mystique of it all; the invisible orchestra placed under the audience, so that nothing intervened between oneself and the stunning sets; the break for an excellent lunch in the middle of each opera, served outside — and the notables in the audience. My mother knew Somerset Maugham, who was there, so we twice lunched with him and his secretary/lover, Gerald Haxton, an American. The latter was most agreeable, but every remark of Maugham's had a satiric or cynical bite to it. His wife Syrie, from whom he was divorced, was a more comfortable person.*

Arriving in Dresden, we spent two nights in the excellent Hotel Bellevue and, finally, left for Berlin, paying a visit to the porcelain factory at Meissen on the way. The first day in Berlin we devoted to sightseeing in the city proper, staying at the Hotel Adlon; on the second we visited Potsdam and Sans Souci and that night saw a memorable performance of *Die Schöne Helene*, staged by Max Reinhardt. On the evening of the third day we entrained for Paris, arriving on August 8th.

The trip was on the whole a great success.

During his last year at St Paul's school, 1931–1932, Dallas won the school's Keep History Prize with an essay on *The Effect of the Labour Party on British Politics*. More like the work of a promising university student than a sixteen-year-old schoolboy, it shows an impressive grasp of events since the election of the first two Labour MPs in 1874, and of the current Labour government's economic, foreign and colonial policies. It is also noteworthy for its extreme right wing slant. Perhaps its young author had some help from his great uncle Urban, Aunt Cara's husband, a former Conservative MP. He may have been trying to distance himself from the views expressed when he signed it not Dallas Pratt, but Jonathan Tory. The teacher judging the essays wrote on it "unquestionably the best."

His school days over, Dallas sailed for Europe on the liner *Europa* and, at the same time, embarked on writing his journal, which he kept up, off and on, for the rest of his life. He wrote daily on the crossing and continued during a stay at 28 Curzon Street, and as he travelled across Europe on his own. Here are a few early passages to give an impression of the journal and of its author. First its opening words:

> I have recently read some selections from Emerson's *Journals*, and this reading has impelled me to imitate, humbly it is true, this practice of confiding to paper any thoughts or incidents which seem worthy of recording. It may be that these pages may prove of use to me in later life, certainly they will if I take up the profession of writing.

Then a poem, written while he was staying at Curzon Street that summer:

> ### To My Mother
> Into the silent river of life
> A star from heaven fell;
> It cleft the flood like an arrow sent
> From a magic bow, for it left no rent
> In the mirror'd water nor broke the spell
> That lay on the river of life.

> Over the silent river of life
> A deity from afar
> Threw the mantle of winds that the morning wore
> Till the charm was snapped; then into the shore
> Born of the beauty of wind and star
> *You* stepp'd from the river of life.

Then, at Triberg in the Black Forest, a set of maxims which he seems to have taken to heart. They could be a description of him throughout his life:

Maxims from Balzac's *Le Lys dans la Vallée*

1. Follow custom and the laws of society, the least well known of which are often the most important. Originality which is like to offend the common taste is useless; conform in externals, but develop your own personality in the world of the spirit if you will.

2. Never be zealous. A zealous man can easily be duped. Zeal never strikes equal fire from your superiors.

3. Rarely talk about yourself, if you wish to keep people interested in you.

4. Criticism is rarely merited, for at the bottom of all men's actions there is a labyrinth of different causes and reasons. Be severe only on yourself.

5. Be witty if you will, but not at the expense of others or of yourself. Never lower yourself to amuse the mediocre.

6. Keep cool and distant, all men respect those who disdain them.

7. Never have disreputable friends. Choose your friends only after long and cool judgement, once having decided one way or another, let the decision be irrevocable.

8. If you set out towards some goal, never give up before it is reached. Don't waste your forces on the non-essentials, but win the essential points conclusively, using all the power you possess to do so.

9. Take as little as possible from others

10. Remember: *Noblesse oblige.*

At Hohenschwangan in Bavaria, an essay on patriotism. And then, after a lyrical description of the mountain scenery of Cortina d'Ampezzo, Italy:

> August 3 1932   Venice
>
> As long as I can remember I have longed to visit Venice and Egypt. And now I sit on a balcony overlooking the Grand Canal, while the songs of the Venetian watermen fill the air.

In the middle of that first night in Venice he was woken by a mosquito, inside his mosquito net:

> A few feeble thrashings and flailing with the hands only angered the beast — I felt it was growing distinctly antagonistic. In fact I felt it in several places. This, I decided, could not go on; Venice lay before my window, bathed in the half-light of dawn. The solution was obvious, and a plan was no sooner formed than put into effect. Fifteen minutes after the opening of the eyes and the first awakening yawn, I found myself creeping down the hotel corridor, fully dressed, and armed with a camera. It was four o'clock in the morning.
>
> My purpose was to see the city, and perhaps take some unusual photographs of Venice at an hour when the streets would be deserted, when I might admire Saint Mark's and the Ducal Palace at my leisure, and alone. With some difficulty I discovered the staircase, and at last found myself in the hall of the hotel. There a weary porter eyed me with mingled distrust and amazement. Conversation was difficult,

and the porter at least seemed to find my breezy "good-morning" rather too nonchalant. Finding, however, that I had stopped and was feebly making signs at the locked door, he growled "What is your room-number?" With a sheepish smile I answered his question, and he opened the door-way, obviously still a prey to the greatest suspicions.

Alas for my illusions! On entering the Piazza San Marco, I found that I was not alone. A number, perhaps ten, of gentlemen were engaged in walking around the vast square and picking up cigar or cigarette butts; they were obviously not connected with the street-cleaning department. After some minutes of avoiding the glances of these gentlemen, who seemed mildly surprised at my presence among them, I moved away. After strolling along the water-front, and trying to forget the odor in contemplation of the architecture, I shortly reached my hotel, again, having received distinct proof of the public disapproval of my appearance in the form of a loud jeer uttered by one of the more unpleasant element.

There was hostility in the air, the scars of sordid poverty and filth. I had seen what was not meant to be seen by the casual visitor, and Venice, like a vain woman, resented the intrusion.

Later, in St Mark's Square, a photographer took a snapshot of the seventeen-year-old Dallas, wearing a double-breasted suit, standing feeding the pigeons. The picture was in the form of a postcard, and Dallas posted it to his sister. She had married on 16 February of that year, 1932, so the card is addressed to Mrs W. Laughlin. What he wrote to her shows another side of his life from the one he was recording in his journal.

Here I am, caught at a pensive moment, outside St Mark's Venice. We are having a glorious time here with the Robertsons and Dukes. Dorothy Caruso is staying with

Queen Aspasia of Greece, and we see them all the time. I sat beside the queen at lunch and she was charming, and she has invited us to tea to-morrow at her house. D.

These people were of his mother's world but were also a part of Dallas's life at this time.

After Venice and a drive through the Veneto and Umbria, Dallas spent the rest of the summer at his mother's house in the South of France, the Casa Estella. She wrote to her brother "Dal loves it there, bathing and lying about on mattresses and relaxing." So relaxed was "Dal" that he neglected his journal and the next entry after Venice reads in its entirety:

> August 22 1932   Cap d'Antibes, France
> Yesterday was my eighteenth birthday.

In a letter to her brother, his mother wrote "I gave him a pearl scarf pin and a cheque on his eighteenth birthday and he was *thrilled.*" In another of these letters, now referring to her husband as Charlie, not Carty, she wrote "Charlie came for a week's stay but really didn't like the heat, late hours for meals (as no one is on time for lunch or dinner there), then the mosquitoes bothered him too and to cap the climax, one of my best women friends told him one of the men staying with us was a "Fairy" and shouldn't be in the same house with Dallas! He was an Englishman I had known seven years. It all disgusted and upset me and when Charlie decided to return after only four days stay, I asked Schuyler White to tell the man my husband had taken a dislike to him and I felt under the circumstances, it would be better he leave the same day as Charlie. He was awfully cut up about it, but did so. I couldn't explain to him *any* details as I was afraid he might decide to retaliate on Charlie and the woman who started the row, by suing Charlie for libel. The libel laws are *very* severe in England. It leaked out to our nearest neighbours, the Boissevains and Somerset Maugham, who are old friends of mine and the man — and in consequence, they were indignant at Charlie's attitude and his rushing home and sympathetic with me.

"Charlie has aged so and become so set — marriage with him is pretty grim, as he seems to have lost the sense of humour he had when I first married him.

"Dallas has been a great comfort and a perfect companion. I have the heart-ache for days when he leaves."

She and Dallas were getting on well. Although when he was a small child she had, in his words, "rejected him", he had never rejected her and, now that he was an articulate and charming young adult, she enjoyed being with him. Also, he was a most presentable escort for her when she was between husbands.

Her marriage to Charles Cartwright was to all intents over. "Aubrey stays at 'Sludge'", she reported in the same letter. Her son Aubrey Cartwright was three, a year younger than Dallas was when she parted from her first husband, his father. The Cartwrights' divorce took several years to complete and by the time it became absolute, in 1938, she had lost custody of Aubrey and, indeed, any contact with him. Aubrey was made a Ward of Court, with an official guardian who saw to it that, when not at boarding school, he was with his father or with Cartwright relatives.

As he lay in the summer heat of 1932 at the Casa Estella, Dallas's journal writing had, temporarily, petered out: there is no mention of his stepfather's visit to Cap d'Antibes, nor of his own return to America. Nor did he write of his arrival as a freshman at Yale a few days later. As it happens, somebody else did. The New Yorker writer, Brendan Gill, contributed an article to the Yale alumni magazine in November 1981 that includes the following:

"Four of us had come down to New Haven from Kingswood, a small country day-school in Hartford, Connecticut, where our families lived. We took up adjoining quarters in Bingham Hall, aware that we were unknown and that the corridors of power within our class and perhaps within the university as well would resound to the tread of graduates of Andover, St. Paul's, Hotchkiss, Groton, and the like. On our very first evening in Bingham, from an upper floor of our entry descended a handsome apparition, in elegant dressing gown, pyjamas, and slippers. His sartorial splendor struck us as resembling that of some sort of Aztec sungod; his right hand held aloft what I mistook at first for a ritual object, which turned out, at second glance, to be a toothbrush. 'Does anyone here have some toothpaste I could borrow?' he asked — not, after all, a sun-god, but Dallas Pratt, the first of the large number of St. Paul's boys whom I was to encounter and make friends with over the next few years."

In his first weeks at Yale, Dallas filled twenty pages of his journal with character sketches of some of his contemporaries there, several of them friends from his school days who remained his friends for life. They are too long to include here in full, but brief extracts convey their flavour. First, his Yale room-mate Alexander Vietor: "Alec is like a strong wind and a sail boat driving before it. He has not a complex character." Then August Heckscher 2nd: "Augie was born old." Gilbert Lea: "I do not know Gil Lea as I know the others about whom I am writing here. I admire him more than anyone I know: perhaps if I knew him better I should admire him less." Whitelaw Reid: "He always wears subdued ties in one colour. He thereby reveals his whole personality." Hugh Chisholm:

Hugh's case is one of two disassociated personalities. One of these personalities is the true one, but the other is becoming more and more predominant, and may completely subdue the first.

It all comes from being *with* people. When one is alone with Hugh, there is no one more sympathetic or pleasant, but as soon as a number of people gather together he attempts to become the "Life of the party".

Dillon Ripley was the member of this group who became the most distinguished of them, as Secretary of the Smithsonian Institution, co-author of the ten volumes of *The Birds of India*, and writer of many other books.

Like Miniver Cheevy, Dillon Ripley was "born too late". He would have been an ornament to the court of Napoleon III during the sixties. His mother lives apart from her husband, and Dillon can play the country gentleman in the spacious estate at Litchfield. He fences, he collects guns and swords, he is interested in pheasant raising and other agricultural matters. Besides this he is a good actor, an amateur ornithologist, and dabbles quite successfully in music and writing. He has very many interests. He is generous and considerate of others' feelings, and a very loyal friend.

He will go through life calmly and graciously, I think, bending his tall body with innumerable old-fashioned bows, and raising his distinctive Lock hat with a grand air. And in his declining years be named the grand old man of Litchfield.

Finally, Sheldon Prentice:

I have known Sheldon longer than any of the others here written about, with the exception of Hugh, and yet I know him hardly at all.

He is vain, but he is the most handsome boy in the school. He is conceited over his polo-ponies and wealth, but he has both in abundance. He lives fast, but his friends use him and egg him on. Underneath all this, however, there is a different man. Let me describe him.

He is intelligent and extremely courteous, always grateful for favours conferred. He likes to read good books. He is by no means blind to the beauties of Villa Palmieri at Fiesole, which belongs to his father. To the few he really likes he is loyal and considerate; an enthusiastic friend.

Here, then, are two distinct characters side by side in one personality, and often at odds. He will have a stormy life, and an unhappy one perhaps but his imagination will save him much.

Later, Dallas added to these words on Sheldon Prentice: "He was killed in the bombing of a battleship, Pearl Harbor, 1941."

On 20 November 1932, midway through his first semester at Yale, Dallas wrote:

I am being reclaimed by the land of my forefathers. I am finding once again in these rocky hills and wooded tracks a "goodly heritage". Let no one say the English countryside, or the Italian, is the most highly individual — or the most beautiful. Who does not rejoice at the thrill of a clean, sunny, cold day in an American autumn? The gorgeous coloring of the foliage, unequalled in the world; the sting in the air, what land has these? My heart is constricted on days like this (like *to-day*) the grandeur of dying leaves and a world falling asleep, the birds overhead, winging south to warmer haunts, the film of ice on the pond, the crackling of the leaves underfoot; changed soon to the crackling of the fire — these things are ours, fellow countrymen! These are *my* loves.

The next entry reads:

January 22, 1933

Two months have passed since I have written in this journal.
Well, journal-keeping is a talent, I suppose, and one difficult
to acquire. One reason I have found it difficult is that I
never can sit down to write without becoming quite
absurdly literary and high-flown. Just look at the entries in
this book! All of them are desperately striving to be literature, and in consequence most (all?) are terrible — strained,
self-conscious, false, worthless. Next to writing at all, the
hardest thing for me is to write simply.

Emerson, I am glad to be able to note, had that same
difficulty. His earlier entries in his *Journals* are very stiff and
conscious; it was the influence of his age, which he was later
able to shed in some measure.

In a long essay and the text of a speech for a student debate
that come next in his journal, Dallas theorised on the theme of a
future when all work was done by machines and mankind could
devote its time to philosophy and the arts. The speech is an
eloquent defence of socialism and puts very different views from
those expressed in his Keep History Prize essay written a few
months earlier. As a contribution to a debate, it, too, may not
express his actual views.

By June 1933 Dallas had completed his first year at Yale. For
several pages his journal described the trivia of daily life in the
style of Samuel Pepys.

Was lured this evening against my will to *Gold Diggers of
1933*, which, contrary to all expectation, I did enjoy hugely.
But in truth, Mistress Keeler, though a comely wench, did
move me not a jot, and I have never seen before such
simperings nor cooing, nor hope to again. Yet I am not
surprised that she be the secret passion of Alec Vietor, for
she is the type which he doth dote on.

Their freshman year over, the two Yale room-mates, Dallas Pratt and Alec Vietor, set out together in a thirty-two foot cutter that Alec had chartered, *The Hotspur*, for a four-and-a-half-week sail along the New England coast. Thirty pages of the journal describe in detail the voyage from Cold Spring Harbor on Long Island Sound to York Harbor, Maine, and back. They endured their ups and downs with cheerful fortitude: rain, fog, a storm that shattered the bowsprit, after which they were becalmed, seasickness (Dallas), food poisoning (Alec Vietor), but mostly beautiful days ending with glorious sunsets. At Newport, Rhode Island, Dallas revisited Reed Cottage, last seen when he was four, and recorded some of the memories quoted here in Chapter One (see page 17). Passing Cape Cod, Dallas wrote, "I am looking for an island to buy secretly and so I plan to investigate any likely islands along the coast we may run upon." If he did in fact buy an island, the secret has never been revealed. What were his thoughts as he sailed? "I was thinking about death the 'undiscovered country, from whose bourne no traveller returns'. That country will remain undiscovered: of this I am sure; for such a land beyond the grave does not exist." And as the journey ended?

> When friends have separated they are dead to one another — only at the next meeting are they born anew. The tragi-comedy of all life is played in the Valley of the Shadow of Death. These are solemn thoughts for youth, but the experiences of existence are not the prerogative of nor peculiar to the mature, and the secrets of existence are unfolded as experiences themselves unfold sorrow, love, hate, joy: these are emotions which any child has known, and he who searches behind them, may clasp many a strange key in his hand.

After two weeks on dry land at Southampton, Long Island, Dallas continued his summer vacation by setting sail yet again, with another Yale friend, Dillon Ripley, on the *Aquitania*, bound for England. "This is about the twenty-fifth time that I have crossed the Atlantic. It is the first time that I have tried Tourist Class." It was also the first time that he described in his journal making friends with another passenger. Mr Barambia, a "Turkish-Palestinian Jew with a real enthusiasm for Palestine and the Zionist movement", taught Dallas some modern Greek and some Egyptian mythology. Dallas made the discovery on this crossing that the people he found most interesting and congenial did not all travel First Class.

He also wrote on the *Aquitania*:

> I want to be a writer! O presumptuous desire! And not just one of the "mob of gentlemen who write with ease"! One thing is certain — I don't write with ease!

After leaving the ocean liner, Dallas and Dillon Ripley crossed France and Northern Italy to Venice. There they joined Dallas's mother and a group of her friends for a cruise along the east coast of Italy and the coast of Yugoslavia on the liner *Oceania*. The party did not include Charles Cartwright nor the baby, Aubrey. In December of that year, 1933, the magazine *Town & Country* published a description by Dallas of this trip, "The Dalmatian Coast". Here is one paragraph:

> In Zara, an Italian freeport, after you have loaded up with cigarettes and perfumes, and have visited all the twenty-three churches (my advice is: don't), stroll around the market square and look at the interesting peasant types. The men wear untidy but picturesque costumes; brightly figured socks, embroidered breeches and vest, a jacket with ribbons and silver ornaments, and a perfectly useless little pancake

hat with black fringe coming down in a tuft over the ear. The women are as colorful, but don't make the mistake of trying to take their pictures free!

Writing in his journal during the cruise, he recorded some of his thoughts. At Ancona:

> We visited the archaeological museum where were some Greek vases. Evidently the Greeks had not our modesty in artistic work: I saw some pictures in red on the typically black vases that would shame the most daring of modern illustrators. Still, it is not for us to criticise the Greeks. They were as a whole a better balanced race than any one of modern times: their code and customs in sexual matters are no worse, for being different than our own. The dissimilarity lies in that they were unashamed of matters which to us are unspeakable. *"Honi soit qui mal y pense."* They had no conception of the modern and mediaeval ideas of sexual matters, intercourse was the natural expression of love, marriage and sex made no difference so long as love existed. I think the distinction we make between "friend" and "lover" is a wholly artificial one, the Greek had one word for friend, for acquaintance, for lover "philos", one word too for like, for love "phileo". We have not improved upon this usage by introducing a host of new words with as many meanings. I should rather say I *love* my relations, my friend, my lover, because I have towards each the same general feeling; as for endeavouring to distinguish between the thousand different ways in which I love, and as for reserving my love for some, and denying it to others that I cannot do. I am not ashamed to admit it that the feeling I have for my friends is as much love as the feeling I have for my sister, or will have, I hope, for my wife. As a matter of fact, I do not even believe one can find many modern languages (besides, of course, English) that stress the distinction so carefully between *like* and *love*.

At Ragusa:

August 22, 1933

I was nineteen yesterday. The time when I must decide what occupation I am going to take up is drawing closer. There is no question in my mind, as there has really never been, that writing would be my chosen vocation. But suppose, as is only too likely, that I cannot develop into a good writer? What then? It seems that I must have a second choice:

Architect: interesting but unsatisfying, and one must be artistic.

Doctor: Not for me, though it is interesting.

Business man: I do not need to make money, I have no business ready made by my father to step in to, I don't want to live in New York — why, then, be a business man?

Diplomat: the opportunities of travel and writing are here, but the preliminaries are long and wearying, and the rewards are all political plums and out of reach.

Lawyer: the field is overcrowded, and New York would have to become my home. Ugh!

Scientist: unexplored field — but strangely *fascinating*.

Archaeologist: this sounds entrancing but in reality it is the pursuit for the professor and entails years of study. Besides, it is only concerned with the past. It is a *dead* subject.

Hitler became Chancellor of Germany in January 1933. Dallas's response marks the beginning of a new strand in his preoccupations and a new tone in his journal-writing:

It is my unalterable conviction that the infliction of unnecessary suffering, of suffering unprovoked and avoidable, is the one crime of which men may not be acquitted before the tribunal of reason. Sadism is the unforgivable offence. The Nazis, if we are to believe well authenticated reports, have unloosed the sadistic desires of a certain pathological type all too prevalent in the world, and by the legalising and giving free rein to numerous mobs of bullies, otherwise known as "Storm Troops", have started a veritable terror in Germany.

For this I can never forgive them. Whatever this movement may develop into in the future, I shall remember on what a bloody basis it stands, and I shall not admit that any real good can spring from such undeniable wrong.

Collecting continued to interest Dallas. In January 1934, at a New York auction, a young woman outbid him for a lock of George Washington's hair, presented by Washington to Mrs Alexander Hamilton.

I never suspected a rival in the shape of the lady sitting so quietly in front of me — the young lady in the necklace of flowers; with the cheap beret and the untidy coiffure. It was most provoking, I thought, to be conquered by a mere slip of a girl with untidy hair.

A little later he listed some ideas for his future as a collector:

Collections
1. Early American maps
2. Curious bibles
3. Literary relics

At about this time, he developed another of his lifelong enthusiasms. This was for John Keats. Dallas seems to have wished he could *be* Keats, or a re-incarnation of him. He read the poems, the letters, a life and several critical works on Keats. He imitated Keats in verses of his own, but then resolved:

to read modern poetry for a change. I am hopelessly out of touch with it, having been living in the past for so long. Keats in his letters is always referring to contemporary works which he has read — such as Byron's *Childe Harold* or Shelley's *Laon and Cythna*, and no doubt he could converse intelligently on them in company. How stupid it would have seemed if he had never read any of his great contemporaries — Wordsworth and Shelley and Scott for instance!

His main preoccupation at this time remained the question of his future career. Poetry?

I don't know why I feel so effervescent — this is a kind of spiritual New Year — reviving old desires and creating new ones. Here is one: to write a long poem in the old style (Keats perhaps).

Science?

Spring came to-day — two months too soon. As I walked to the laboratory and looked up at the clouds and the blue sky I felt the sap rising in me and new horizons opening ahead. I rebelled at the shackles of chill science, at the hours ahead of me in the work-room over my microscope.

February 5th 1934

Sometimes I think and think about the future until my mind is a slough of indecision. All the momentous problems to be faced and decided make me feel like a bent twig.

February 6th 1934

How I wish for the careless happy days I knew at Saint Paul's: "when every morning brought a noble chance."! They are gone forever, and college life has usurped their place. If college is indeed a foretaste of the world, it must be a bitter place towards which our faces are turned. There seems to be some blight in the air: the old joyousness, the outspoken criticism or commendation, the enthusiasm and the spirit is gone, and in the place of these comes suspicion and selfishness, unscrupulous competition or cynical apathy as the case may be. My friends are changed: most of them seek their own good and take me or leave me as I prosper or harm them in their desires, some few draw away and follow the rising stars, one or two stay by me, perhaps, but that atmosphere of ruthless competition is not to be escaped, and we all come under its influence to a greater or lesser degree.

To me the influence of Yale is harmful. I am non-competitive by nature, yet all around me there is competition, and sometimes I am envious of the success of others. I want the country again, the city with its noise and dirt and strong impassiveness is hateful to me. I want the smell of the earth after the rain, and the sounds of woodland, and the breadth of open fields. Here the eye grows weary, it cannot look into the hazy distance to the horizons, but always its view is blocked by the limitations of city streets and repulsive houses. What satanic instinct is it in man that impels him to imprison himself and his fellows in the small and sordid compass of a town?

There are many pages in this vein but, increasingly, he comes back to the same thought, "I might turn to the sciences — medicine probably." And again:

> May 20th 1933
>
> I'm suspicious of youths who decide prematurely on life careers. God knows, I've given more than enough thought to the question, and although I've at last reached a conclusion which seems inevitable which ever way you look at it, I refuse to call it final. Still, I can think of no career more satisfying and stimulating than that of a scientist.

As his second year at Yale came to an end, he seems to have made up his mind. For all that, science does not figure in this part of his journal. Instead, there are notes on the painters and sculptors of Florence under the Medici, commentaries on almost every Shakespeare play, and an outline of the reign of Queen Anne.

Dallas and his room–mate Alec Vietor had planned to explore the American Great Lakes together in the summer of 1934. Dallas was deeply upset when Alec Vietor decided against the trip. Little mention is made, in this part of the journal, of personal relationships but this disappointment triggered page after page on the subject of friendship, with literary quotations on the topic from Montaigne, Bacon, Theophrastus, Confucius and ending with the Bible's account of David and Jonathan.

To Dallas's great relief, Alec Vietor agreed to go on a different trip. At the beginning of July 1934 they were sailing together on a liner, the *City of Los Angeles*, from the West Coast of America to the South Pacific.

Tahiti, July 18, 1934

I read somewhere in O'Brien's *Mystic Islands of the South Seas* that Gauguin's house was next to the Ecole de Punaauia, whose wooden gateway bears the naif legend: 2 + 2 = 4. Alec and I stopped there this morning, and inquired of a native woman if the rather tumble-down native house in which she lived was the home of the painter. Yes it was, she replied in French, but showed us another nearby where he had lived for the main part. When we approached, a dark-skinned man with an enormous forehead and a fringe of grey white hair came out and greeted us in good but accented English. He said that his house was formerly Gauguin's, but that the studio was no more. "When I came here I was superstitious, and I burnt all the paintings and wood carvings he had left. The house was surrounded by wooden gods and other carvings". I asked if any paintings were burnt. "Oh yes, he left numerous panels that he had painted. A few things remained, which I sold for practically nothing. Some of the statues I used for targets, and some I threw into the lagoon. No, I don't think there would be any point in looking for them. It was twenty years ago — or thirty — that Gauguin left for the Marquesas. He died there — he was off his head at the end".

After three weeks on Tahiti, Dallas and Alec Vietor sailed on the RMS *Malucca* to New Zealand. There they spent a week of intensive sightseeing, organised by the government tourist bureau.

A genial and distinguished Spaniard, Senor de Amezua, who travelled out in the *City of Los Angeles* and stayed in Tahiti while we were there, joined us for the New Zealand jaunt.

Together, the three of them saw miles of grazing sheep, Maori dancing, and English-looking towns of stone-built houses. Both Dallas and Alec Vietor bought Maori carvings, each claiming his own as ancient and the other's a tourist-trade fake. Dallas recorded his impressions at length. A few brief extracts:

In New Zealand, that remote but highly civilised country, everyone drinks tea, and drinks it incessantly. The trains stop so frequently for refreshments, i.e. tea and sandwiches, that our trip assumed the aspect of a Mad Hatter's party. Around the refreshment table the New Zealanders throng, gallons of tea are consumed, then, a bell rings, and "move on, I want a fresh cup" is the cry. Before we know it, the train has stopped again for refreshments.

In New Zealand the food is uniformly good — oh! the rich cream and delectable desserts! — and the service equally excellent. The maids have stiffly starched dresses, which crackle as they walk, and always are spotlessly clean. Another thing that struck us in the dining-rooms was the amount of cutlery on the table. Knives, forks, and spoons for every dish imaginable tempted one to range widely through the extensive menus. A steak for breakfast became a commonplace for some of us before long.

The Maoris were originally cannibals, which seems strange when one sees how gentle a people they really are. But it is easily explained by the fact that before the coming of the whites, New Zealand had practically no wild life of any sort. Thus, for a balanced diet, it was necessary that cannibalism be practised.

The climax to our trip was undoubtedly the glow-worm cave at Waitomo, in which the guide directs by means of an invisible overhead wire. The cavern is quite dark except for the glow-worms attached to the roof. The first chamber is a revelation, but the second is beyond description. The spectacle has been compared to that of the Milky Way on a dark night but why compare it with anything? Sitting silently in that soft-gliding boat, seeing nothing but a million points of fire hung in the impenetrable blackness overhead, or the merest glimmer of daylight as we rounded the farthest bend — light that outlined with a delicate precision the shapes of ghostly stalactites, and lay on the surface of the water like a torn cloak of silver.

Dallas's journal does not mention that his second day in New Zealand was his twentieth birthday.

Chapter Four

1934–1944

Twenty to thirty

The South Seas trip with Alec Vietor continued with visits to several of the Samoan islands and to Fiji. Dallas was disappointed. He had not expected to see "gasoline buggies", corrugated iron roofs on houses and, worst of all, a small office building, even though "I daresay it is the only office building in the South Seas". Everything fell short of the expectations evoked by the magical place names. And it rained much of the time they were there.

Back at Yale for the third of his four years, he and several friends were appointed columnists on *Yale News*. August Heckscher was given *Bread and Circuses*, Dillon Ripley and Hugh Chisholm shared *The Play's the Thing*, and Dallas had *The Bookshelf*. He wrote lively notices of the books of the day, such as *National Velvet* by Enid Bagnold, *Claudius the God* by Robert Graves and *The Nature of Capitalist Crisis* by John Strachey. For example, his review of *The Primrose Path* by Ogden Nash begins:

> A poem by Ogden Nash is as shapeless as an amoeba,
> Being *vers libre*.

In March 1935 Dallas and Dillon Ripley made a trip to the Deep South, spending "two delightful days in Charleston on our way to the ornithological high spots of Florida". With Dillon Ripley again, on 21 August 1935, Dallas celebrated his twenty-first birthday at the Ripley family home at Litchfield, Connecticut. The day began with a housemaid bringing him piles of letters, parcels and telegrams to open in bed. From his mother's letter "out fluttered a cheque", Grandpa Benjamin's wire said "a handsome deposit of funds awaits you at the office". It came as no surprise to Dallas that the day ended with a "surprise party" of friends and family. In his journal he wrote:

> Last night I was a negligible quantity in the eyes of the law and of all man-made institutions, I thought, but this morning I am eligible to vote, to be cast into prison, to marry without parental consent, to make a will, to wage a law-suit, and to buy and sell property; furthermore I am the sole recipient and ruler of so many thousand dollars of income a year and (theoretically at least) I can now flout the family.

As well as the cheque, his mother's letter contained the news that Aubrey, then aged five, had been seriously ill. Dallas reports:

> It was not infantile paralysis, but something akin. Bloodshot eyes, fever, delirium, and for a few hours, a *dragging leg*, threw Carty and the nurse into a panic. Mamma came hot foot back from Baden-Baden, where she had been enjoying(?) a cure. Then everything but the blood-shot eyes disappeared and Aubrey is now almost as good as new.

The Cartwrights' marriage was over, though they were not formally divorced, on the grounds of her desertion, until five years later. Without an English husband, she no longer needed a big London house. Two stars of the London theatre, Jack Hulbert and his wife Cicely Courtneidge, bought 28 Curzon Street. After this, Dallas's mother's London base was a flat in Upper Brook Street.

When Dallas started at Yale, his New York home was still his Benjamin grandfather's apartment.

> On a wall of the dressing-room was one of the original plaster casts taken from Benjamin Haydon's famous life mask of Keats — Grandpa B. had bought it at the estate sale of Robert Louis Stevenson. When I started my own Keats collection in the 1930s, grandfather kept saying that someday he would give me the mask. For several years he tantalized me with this remark, but the gift never materialized. Finally when I was telling him about a Keats manuscript I had recently acquired from A. S. W. Rosenbach — 31 lines from the first draft of "I stood tip-toe upon a little hill" — he said, "I really *must* give you that mask." He went off on another tack but before he had finished the next sentence I marched into the dressing-room, lifted the mask from the wall, and with much feeling thanked him for the wonderful gift.

Dallas was beginning to learn how to stand up to his domineering grandfather.

Soon after this, Dallas's sister Cynthia, and her husband William Laughlin, gave him a room in their Manhattan apartment. It was his first New York home with his own generation, rather than parents or grandparents; a most convenient place to spend time in New York during his Yale years. The couple had their first child in 1934, a son whom they called William after his father. Dallas was always on friendly terms with his brother-in-law and nephew, but did not form a close bond with either of them, then or later. They scarely figure in the pages of his journal, nor of this biography. His sister Cynthia, on the other hand, and her second child, Linda, born in 1939, became ever more important to Dallas, and he to them.

If Dallas went abroad in the summer of 1935, he made no mention of it in his journal. After the account of his twenty-first birthday, it lapsed until the following February. He had many other claims on his time including, first and foremost, working for his degree. Soon he had to make a commitment about his future. More difficult still, he had to square it with his family.

In his article "Six American 'Princesses'", Dallas describes how, in the super-rich world of his birth, a man's role was clearly defined: for the older generation it was to work hard to make even more money. Dallas was subjected to the authority of this older generation in the person of his Benjamin grandfather who had long-since assumed the role of father to him.

In many ways William Evarts Benjamin was a most cultivated man, a collector of rare books and works of art, but in matters of money his attitudes were those of the world he had married into. As he saw it, however much wealth the family had accumulated in the past, it could never be enough. He regarded a Wall Street office as the only practical and socially acceptable place for a young man like Dallas. By his standards, compared to the noble calling of making money, a lifetime spent as a medical doctor was contemptible.

After many months of no journal writing, Dallas expanded on his career choices for page after page. The extract that follows recalls the early years of Franklin D. Roosevelt's presidency when many wealthy people, like Grandpa B, regarded him as "a traitor to his class", and felt threatened by his policies:

> February 8th 1936
> For the past year I have been living in a story-book atmos-phere. The situation consists in the choosing of my career,

the villain is Grandpa, the injured hero is myself. I am a bird in a gilded cage, bound with golden chains, surfeited with comfort, well nurtured and strongly protected, but denied the most excellent gift of freedom... You see how easily I can dramatise my problem!

I should like to review the difficulties and see why I am so concerned over what an old man, two generations removed from me, and mocked by the rest of the family for his selfishness, says about my choice of career, the one prerogative which is peculiarly and wholly mine — in theory at least.

1. He claims that it is my *duty* to care for the family fortune: my duty to him, to my mother, to my sister, to Aubrey and to myself.

2. He says that *in view of the present situation*, which seems to carry the seeds of a future levelling of classes and incomes, the fortune is threatened, and I must see what I can do to outwit the government in order to retain a modicum of money.

3. He says that *he is likely to die* at any time, and that the fortune would be in a frightful state, and might be swept away. If I am there, however, these things will not occur!

4. He particularly objects to *my going into medicine, and research*, in that he sees in this the possibility that I will isolate myself from the world, and become absorbed in specialisation to the exclusion of everything else.

5. He suggests as an alternative that I "*do not personally* go into research, but join a laboratory and *support several young men, guiding their research*".

My answers to his objections, and further arguments for my point of view, are as follows:

1. My first *duty* is to myself. I have one life to live, it is my own life, it is for me to live as I conceive I can live most

happily. I should take advice from my elders, but I should not force myself to enter upon a career which is hateful to me. If my family was destitute and really needed my help the case would be different, but as, on the contrary, it is enormously wealthy, I cannot see that my duty lies in that direction, particularly as the uses which my family makes of its money are essentially sterile and selfish.

2. If the government carries out a levelling of fortunes, I cannot prevent that levelling from affecting our own pile. Indeed, if such a trend can be discerned (and I believe it can be) it is imperative that I put myself in a position of being able to earn my own living if need be.

3. If he has arranged matters so badly, and has so complicated our affairs, that on the death of himself we are in danger of losing our fortune, he is severely to blame. I do not believe that such a situation really exists, since I have been assured by Grandpa himself that everything is in excellent control.

4. I have always maintained that I am not going into medical research with the idea of devoting myself exclusively to it. I have even said that after I have gotten started, I shall continue it as something of an avocation. I have never shown the slightest indication of being a born specialist. I have a wide range of interests, and probably take a more varied course than anyone else in the University. I do not look upon medicine as a collector looks upon his hobby, but am myself fascinated at the thought of personally engaging in it. For *selfish* reasons I wish to engage personally in the pursuit. If it comes to the point, as I suspect it will, where Grandpa offers generous support to research as long as I do not engage in it, or no support at all if I persist in participating myself, I must choose the latter, even though it would seem to show me more selfish than altruistic. But even if I did not

make such a choice, I would be doing right, I think, for the time will probably come in the future when I shall have money to promote research and have my own laboratory and assistants. How much better shall I be able to direct the enterprise then, when I am myself grounded in the essentials of the thing!

5. I am not a competitive person, and research offers me a career which is purely individual.

6. I am cynical of the essential value of most things in this world; the only thing which seems to me to be in the last analysis undoubtedly worthwhile is the relief of human suffering: the only knowledge which seems essentially important is knowledge of the human body and of its manifestations.

7. I am conscious of the injustice of the system under which we live, and while I am weak enough to continue to enjoy without protest the fruits of the inequalities of that system, I cannot pretend that I could spend my life working to increase these inequalities. I could do it, but I should be lacking in enthusiasm, and ashamed of myself for doing it.

8. I feel that I must justify my parasitical position by working for others.

9. I think that I should divert as much as I conveniently can to useful channels, seeing that the other members of my family seem determined to spend their share only for their own selfish comfort.

10. I have made my desires clear on this subject to so many people that I have pretty firmly committed myself. I can only go back on my intentions now with considerable loss of respect for my character.

11. If I give in, I shall know in my heart that I do so through cowardice. If I am a coward now when I am confronted with the first real battle of my life, I shall be a coward

henceforth and forever. Grandpa's attitude has virtually made it impossible for me to retreat.

12. I am enough of a bourgeois American to feel ashamed of being a man without a real career. I do not wish to spend my life explaining that I am really working, and not just cutting coupons and trying to evade the income tax.

13. I am of the opinion that wealth, although tending to control the owners of it, can be nevertheless subjected and made into a useful implement, whereby happiness and power may be secured. Wealth to me is an opportunity, not an obligation. If it imposes upon one's happiness, it should be cast away.

14. I personally revolt at the kind of life which should be mine if I entered Grandpa's office. It would be lacking in adventure, in interest, in even enough activity to fill the day. It would be an office life, which one would be condemned to spend in New York, poring over columns of figures and financial reports. And when one was through with it, it would not be easy to look back upon it and say, "that was a life well spent! I have lived nobly, and I leave the world a better place than I found it!"

In April 1936, seven friends who were fellow members with Dallas of the Phalanx Senior Society at Yale assessed each other. His fellow students were not in complete agreement about his "good traits". Five of the seven put "intelligence" top. But they were unanimous on his "bad traits". All seven put "Reserve" as number one. Had Dallas gone to school and university in England, his classmates there might well have rated his reserve amongst his good traits. There was an element of this reserve even in his journal writing:

This journal is myself talking to myself — "Myself coming home to myself". I must write in it only those things which are what I really think and believe. Only in this way can I straighten out my ideas on vital questions, and make the following pages valuable and interesting. In this connection, I resolve to write for myself alone — this, after all, is not for publication! The *whole* truth, and nothing but the truth. There is one side of me which I cannot reveal here, but with this one to-be-regretted exception I hope I shall be able to talk without reserve.

In the event, what he mostly wrote about at this period was his reading, and the thoughts that this provoked.

Dallas majored in English but, with medical school in mind, he also studied physics, chemistry, biology and mathematics, a far more demanding programme than most of his contemporaries. There can be no doubt that he did well, but how he did in each subject cannot be revealed until 2011. For reasons that it does not offer to explain, Yale University keeps secret the grades of former students, even if they are dead, for seventy-five years from the date of graduation.

His four years at Yale finished, Dallas took a year off from academic studies. He devoted the months from July 1936 to the summer of 1937 to travelling round the world. He went westwards, mostly on his own but accompanied for sections of the journey by one or another of his school and college friends. He started in the company of Ted Woolsey, sailing from the west coast of America to Hawaii, Honolulu and Japan. These places are scarcely mentioned in the journal. As they travelled, Dallas read and read, concentrating on philosophy, especially ethics, filling many pages of the journal with notes on Spinoza. He wrote, too, about Plato, Blake, D. H. Lawrence and, again and again, Keats.

In 1990, in his mid-seventies, remembering his 1936 visit to Japan, he wrote:

The reason that my journal entry on Japan was so brief was that I was disappointed with the place. I had arrived primed with Lafcadio Hearn's romantic descriptions, as in his *Glimpses of Unfamiliar Japan* (1894). Forty-two years later, when we were there, there were so many discordant notes, mainly the result of the eagerness of the Japanese to "westernize", that I couldn't overcome a feeling of disenchantment. However, the setting of many of the temples was unimaginably beautiful, especially Nikko and its cryptomerias. That I loved, and still remember with much appreciation.

Besides his reading, Dallas wrote about collecting. As he travelled he made many purchases. Again in 1990, he commented on this:

In Japan I was preoccupied with buying scroll paintings. These purchases represent the first fruits of my art collecting, which continued throughout my trip around the world, and included such treasures as a Coromandel screen, several Gandhara sculptures, a jade and gold cup, and two finely decorated boxes from Isphahan, a bronze image of "Buddha in the Lotus", and a Nepalese crystal and brass image of Shiva, which I bought in Srinagar.

After parting from Ted Woolsey in Japan on 12 August 1936, Dallas was on his own in Saigon in September, and the Bay of Bengal in October. In Srinagar he rented a houseboat for two weeks, cared for by a crew so numerous he never made out how many of them there were, but at least eight males and an indeterminate number of females. Dallas's quarters occupied the whole of the upper deck. The twenty or so crew shared the deck below.

On 3 November 1936 Dallas was speculating about the presidential election happening at that moment in America. He wrote at length about politics and economics, fearing the extremes of either capitalism or communism, and wondering if he might have to "give up the many advantages which accrue to me personally" under the present system.

The houseboat was towed by hand along the waterways to Nazim Bagh. Dallas enjoyed the beauty, peace and solitude as he read and wrote. He devoted eighteen pages to an ingenious analysis of Hamlet's "To be or not to be" soliloquy. In Dallas's interpretation, argued with determination and erudition, Hamlet is not considering suicide, weighing up "to be", meaning to live, against "not to be" meaning to take his own life. He is choosing between "to be" meaning to do nothing about Claudius and survive dishonourably, and "not to be" meaning to kill Claudius and be executed for the crime.

One of the many books he read on the journey was *Lalla Rookh*, the volume of oriental tales by the Irish poet Thomas Moore (1779–1852), who only knew the land from books.

I came on these lines:

"Though sunny the Lake of cool Cashmere
With its plane-tree Isle reflected clear —"

This fitted the picture perfectly: it was sunny, it was cool; and there, hardly a stone's throw away, was the actual "plane-tree Isle reflected clear". It would be fun to be able to read certain books and poems, which rely in a great measure for the effect on their setting, in that setting. I should like to read the first chapter of *Kim* sitting in the square before the museum at Lahore, or even on the big cannon which Kim used to bestride; *Life on the Mississippi* would make good reading on a Mississippi river-steamer, the more old fashioned the better; *Endymion* should be read on Mount Latmos; the first part of *Peter Pan* in Kensington Gardens; *Wuthering Heights* on the Yorkshire moors; Ainsworth's *The Tower of London*, of course, in the Tower (hair-raising experience!), Verne's *20,000 leagues under the Sea* in the bathysphere; and *The Specialist* in — !

The houseboat took him as far as Islamabad, where by night he slept on board and by day toured on horseback, accompanied by a guide and a "running footman". At Achibal the gardens seemed "more attractive than any I had seen… the fountains were turned on for my benefit. I next rode across country to see the ruins of Martaud, the largest temple in Kashmir", and at Bawan "some uninteresting caves". Pine woods at about 6,000 feet, near Bijbiara, reminded him of St Paul's or Aiken: "Imagine my surprise at having my illusion of being in the Adirondacks shattered by the appearance of a troop of yellow monkeys!" Dallas's two weeks in Kashmir ended with the return journey on the houseboat to Srinagar, enjoying superb views of distant snow.

At Kewsing he wrote about the circulation of money. At Nomchi, in a long essay on President Wilson, he tackled the questions of good and evil, and of whether ends justify means, with reference to America's participation, first, in World War I, as we now call it, and then in the League of Nations. His essay points out the irony of the League's slogan "to make the world safe for democracy" at a time when "the world is about as unsafe for democracy as it has *ever* been. Dictatorships in Germany, Italy, Russia, Greece, Turkey and, I suppose, by this time in Spain; a professed Socialist government in France, Fascist riots in the East End of London, Roosevelt labelled as the 'Kerensky of the American Revolution': surely these things — and many more of them deriving more or less directly from the War — cannot inspire Democracy with any great feeling of security". At Badantam on 2 December 1936, the news of Roosevelt's triumph (46 out of 48 states), pleased him because he believed that the nation's "principal problem is the existence of ten-million unemployed, whom Roosevelt would be likely to help". The electoral landslide also saddened him because "the decline and fall of the Republican party is an evil portent. Unhappy is the land whose opposition is meagre!" In Darjeeling, a visit to a Lama monastery inspired a thoughtful essay on Buddhism and Lamaism.

On 5th December 1936, he reached Cooch Behar, where he stayed for several days as the guest of the Maharani. She was a friend of Dallas's mother. Her home was "an Italian Renaissance palace set in the middle of jungles and native huts". Soon after she had welcomed Dallas, and he had been shown to his room:

> she came rushing to my door, brandishing *The Statesman*. "Have you seen the news?" she cried. It was the announcement of the proposed marriage of the King, with Mrs Simpson, an American divorcée with two living ex-husbands. Of course everyone had known that she was the present incumbent of the position formerly held by Mrs Dudley Ward and Lady Furness, but despite rumours which had come to the Maharani's ears (though not to mine) no one had imagined that the king wanted to *marry* the lady. Her Highness was filled with excitement and enthusiasm, and we bewailed in chorus the fact that we were not in London to read all the papers and listen to "what people were saying".

The young woman Dallas's mother first knew in California as Wallis Spencer, had achieved world-wide notoriety as Mrs Simpson.

Dallas had not yet given any serious thought to the cause of animal welfare and, when the Maharini suggested some big-game hunting, he looked forward to the excitement:

> A leopard shoot, or shikar, had been arranged for me in the afternoon, and immediately after lunch we started out in a bus. There were about ten of us. A shikar is only organised

after reports have come in during the morning that a leopard has been heard growling in such and such a locality, or has killed a goat or other domestic animal; whereupon the Maharajah or his family or guests organise a hunt in the afternoon. Thus it will be seen that compunctions over the sufferings of the leopard are foolish, as the beast is a decided menace to the farmers and their stock.

Dallas was mounted on an elephant with Mr Gupta, the aide-de-camp in charge of the palace. Beaters, also on elephants, drove the leopard towards them. Dallas, with some help from Mr Gupta, was the first to shoot the "fine big yellow beast", though somebody else delivered the fatal shot.

As it is the custom that the leopard belongs to whoever draws first blood, this particular animal is to come to me. He measured seven feet and three inches from tip to tail, and is considered a fine sized specimen. I enjoyed the hunt very much: the minute or so when one is standing up in the howdah with gun ready, while the noise of the beater elephants thundering through the jungle towards one and the shouts of their mahouts reach a crescendo, is exceedingly thrilling; and when the leopard himself suddenly glides into view among the grasses the excitement is almost paralysing!

Dinner was a rather formal affair, and the Maharani explained why she was not keen about the proposed Indian Federation, as States are represented by population. Cooch-Behar's half-million gives her too little influence when compared with such a state as Hyderabad-Berar, with a population of nearly eighteen million. Some states even have to share a deputy between them.

After dinner we played backgammon, to an accompaniment of the howling of jackals and the hooting of bats. The Maharani, with her Rue de la Paix jewels and her air of European elegance, lorgnette and long cigarette holder completing the picture, was a hundred miles apart from these naive and primitive natives, over whom she has exercised despotic power for so long. No matter how much time she may spend doing the fashionable things in London and Paris, she must come back in the end to Cooch Behar. And despite her seeming apartness, despite the foreign style in which she lives, there are bonds to her native land which she cannot or will not break. After dinner, for instance, she excused herself with the announcement "I must go and say my prayers"! Tomorrow she is going to observe an all-day fast, a religious requirement which she as a widow is expected to carry out. "So enervating, don't you know, but so good for the figure".

Dec. 7. 1936

Her son, the Maharaja, arrived this morning from Calcutta, where he has been playing cricket. I found him very hard to talk to. He had three topics of conversation: horse-racing, polo and cricket. I have absolutely nothing to say on any of these subjects.

He is a bulkily built young man, with a decided tendency to a double chin. He speaks flawless English, with no accent; this he owes to five years at Harrow and one at Cambridge. He is quite unaffected, still has something of the schoolboy's shyness, but has perfect manners. He is just twenty-one, having been installed as *reigning* Maharaja only this year. He has been Maharaja, however, since 1922, when his father died, and during his minority his mother has been regent. Now that her son has reached his majority, she must retire into the background, but she seems to be taking her time about it. While I was staying at the palace it was she, rather than the Maharaja, who was studying the files relative to the coming Federation, and I noticed that the red lantern, on the top-most pinnacle of the palace, which is supposed to indicate the presence of the *reigning* prince in Cooch Behar, was kept lighted even when the Maharani was in residence alone.

As he left the subcontinent, Dallas listed his purchases in Indo-China and India, mostly statuettes of Buddha and Hindu divinities, as well as some pieces of ancient jewellery and "a coat made of Pashmina (wool from Tibetan goats)".

Writing essays on Communism, Hinduism, Buddhism and, again and again, Keats, Dallas travelled on through Persia. A college friend, Henry Wolcott, joined him for part of this journey. Bushire "seemed a horrible place", Shiraz "was disappointing", but at Persepolis the decorative bas reliefs "surpassed anything I have ever seen of antiquity, with the single exception of the Parthenon frieze". Dallas decided to make a side trip to Isphahan but it had to be without Henry Wolcott who could neither afford it nor agree to be subsidised by Dallas, who suspected:

> he probably wants to get rid of me. There's no denying the fact that we're completely different types, and my "Continental Patina" is no doubt as irksome to him as his "100% Americanism", Buffalo, New York variety, is to me. But despite all, he's a very good sort, though too easily upset and discouraged to be a good traveller — O that *rara avis*!
>
> I arrived at Isphahan towards sunset. It has three of the most beautiful buildings in the world: the Sheikh Lotfollah, the Madresseyeh Chahar Bagh, and the Shah's mosque. These mosques are completely covered, within and without, with enamelled bricks in blue, yellow, and green. The bricks fit together to make elaborate arabesque designs, and the effect is surprisingly beautiful. I am now going out to see how the Madresseyeh mosque looks under the full moon.

As Dallas travelled, he wrote in similar vein about Teheran, Jerusalem and Bethlehem. His descriptions can only make a modern reader envy him seeing all these places as they were in the

1930s. On 23 February 1937, he was in Cairo. His thoughts turned once more to his position in the world, and his future. This, again much abridged, is what he wrote:

> I have the instincts of an artist, but I lack the ability. I have a strong creative urge, and a sharp mind — but these are not enough.
>
> First and foremost, I have tried literature. Poetry and prose. Despite what some (whose affection outshines their discrimination) say, I shall never be good enough as a writer to satisfy myself. Unfortunately, I am too good a critic to delude myself on that score.
>
> As a critic, perhaps, I could succeed. But literary criticism is not creative enough.
>
> There is music, of which I am very fond. I have taken piano lessons for years, I have tried the flute, the drum, the recorder, and the mandolin-banjo, but I am still unable to play a note. My friends tell me I can't sing — I think they exaggerate, but I shall certainly never tread the boards of the Metropolitan!
>
> Painting and sculpture I appreciate profoundly, but the sad truth is that I can't even draw.
>
> There are other modes of creation, beside those included in the field of art. Most people, especially women, create a family, and find this sufficiently rewarding. But this is impossible for me. There is the creation of a fortune. In my case this would be something of an attempt to pile Pelion on Ossa.
>
> I have tried acting and public speaking: both lead to creative spheres. But the theatre does not seem significant enough nowadays to devote one's life to, and as an actor, as has become apparent to me at school and college, my success has always been due to my power, such as it is, of interpretation, of treating a part with subtlety and intelligence, but not with creative genius. And as for public

speaking, as a preliminary to public life: my whole nature is a solitary independent one — I could never associate with or influence other people to the degree demanded of the politician.

There remains the study of economics, of history, or of the law. The first two appeal to me, the last does not. But in these cases, the work is analytical again, and by no means creative.

I have pretty nearly eliminated everything, and it begins to seem as if I am to remain permanently unsatisfied, seeing that I *can't* do anything really creative well enough to satisfy myself, and I *won't* do anything which is chiefly interpretative. I think, however, that I have discovered a line of activity which suits my type of mind but which is also creative. I mean medical research. Now in this, it cannot be denied that the actual work to be done is chiefly analytical and synthetical, but the results, obviously, are neither destructive, like bad criticism, nor conservative, like Grandpa's brand of finance, but are actually creative, and immediately so. For the medical sciences are so closely knit that an apparently insignificant discovery in the realm of veterinary medicine, such as Pasteur's, can change our whole conception of disease and profoundly affect and benefit mankind. Science seems especially designed for such people as myself: it is the short cut to creative expression.

He wrote appreciatively about Luxor and Memphis in both prose and verse. By the end of March he was in Rome, and back in familiar company. His school and college friend Hugh Chisholm was spending his Easter vacation there from Cambridge University, where he was doing two years of postgraduate study at King's College. Dallas's mother was also in Rome. So was Natalie Coe. From the age of seven to ten, Dallas, along with his sister Cynthia and their governess Dear, had been a frequent guest at the Coe's Planting Fields estate at Oyster Bay, Long Island, and once at the Coe's Wyoming ranch. In 1934, aged twenty, Dallas visited Planting Fields again, for Natalie Coe's wedding, conducted by the Papal Nuncio. She married Leonardo Vitetti, an Italian politician. "Leonardo, a cultivated and ambitious man, shot like a meteor to the position of President of the Council, and right-hand man to Ciano". Ciano was, in turn, right-hand man to Mussolini and married il Duce's daughter Edda, after which Mussolini elevated both Ciano and Vitetti to the nobility as counts. "Natalie was transformed from the frumpish hoyden of Planting Fields into a Roman countess, glittering in the splendid setting of Palazzo Orsini (where their apartment was). With her money and his brains, all doors were open to them".

Dallas escorted his mother to an evening reception given by the Vitettis. "All Rome" was there: the Queen of Spain and her daughters, the Infantas Beatriz and Christina, "these girls were the first royalty with whom I have felt perfectly at my ease", Prince Christopher and Princess Marie of Greece, Princess Juliana and Prince Bernhard of the Netherlands "just returned from their Indonesian honeymoon", the Duchess of Sermetta, the Duke of Alba, the Duchess of Westminster and the Duke and Duchess of Melitto. The rest of Natalie Vitetti's extraordinary story, is told in Dallas's article, "Six American 'Princesses' ".

While in Rome, on 2 April 1937, Dallas attended the Easter Pontifical High Mass at St Peter's:

> Hugh and I arrived at the church at 9 o'clock, both of us feeling very odd in tails and white ties (mine had been borrowed from the head waiter at the Grand!). Natalie had secured two seats for us in the Diplomatic Tribune, on the left of the Papal Throne. Most of us in the congregation had at one time or another during the last few months given up

this man for dead, and to see him once more performing his wonted duties with apparently unimpaired energy was like watching someone resurrected from the dead. As he slowly approached, borne by twenty-four chairmen clad in costumes made of traditional red damask, and followed by the two beautiful fans of white ostrich plumes, the mind was stunned by the grandeur of the scene, perhaps the most dramatic and the most awe-inspiring that the fertile mind of human beings has ever been able to conceive.

The service began with an impressive paying of respects to His Holiness by the cardinals. Each one in turn swept up to the throne, scarlet train trailing far behind, bowed to the Pope, kissed the ring *through* the vestments, bowed again to the Pope, bowed to the cardinal on the left of the throne, then to the one on the right, then turned, and received his train over one arm in a huge bundle hastily collected by an attendant ecclesiastic, and proceeded back to his place. I was amused to see how everyone from the Pope down was completely under the thumb of the Master of Ceremonies, who stood to the left of the Pope's throne, and directed by gesture the cardinals' manoeuvres: indicating when they should cease to advance, when kneel, when rise. This personage even instructed the Pope when to bless the congregation, and the Pontiff meekly obeyed his Master of Ceremonies' whispered commands.

Fascism and the Papacy, however little they appealed to Dallas, provided spectacle. But for him the significance of Rome lay in its Keats connections. The house on the Spanish steps in which the poet died in 1821 was opened as the Keats Shelley Memorial House in 1909. In 1937 Dallas met its young director Vera Signorelli and they became lifelong friends.

By then Dallas had been travelling for nine months, taking in the sights and customs of a dozen countries, as well as doing a lot of reading, writing and thinking. Now he was about to become a participant in life as well as merely an observer. It seems as if in some way he anticipated the transformation of his existence. He completed one volume of his journal at about this time and started a new one. On the title page of volume four he put a quotation from Milton's *Comus*: "How charming is divine philosophy!" Predicting what was soon to happen, he began volume five with the final words of Keats's *Ode to Psyche*:

> "A bright torch and a casement ope at night
> To let the warm Love in!"

Love had so far played no part in the self-portrait Dallas sketched in his journal. Apart from his sister Cynthia and some of her friends, all of them scarcely more than acquaintances, the people he spent his time with were male, mostly the little group who had come through school and university with him. In his journal, such feelings as he had for his own gender are implied rather than explicitly described: the intensity of his disappointment in 1934 when his Yale room-mate Alec Vietor called off their tour of the Great Lakes; a lyrical description of a blue-eyed, fair haired boy diving for coins in the Persian Gulf who reminded him of Kipling's Kim; his response to the Greek red-figure vases at Ancona; the reference, written many years later, to his mother's Adonis of a footman whom Dallas "worshipped from afar". All of these seem to belong to "the one side of me which I cannot reveal". He can hardly be criticised for his discretion at a time when departure from the norm was generally regarded as abhorrent and was also criminal. There is no reference throughout his journal to any intimate relationship with a woman, let alone any thought of engagement or marriage, nor to any pressure from his grandfather to follow his example and marry an heiress. But now, near the end of his round-the-world trip, his feelings were to come out into the open. During his first week in England, he met John Judkyn, an event that completely transformed his life.

Yet the journal makes no mention of their first encounter. The name John Judkyn appears for the first time in an entry dated 19 April 1937, in a list of some fifty people Dallas had met in the week since his arrival in England. It must have been a crowded week as, during it, Dallas was with Lord and Lady Sackville at Knole, several members of the Howard family at Castle Howard, as well as inspecting Keats manuscripts in the British Museum library, and visiting Grasmere in the Lake District.

He met John Judkyn through Hugh Chisholm. Dallas visited him in Cambridge and, in his rooms there, met several young men who were exactly the sort his stepfather Carty feared he might encounter at Oxford but believed did not exist in Cambridge. They included Michael Pitt-Rivers, Charles Fletcher-Cooke, Robin Maugham and John Judkyn. Many years later, the first three of these men, whom Dallas seems to have met just this once, each made sensational headlines in the London newspapers as a result of their involvement with young men. In 1953 Michael Pitt-Rivers was sent to prison, in a blaze of publicity, one of the three men convicted in the Lord Montagu trials. In 1963 Charles Fletcher-Cooke's rapid rise in British politics came to an abrupt end when he let a young man, with no driving licence and no motor insurance, drive his car — and crash it. The young man, who had a criminal record, had been introduced to him by Robin Maugham. The newspapers made so much of the incident that Charles Fletcher-Cooke resigned his ministerial post and was never offered one again.

All this was well before the start of some degree of tolerance and acceptance following changes in the law in 1967. When

Dallas met these well-to-do former public school boys in 1937, amongst the brightest of their generation, they had to conceal their true nature or risk, at the least, blighted careers or, at worst, imprisonment. They presented themselves to the outside world as the essence of respectability.

The subjects covered in the journal for this period are far removed from the personal. Dallas wrote in May 1937 at some length on Zionism and Buddhism, and on Keats and Blake, as well as notes on some early sixteenth-century maps he bought at Maggs, and a recipe for Crème Vichyssoise. The only hint that his friendship with John Judkyn was progressing comes in another, supplementary list, made on 23 June 1937, of people Dallas met in London and Paris, which includes John's mother, who was called Mrs Herbert Judkins. John had adopted an ancient spelling of his family's surname while he was in his teens. This may have been simply from a love of the antique, or perhaps to assert that he was different from his relatives.

Any details of the meeting of Dallas and John would not have been recorded at all, except that near the end of Dallas's life, when he was on what he seemed to know was the last of his many yearly visits to Ben Duncan and myself, Dick Chapman, in our house near Cambridge, we drove past Newnham Terrace, a row of pleasant old houses near the colleges. Dallas pointed to No.3 and said, "I first met John Judkyn in Hugh Chisholm's rooms in that house". He then described the circumstances with some intensity, as if he wanted what he said to be remembered.

They had met there that day, in May 1937, and arranged to meet the following weekend. John worked for an antique furniture dealer in Mayfair and was about to make a business trip to Salisbury and Broadway. He suggested Dallas accompany him. Dallas, mistakenly thinking John's plan was that they spend the night together, arrived at John's flat with a suitcase. John saw it, said nothing about it, but excused himself for a moment, and reappeared with his own overnight bag. This, Dallas explained to us, was an example of John's tact and niceness. John had recognised in an instant that Dallas was eager to embark on an intimate relationship, and that it was what he wanted too. They stayed in Salisbury and returned to London the next day as a committed couple.

Three months later, on 21 August 1937, Dallas's twenty-third birthday, John commemorated their trip by giving Dallas an eighteenth-century engraving of Salisbury. On the back of it John pasted what looks like a Victorian valentine. It reads:

> *TO ONE I LOVE*
> Thou may doubt there is a sun above
>   Or doubt there is a sky,
> But doubt not, dear, that I do love,
>   With true sincerity,
> And when my love for thee shall cool,
>   Or sense shall from me part,
> Twill only be when death shall rule
>   And still shall be my heart.

Many years later Dallas added one word to this: "Prophetic…"

In the more tolerant days of the early twenty-first century it is hard to appreciate quite what a courageous step the young Dallas and John were taking. Looking back in the 1980s to the time when he "had met John and we had agreed to 'Marry'", Dallas thought about how they had "defied convention" and wondered if this might in part be attributed to lessons learnt from "my mother's defiance of convention — divorce, marriage to two 'playboys', friendship with nightclub entertainers, and with gay young men, etc. Especially the last!" He might also have mentioned the toughening process of learning to stand up to his grandfather.

It seems that Dallas's mother soon came to terms with John as a member of her family. Similarly, John's mother accepted Dallas. In their different ways, they were both characterful women, not ruled by the conventions of their time. Perhaps, too, at some level, each of them was glad to be spared having a daughter-in-law. It is hard to picture Dallas's mother being at ease with one. John's mother got on badly with the only one she had, the wife of John's older brother Myrton.

John and Dallas shared many interests and enthusiasms, in particular humane causes and the decorative arts. But as individuals they were complementary rather than similar. Dallas was highly educated. He spent years of his life studying philosophy, history and religions and, as he put it, "thinking deeply". Dallas was a perpetual reader. He claimed that he had never known John look at a book but that John had an extraordinary gift for absorbing knowledge without reading and knew more than Dallas about most subjects. Dallas was analytical and a non-believer. John was instinctive and religious. He was an active member of the Society of Friends. John had many of the qualities generally associated with the Quakers, such as hard work, a questioning of established truths, a readiness to stand up for unpopular opinions, a highly developed sense of individualism, and a disregard for ostentatious display. Yet the simplicity he appreciated was not that of plain living and high thinking; it was the very different simplicity that belongs to the ultimate degree of style and comfort.

John had a set of simple precepts, formed by intuition, by which he lived and which he liked to recommend to others. Dallas called them "John's *Dos* and *Don'ts*", and they ranged from the trivial to the serious. For example, he said that when you visit anyone you should always park facing outwards. If the visit goes well, this spares encumbering your farewells with awkward reversing and manoeuvring, and if things go badly you can make a speedy exit. He had no time for self-martyrdom. "Don't suffer in silence" and "Don't be a drudge" were two of his maxims for himself and others. Another was "If you don't know, keep your mouth shut". He believed that if you could afford it you should employ help. He liked to have a secretary and an assistant and, in any establishment he was running, housemaids, a cook and a butler. Dallas, who grew up with too many servants liked to do things for himself. John eager for a long life and not to damage his arteries, ate margarine instead of butter long before this became at all general, though he did not impose this on his guests.

John, born in 1913, was about a year older than Dallas. He attended Repton School from 1927 to 1931 and left early because of ill health. The exact nature of his illness is not on any record that I have been able to find but it was serious enough to end his schooling and any thought of university. It was said to be rheumatic and to affect his back. During the years I knew him, he wore a support around his abdomen, sat and moved rather stiffly, and seemed some of the time to be in pain. This he did suffer in silence, and it may account for the stiff posture and set facial expression he shows in photographs, quite unlike the warm, cosy, bubbly and joky person his few surviving friends remember.

After leaving school, he went to live for about a year in Paris with Cunynghame relatives, that is, from his mother's side of the family. Many years later, Dallas wrote:

> In Paris, his interest in decorative arts first manifested itself. He studied at the Ecole des Beaux Arts, and worked for a time with the distinguished interior designer, Monsieur Boudin. Returning to London, he worked for several years

with Acton, Surgey, a firm which specialised in furniture
and artefacts of the Gothic and Elizabethan periods, bringing John into contact with such clients as William Randolph
Hearst. Another formative influence in the 1930s was his
friend Sir Philip Sassoon. Sassoon was accustomed to stage
annual exhibitions, drawn from his own collections, at his
Park Lane, London residence, and John helped with the
cataloguing and arranging of several of these.

No one in John's immediate family was particularly
interested in collecting antiques or objects of art, although
the family was affluent for generations through ownership of
land in Northamptonshire and of a rich granite quarry,
developed under the corporate name of Judkins Limited, in
Nuneaton. His mother, née Florence Cunynghame, was the
descendant of a Scottish baronet, and his great-uncle by
marriage was the benefactor of Dublin's National Gallery,
Hugh Lane (drowned in the sinking of the *Lusitania* in
1915).

In 1937, when John and I met, he had not yet visited the
US, but wanted to, and after we became friends we agreed
to share an apartment in New York. He already had some
close friends among Anglo-American families in England:
Eshers, Camoys, Lebuses, Gainsboroughs and others. Having
secured a job with Stair and Andrew, London dealers
specialising in antique eighteenth-century English furniture,
he arrived in New York in the fall of 1937 and went to
work in their gallery on East 57th Street.

Before long he had made a contact with the Cooper
Hewitt Museum, where, as a volunteer, he undertook to
"vet" this collection and prepare an informal catalogue.

While still in England, John had started to form his own
first collection of antiques. There were soon enough largely
to furnish the residence known as The Bishop's House, at
Henley-on-Thames, which he and his mother acquired in
the mid 1930s. He also started to deal in a small way, at one

time sharing a small shop with Jane (Mrs Charles) Toller, in St. Christopher's Place, London.

John used to say, semi-jokingly, that he had been converted to Quakerism by the Archbishop of Canterbury. The Archbishop was Geoffrey Fisher, Headmaster of Repton School while John was there. After John's death, writing to a friend who was preparing some biographical notes about John, the Archbishop (by that time retired, with the peerage of Fisher of Lambeth) had this to say:

"I knew him well but, if I may say so, on the narrow front of casual conversations, while he was at school, and once or twice after he had left. My impression of him is absolutely clear. He won my great affection and my deep respect. I cannot recall much about his parents but he had an elder brother who was a typical public school boy, something of an athlete and with all the somewhat commonplace interests of the ordinary public school boy. John was quite different: where his elder brother was obvious John was original and one could not talk to him without realising at once that the main spring of his life and interest was hidden, as St Paul says, 'in Christ', and more obviously hidden too in subtle spiritual and aesthetic enthusiasms.

"It is less easy to talk about that part of his life which was hidden in Christ. I have a recollection that he talked to me at one time about ordination: and I think I remember that I told him that his religious experience was too diffuse to be fitted into the channel of ordination and clerical ministry. I think any thought of a channel was really uncongenial to him, and the fact that he became a Quaker was really the right thing for him. For the Quakers live in the spirit

105

in a freedom which is unfettered, wherein lies both their strength and their weakness."

The conversation about ordination took place in the mid 1930s, when Fisher was Bishop of Chester; he became Archbishop in 1945. As a result of his suggestion, John attended several Quaker meetings in England, then joined the New York Society of Friends. John enthusiastically entered into strengthening the links between the American Friends Service Committee in Philadelphia and Friends House in London.

By 29 June 1937, ten weeks after meeting John, Dallas was on board the *Berengaria* en route for New York, knowing that John would soon join him there. This crossing completed the voyage around the world he had started the previous July. The few pages he wrote in his journal during the crossing, and in New York before John's arrival, are filled with thoughts on Keats, on philosophical questions of good and evil, as well as riddles, puzzles and jokes. Then not another word until the following May: no mention of his experiences as a first-year medical student at Columbia College of Physicians and Surgeons, nor of his family's response to his choice of a medical career; nothing about John's arrival, nor his family's response to that. Perhaps he had given up his ambition to be a writer and no longer felt the need to work on his style. Perhaps with the demands of his medical studies, and with John for company, he had neither time nor inclination for journal writing. Perhaps for the first time since his early teens, he was more engaged with life than letters. By the end of 1937, Dallas and John were sharing an apartment of their own in mid-town Manhattan.

At the end of the academic year, Dallas again set sail for Europe. Once again, he was thinking about his future, and at enormous length. The following passages are much abridged.

I have finished the first year of medical school. The work has been difficult, but not repugnant, some of it has been interesting, much of it has not. I feel that under the circumstances I have chosen wisely and I am determined to go on with it. I am not too sure, however, whether I wish to take up medical research when I am through with my formal education.

Just as I have never wished to practice medicine, so now I do not feel that I wish to devote my life to medical research, whose tools are the test tube and the microscope.

What I have consistently left out of the scheme of things, of course, is the mind. After four years I should have sufficient comprehension of the body to be able to pass on to the mind. Because psychology is somewhat in dispute among medical men is no reason for shying away from it, nor because it is the most intricate and difficult of the medical sciences.

The chief appeal of psychology is its midway position between the materialist world as represented by the body, and the spiritual world as represented by the spirit. By spirit I do not mean soul, but any manifestation of life which seems not to be readily explained by the ordinary laws of the material world, but which appears nevertheless in all the multitudinous activities of the human race. Philosophy I take to be the science of the spirit, and if psychology one day leads to philosophy, as I perceive that medicine will lead to psychology, then so much the better. Certainly I can conceive of no greater training for a philosopher than that which leads from medicine through psychology.

In June he was again in Germany, once more recording his revulsion at the rise of Nazism. He had read Stephen Roberts's book *The House that Hitler Built* (1937) and made extensive notes on it in his journal. Now he actually saw Hitler. He took a snapshot of the Führer riding in an open car, arm raised in a salute to the immense cheering crowd. But Dallas was in Germany to study rococo churches, not politics.

In England in July, 1938 he was joined for a time by John. Together they visited the Scottish ship owner and art collector Sir William Burrell and his wife at their castle in Northumberland, which John was helping them to furnish. Later in the summer, in Antibes with his relentlessly social mother, Dallas listed some eighty people he met there, including the Duke and Duchess of Windsor, formerly King Edward VIII and Mrs Simpson, who had married the previous year. In August 1938, Dallas went with his mother to visit the Windsors who had rented Château de la Croë, close to his mother's Casa Estella. Speaking about it in later years, Dallas recalled how puzzled he was by the intense interest the Duke seemed to show in his medical studies, before realising that, for the Duke, asking questions of this sort was the only conversation he could possibly make with a young man from outside his circle. Six months later Dallas wrote a detailed account of the visit in his journal describing what everybody was wearing and what everybody did and said. For example:

> As we knew the Duke demanded "royal honors" for the Duchess, Mamma had decided that she would curtsey to her, since we had rather put ourselves into their hands by accepting an invitation from them. So Mamma made a little bob as she shook hands with the Duchess, but the two addressed each other by their first names. I bowed when shaking hands. To the Duke Mamma made a deep curtsey,

and the difference between this and the first one, which was rather obvious, made me feel better!

The social niceties at work here are almost impenetrable now, but clearly Dallas approved of his mother's decision not to make too much of the Duchess who was, after all, just another American divorcée like herself.

Apart from this, Dallas wrote little in his journal during his second year at Columbia Medical School: notes on Chinese porcelain and European medieval art; an extremely hostile account of a speech at the Union Club in New York by the reactionary Texas congressman Martin Dies, Jr. who had recently become the founding chairman of the House committee investigating "un-American" activities; and his first detailed notes on early American interiors. Descriptions of stair-rail designs, stencilled walls, and tiles seen in Marblehead and Salem in January 1939 mark the early stages of his and, no doubt John's, interest in American decorative arts. But notes on medical matters fill most of the pages.

In the summer of 1939, Dallas and John rented St Briavels castle in Gloucestershire as a place where they could enjoy the English and Welsh countryside and the company of their friends. John went to St Briavels before Dallas, who stayed at his mother's flat in Upper Brook Street and, on 6 July 1939, attended a debutante dance at Holland House. This occasion later became famous as the last great social event in London before the start of World War II.

> On Sunday, August 20, I was at St Briavels, entertaining a week-end party consisting of John, Jane and McClure Howland, Peter Carter, and Peggy Wagner. We were very much disturbed by the morning papers — not by any news so much as by the editorials, which in the *Observer* and

Sunday Times (two most sedate and non-alarmist papers) were extremely grave, and announced that the long expected crisis was upon us. If war was to be the outcome it might well break out before our sailing date of September 7. If this were to happen there was a good chance that John might be prevented from sailing; so it seemed imperative for us to book an earlier sailing.

Dallas and John packed in haste as soon as their guests were gone. They left St Briavels at 5.30 the next morning and drove to London, where they managed to book a cabin on the *Veendam*, sailing on August 26.

We found that we were one jump ahead of the general panic, which did not begin until later, after which the steamship offices were perpetually crammed with people and no accommodation whatever was to be had on any boat sailing for America. I telephoned Mamma in Antibes on the Monday, and warned her of the seriousness of the situation, but she said that she would not consider sailing until her affairs were settled and the situation had taken a very decided turn for the worse. I said that if Mamma wished we would take Aubrey in our cabin. But his father decided against this plan.

A tremendous number of Americans boarded the boat, for by now people had begun to realise how serious the situation really was. We began our transatlantic adventure with some 850 passengers, many of whom had to sleep on improvised cots — in the officers' rooms, the cocktail bar, and even on planks laid between the running-boards of automobiles.

As we sailed westward, the news bulletins became more and more alarming. Finally on September 3rd came the declaration of war, following Hitler's invasion of Poland and seizure of Danzig. We heard of the sinking of the *Athenia*, but being a neutral ship we took no precautions ourselves, and steamed safely into New York on September 6th, much to the relief of all, and especially of the German-Jewish refugees, of whom there were a great number on board.

John had lived in America for two years by then but, even if he had stayed in England, he would not have had to join the fighting services, both because of his bad back and because Quakers were recognised as conscientious objectors. He joined the New York Quaker Relief Organisation as a volunteer and worked with them until after the war ended.

Dallas was half-way through his training at Columbia's medical school, where he was doing well for somebody so new to science. He averaged 81.5% grades during his four years there, with consistent B grades in Psychiatry. His only A was in Public Health, in which he wrote a detailed proposal for a "Parents' Night Clinic", an institution for "the instruction of parents in the psychology and upbringing of children". His studies displaced his journal writing. Such pages as there are contain jottings on psychiatry; notes on his dreams (Dallas meets John Keats, they pick wild flowers together); and Rorschach analyses of himself and fellow students. They practised their analytical skills on one another, writing lengthy studies of their personalities. Yet, even amongst these people, any question of sexual abnormality would appear to have been so dreadful as to be unmentionable. Photographs show Dallas as a handsome young man but he wrote this about his looks:

> Notes on photographs of myself —
> My left jaw has a peculiar bulge, so that it must not be shown either in profile (head turned to left) or full face. The head should always be turned to right, so that the left jaw is seen more or less full on. Chin should not be tilted down, as this always gives impression of double chin, and adds about

ten years to one's age. It is much better to look directly at camera. Serious is better than smiling, because of assymetry of mouth.

Also some self-analysis:

> That I am afraid to stand on my own feet is true. This is born out by my shyness in groups, my fear of speaking out or upholding my own opinions.

A colleague described how he appeared not exactly awkward but quaint: "By quaint I mean that when carrying a package you look like a little boy with a Christmas present, and when bored you look like the same little boy lost in a snow storm. Hoping to be forgiven, I am, yours very sincerely, Anne Tarnay."

Dallas glanced back to his early childhood:

> My desolate afternoons at school, when I wandered around alone and felt lonely and rejected. I have disliked the afternoons ever since.
> The final rejection is by Mamma. It was not Dear who preferred her to Daddy, it was I as a small child. But she rejected me.

These are the harshest words on his mother in any of Dallas's writings.

The start of the war separated Dallas even further from the lives of his mother, his half-brother Aubrey, and from Aubrey's father, Carty. Dallas's mother was at the Casa Estella on 3 September 1939 when England and France declared war on Germany. She stayed there for another six weeks, spent part of the winter at Nassau in the Bahamas, and was in New York in February 1940 when her father died there. After his death she still had her troubles but they no longer included any lack of money. Nor was there anybody who could prevent her marrying.

Aubrey, nine years old when the war started, was at Summer Fields, a preparatory school in Oxford for boys going on to Eton. As a Ward of Court he was, officially, the responsibility of his legal guardian. He spent his school holidays with Cartwright relatives. His parents' divorce was decreed absolute within a week of the beginning of the war. At the same time, his father rejoined the navy, with his old rank of Captain. A few months later, in May 1940, he was sent to lead a land reconnaissance mission in Holland. The vehicle he was in was ambushed, and he and the Dutch soldier who was driving him were both killed. Whether Aubrey was told of his father's death by his legal guardian, or his headmaster, or an aunt is not recorded. His mother applied to the English courts of law to have Aubrey released into her care but was refused. Mother and son had scarcely seen each other for four years. The war was now to separate them for another four.

In the same month that her third husband was killed, she married husband number four. In March 1940, six months into the war, she returned to France and embarked on this, her final, briefest and most ill-judged marriage. Her new husband was the Australian socialite, playboy and bobsleigh champion Frederick J. McEvoy. He was known variously as Freddy, Freddie or, because of his great strength and piercing blue eyes, Tiger. His closest friend was Errol Flynn, the Tasmanian film star and adventurer, who was then at the peak of his fame. Freddy was best man at the last of Flynn's three marriages. This was the one in which, at the wedding reception, the bridegroom was served with an arrest warrant on a charge of statutory rape.

When Beatrice Benjamin Cartwright married Freddy McEvoy she was in her early fifties, nearly twenty years older than he was, three times divorced, and twice a grandmother. After their wedding in Paris, the McEvoys travelled to Antibes to spend yet another summer at the Casa Estella, despite the war. As Denmark, Norway, the Netherlands and Belgium fell to the Germans, as "the Battle of France" was fought in the northern regions of the country, as the little boats evacuated the British soldiers from Dunkirk, and Italy entered the war, even after France signed an armistice with Germany, Beatrice and Freddy McEvoy stayed on at the Casa Estella. Under the terms of the armistice, the southern part of France was not yet occupied by the Germans. Only in October 1940, when "the season" was over, did they go, via Lisbon, to New York where they settled in an apartment at the Waldorf Astoria. The Casa Estella was unoccupied for the remainder of the war.

In August 1940, when he had just completed his second year at Columbia's medical school, Dallas wrote a long piece in his journal on the progress of the war in Europe and the possible menace from Japan, including this mistaken prophecy:

> It seems unlikely that Japan would care at this time to risk war with the United States. We are probably safe in the Pacific.

He kept up with world affairs and also read about philosophy and psychology, and made notes on Emerson, Bertrand Russell, Aldous Huxley, Freud and Jung.

Dallas and John searched for a country property where they could escape from New York at weekends. In November 1940 they tried, but failed, to buy an old farmhouse with 300 acres in the East Canaan Valley in Connecticut, where many of Dallas's Pratt ancestors had lived.

Dallas graduated from Columbia in June 1941. That autumn, now Dr Dallas Pratt, MD, he started a two-year postgraduate internship at Bellevue Psychiatric Hospital in New York, training to become a psychiatrist. One of the attractions of this course was that, because of the threat of American involvement in the war, it was compressed from its usual three years into two. Dallas worked with neurotic and psychotic patients. Years later, in 1983, he was questioned about his time there by a publisher whom he met at a dinner:

> When he asked how I managed to deal with the disturbed, often violent, patients at Bellevue in the early 1940s, before the advent of tranquillisers, I said "By treating everyone with courtesy".

At about the same time as Dallas started at Bellevue, he and John found the property they had been seeking, at Downington, Pennsylvania, about thirty miles from Philadelphia, in the heart of American Quakerdom. They named it Brandywine Farm after the battle in the American Revolution which was fought nearby. The seventeenth-century farmhouse was surrounded by woods, orchards and fields. The house needed extensive repairs, and Dallas's mother paid for them. Dallas made an arrangement with a local farmer to manage the land to make a profit, which Dallas and the farmer shared. Dallas and John set about furnishing and decorating with a joint enthusiasm for English eighteenth and early nineteenth-century furniture. The only exception was a painting that John bought in a New York auction in October 1942. It is a fine example of nineteenth-century American folk-art, and depicts a train pulling into the station of Ashoken, New York. It was the first piece of Americana either of them bought.

Dallas scarcely mentions Brandywine Farm in his writings, but an impression of life there comes in the published diaries of Christopher Isherwood who, at that time, was often in the neighbourhood with Quaker friends. Isherwood was attracted by Quakerism, and for a time worked for the American Friends Service Committee, though he never joined the Society.

"May 9 1942. To stay with John Judkyn and Dallas Pratt at their home, Brandywine Farm, out beyond Paoli. Judkyn is English. His friend is an American doctor. Judkyn interests me because he has become a Quaker without giving up his urban chic, upper-middle-class tastes: he is still the kind of elegant, well-tailored youngish man you meet at New York cocktail parties. The Quakers are puzzled by him, no doubt, and by Pratt, but they accept them because Pratt is a doctor and Judkyn is very efficient at organising relief work. Nevertheless they don't fit in at all. They are still really outsiders. Socially, Judkyn would only make sense as a Catholic.

"Their dining room is decorated with early nineteenth-century French wallpaper, bought for a stiff price at a New York auction: John and Dallas have a standing argument, because Dallas insisted on papering the room with the pineapple frieze upside down. Their court cupboard. Their Crown Derby. Their pseudo-Chinese chairs from the Royal Pavilion at Brighton."

It was at Bellevue Hospital that Dallas heard the news of the Japanese attack on the American fleet at Pearl Harbor on 7 December 1941. Within four days, the conflict became global as the United States went to war not just with Japan but also with Germany and Italy, which Britain had already been at war with for two years. These developments were bound to have a cataclysmic effect on everybody's lives, especially those of military age. Yet Dallas, far from being cast down, found that his spirits rose.

116

Bellevue Psychiatric Hospital
Dec 9, 1941

Declaration of War

Yesterday war was declared. Today all of us here in the hospital feel a little elated. Several of the interns have started to talk about giving a party — "for no particular reason." Rarely has conversation at meal-time been more animated and amusing. This reaction is unexpected. In the past I have often read with distaste of the behaviour of the people at the commencement of the last war. "War hysteria" seemed something which could not touch one who believed in peace and hated war, and who would only accept war as a painful necessity, a lesser evil and then with a feeling of betrayal, of guilt even; and most certainly, sadly and soberly. Instead we are laughing and joking, while the news comes in hourly of Americans being maimed and killed in the Pacific Islands, and the threat of air-raids hangs over New York itself, in the shape of reports that enemy planes have been sighted off the coast. The schools are let out, sirens are sounded and the population is warned to stay off the street, the hospital is "blacked-out", yet the whole performance seems like a tremendous lark.

Dallas's mother was alone, perhaps, in being concerned only with her own troubles, to the exclusion of world affairs. Things were going badly for her. Early in 1942, fearing that Freddy was associating with other women, she had him watched. When the private detective came to report to her in her suite at the Waldorf Towers, and confirmed her suspicions, she collapsed unconscious, with the first of a series of strokes that progressively robbed her of the power of speech and rendered her incapable of doing even the simplest things for herself. That, at any rate is the story told in Dallas's family. Dallas believed that one of the reasons his mother married so many times was that to her an affair outside wedlock was unthinkable. Monogamy, even if serial, was the rule, and for a husband to cheat on her was more than she could take. In another version, also told in the family, the detective was hired to investigate whether Freddy was misappropriating her money. Yet another, completely different, picture of the couple's relationship is given in Michael Seth-Smith's 1976 book *The Cresta Run*: "A great Cresta character was the Australian Freddy McEvoy. Freddy was kept by Beatrice Cartwright at the Palace Hotel for season after season, and spent her money lavishly. However, Freddy found that Beatrice was getting old — too old to satisfy his amorous activities — so one year he brought a beautiful model to care for his every need! As he explained to everybody — Beatrice included — he must have a younger bedfellow than Beatrice. So Beatrice footed the bill for all of them." At this distance in time, there can be no knowing which of these accounts comes closest to the truth. In any event, she sued for divorce on the grounds of Freddy's adultery in April 1942. On 3 May, Dallas wrote to her from the Psychiatric Division, Bellevue Hospital:

Dearest Mamma:

It was nice to hear your voice on the telephone the other day. I thought you sounded cheerful and rested, so your trip must have done you good, despite the vexations of the divorce and your painful arm. As to Freddy, a quick, clean lopping off is the best way, rather than dragging out a relationship which is all debit and misery as far as you are concerned. I am happy that you made your own decision rather than have it forced on you by others: unless we can feel in our hearts that something is right, or wrong, it is no use listening to the wiseacres who know what *they* would do were they in your place. Especially in a sentimental situation, if your emotions get you into it, then all the reason and intellect in the world won't pull you out, only a "change of *heart*", as the phrase so aptly expresses it.

The divorce was granted in October 1942. She allowed Freddy to keep a 104-ton yacht they had bought together. This led to another catastrophe nearly ten years later. In 1951, the *Kangaroo*, as it was named, a reference, it would seem, to his Australian origins, was wrecked in a storm off the Atlantic coast of Morocco. Three of the crew survived, but six people drowned, including Freddy and the last of his three wives.

In April 1942, straight after parting from Freddy, Dallas's mother acquired a spectacular new home in New York, the entire top floor of one of the city's grandest apartment buildings, 820 Fifth Avenue. Its three elevators opened into a forty-foot-long gallery, off which were the principal rooms, living room, library, dining room and main bedroom, all looking out over Central Park. There were four more grand bedrooms, six bathrooms, seven servants' rooms and a servants' hall. At the same time, she reverted to the name Mrs Beatrice Benjamin Cartwright, presenting herself from then on as the widow of a war hero rather than the ex-wife of a playboy. After the war she had a monument in memory of Charles Cartwright installed in his parish church in Leicestershire.

During the summer of 1942, the newspapers had not only World War II and the McEvoys' divorce to write about but also another scandal in the family, to do with the will of Dallas's grandfather William Evarts Benjamin, the oppressive father of Dallas's mother. A dispute arose between New York and Connecticut over which of them might claim state inheritance tax on his vast fortune. To the delight of the scandal-mongering press, the case brought out details of the private life of this elderly book-collecting widower. Under the headline "Rich Art Patron Was

Also Collector of Girls" the New York *Daily News* revealed that he had paid the rent for one young woman, given luncheons, theatre parties and expensive jewellery to fifteen others and written cheques for at least nine more. According to his accountant, he always carried bracelets, rings and watches in his coat pocket, saying: "When I go out with the young girls I like to have a few articles of jewellery for them to wear; it makes them happy."

Dallas, meanwhile, graduated from Bellevue Hospital in June 1942 and was soon in the US army as First Lieutenant Dallas Pratt, MD. He was sent as an army psychiatrist to Valley Forge General Hospital, Phoenixville, Pennsylvania. Miraculously, this was about twenty miles from Brandywine Farm, so he and John were able to spend weekends there, sometimes with friends, sometimes with Dallas's mother, to stay with them. For the next three years, Dallas treated soldiers who had been sent from the war zones as neuro-psychiatric patients. Much of what he did is beyond a layman's comprehension. For example, he was one of three writers of a paper published in the *Journal of Nervous and Mental Disease* in March 1943 on "Cardiovascular Response to Acetyl-Beta-Methylcholine (Mecholyl) in Mental Disorders". But another scientific study, which he undertook in the summer of 1945, and published in the *Bulletin of the US Army Medical Department* in September 1947, is easier to understand. It shows Dallas defending the patients in his care against any suggestion that they were lesser men than the physically injured soldiers in the other wards of the hospital. He wrote it with the help of a statistician. Its summary reads:

> A study was made of casualties from the open neuropsychiatric and plastic surgery sections, comparing the factors of (1) awards and decorations, (2) total length of service, and (3) length of service overseas. The psycho-

neurotic group received more awards and decorations and had longer overseas service and longer total service than the surgical group. These findings should lead to a better appreciation of the military record of the psychoneurotic casualty in overseas service.

The paper begins:

An impression prevails that the combat record of the psychoneurotic soldier is poor. We observed, however, that these patients had won a fair share of awards and decorations for outstanding service. The psychoneurotic casualty had often been hospitalised only after prolonged exposure to combat. The public is prone to recognise the military service of a physically wounded veteran, but to underestimate the soldierly qualities of the psychoneurotic veteran.

A letter to his mother paints a less formal picture of his work:

We have some seventy-five patients here now in our service and I am working very hard. But it is like a mouse nibbling at a mountain. I have four wards and about forty-five patients directly under my supervision. It is too many, particularly because there are endless details of administration which I have to settle. I am Jack of all Trades, and do everything from censoring letters to tieing disturbed patients down. This latter aspect of psychiatry is one in which I am not at all interested, but comes under the heading of military duty, so must be done without grousing.

The courtesy he displayed at Bellevue must sometimes have been hard to square with army discipline.

A glimpse of life in wartime New York comes in this same letter to his mother written on 28 March 1943. She was in Florida and had let him use her Fifth Avenue apartment for a weekend.

I enjoyed staying at the apartment during my week-end in New York, and had two tea parties without any trouble.

Miss Murray got some delicious sandwiches in, and these, supplemented by cakes from Dean's, made a delicious tea. Lucy served beautifully, and all in all it was one of the nicest parties I've ever given, despite or perhaps because of the absence of alcohol!

When escorting Leta home in a taxi late that evening, a soldier darted out from the curb and ran into us. He fell like a log, and we pulled up of course. I found that he had a fractured skull. I took him to Metropolitan Hospital in an ambulance but he died a few minutes after we arrived. The sequel was that I had to return to New York on Tuesday and testify. The cab driver was acquitted, and the magistrate pointed out that such accidents were frequent because of the dim-out. It was very tragic, and made a sombre ending to an otherwise merry week-end.

By then, John had been working for three years as a volunteer for the American Friends Service Committee in Philadelphia and New York, and liaised between them and Friends House in London. At the end of 1943 the Service Committee appointed him their representative to the British Friends Relief Council. On 1 January 1944, he arrived in England. He found himself a service flat, in Chesham Place in London's Belgravia, with meals provided; and spent weekends with his mother at Henley. He was upset when he saw that a bomb had destroyed the shop where he had worked before the war, Acton, Surgey, on the corner of Bond Street and Bruton Street. (After the war its site was filled by the Time-Life building). The West End looked "a very sad place".

John and Dallas's letters to each other are lost, but long letters survive that passed between John and Dallas's mother, he signing "Affectionately", she "With love". She sent him lists of tasks to perform for her. The most outlandish was to ask Jack Hulbert and Cicely Courtneidge to part with the panelling from the dining room at 28 Curzon Street and have it shipped to Palm Beach, Florida for her new house Estella, which she had recently bought to take the place in her life of the Casa Estella on Cap d'Antibes. He tactfully made it clear that, in the unlikely event of the Hulberts, then at the height of their fame, agreeing, wartime restrictions would prevent anybody being available to do the work.

In one of her letters she refers to Aubrey, now thirteen and at Eton: "Poor Aubrey has had a boil in his mastoid ear, and was so seedy that he lost three weeks of the summer term, which delayed his return. He is awful about writing — seldom writes anybody. I have protested to his aunt-in-law, Lady Watson and his housemaster as well as Aubrey. Guess his time is very much taken with study and games. However, I don't think young boys ever want to write letters". John also wrote to her about his work. It was the summer of the "second blitz" on London, the V1 pilotless bombers and the V2 rockets. Wearing a "tin hat", John visited the large underground shelters in the basements of docklands warehouses in which thousands of Eastenders spent their nights. The Friends Relief Service provided canteens and arranged medical care for anyone who needed it.

Hundreds of thousands of American troops were arriving in England to take part in the liberation of Europe that began with the D-Day Normandy landings on 6 June 1944. Dallas, after two years at Valley Forge General Hospital, applied to be sent to England, but without success. He was still working at the hospital in Pennsylvania when he reached the age of thirty, as Captain Dallas Pratt, MD, on 21 August 1944.

Chapter Five

1944 – 1954
Thirty to forty

Paris was liberated on 24 August 1944, three days after Dallas's thirtieth birthday. The devastation of warfare, and the years of German occupation, left France in even greater need than England of the help of the American Quakers. A team organised by John is said to have been the first civilian group to land in Normandy after D-Day, bringing to the French people clothing, food and medicines, donated by American Quakers. Early in 1945, John established a Friends Relief office in Paris. He and a friend, Bob Sherwood of the American Red Cross, were fortunate enough to be able to rent, for themselves to live in, the apartment of Gaston Palewski, *chef de cabinet* in de Gaulle's post-war government, and the model for Fabrice in Nancy Mitford's *Love in a Cold Climate*. "It was on the second floor with a suite of magnificently proportioned reception rooms, each one panelled and with walls hung with old silk", wrote John. They shivered in these elegant surroundings because of fuel shortages, and wore overcoats indoors. He worked in Paris, Marseilles and Toulouse until the beginning of 1946 when the Quakers closed down their services in France, "not because there will no longer be any need for further help but because we feel that the French can help themselves and it would not be appropriate for American Quakers as a foreign group to continue to stay in France doing jobs which should be done by local French agencies." This is from a letter of 8 February 1946 to Dallas's mother in which he also wrote:

> "I am definitely leaving the staff of the Quakers as soon as I get back to Philadelphia in the spring. I have worked with them for six years and that is a long time to work as a volunteer in that type of service. I find myself too often looking at human problems and tragedies as a hardened 'professional' and reaching quick and unsympathetic decisions. There is no place for this in Quaker service which should have deep religious motivation and when one feels that the sympathetic and understanding spirit is lacking, it is time to move out.
>
> "I don't quite know what I want to do next. I should like to find some work in the field of Anglo-American relations in which I've had considerable experience these last five years. I feel that among other things, the promotion of deeper understanding and fellowship between England and the US is absolutely basic to any sort of world peace in the future."

He returned to New York in the summer of 1946.

The war in Europe had ended with VE Day on 8 May 1945 and in the Far East with VJ Day, 15 August 1945. Eager to bring back servicemen from the Pacific, the American army replaced some of them with men whose war service had been in America. In October 1945, Dallas was sent to Luzon in the Philippines, more than doubling the distance between him and John. Dallas spent three months there, enjoying the scenery, reading Tolstoy's

War and Peace, and making notes in his journal on philosophy and paleontology. There he wrote his only war poem. His response to the atrocities of war, expressed in the poem, was based on what had happened in Luzon during February 1945, about eight months before he arrived there. General MacArthur's troops, approaching Manila, met fierce resistance from the Japanese, who were cornered but unwilling to surrender. The Americans launched a massive bombardment along the shore of Manila Bay, and took possession of the city, but with enormous loss of life. About 1,000 Americans, 12,500 Japanese and 100,000 Filipino civilians were killed, and far greater numbers wounded. Much of the city was destroyed, including most of the ancient, walled Spanish enclave Intramuros. Of the many churches, only San Agustin survived, almost unharmed.

24 Replacement Depot, Luzon
12 November 1945

Intramuros

I

Softly, over the patient sundial-face
Glides the wraith of unremembered years,
And gently, through the cloister, the rapt nuns pace,
Burning in ecstasy, or drowned in immemorial tears.

This was Intramuros — within the walls, —
A drowsy city, dreaming beneath the sun;
No sound or movement — only the footfalls
Of circling nuns, the glide of shadow on the stone.

II

They heard a murmur like the wind, like the surf breaking,
Like distant thunder... Guns! and the air
Suddenly rained tremendous death. Shrieking
They started from the noonday dream to the nightmare.

After terror came peace, like a penitent. Curfew and reveille
Measured no more the bloody pantomime
Of day and murderous night. Halting and heavily
Over the shattered walls crawled the long shadow of time.

III

But the heart of Intramuros is beating yet:
Victorious, inviolate, the church of Augustine
Stands in the ruins, bucklered from wreckful threat, —
The mystic lamp still flames, the saints from their altar lean.

The heart of human-kind is beating still
Within these mortal walls of dust and dreams.
Even in the slayer at the kill —
Even in you and me — the light within still gleams.

Dallas was promoted to the rank of Major and, in November
1945, was sent to Okinawa as Chief of the Neuropsychiatric
Service at the Ninth General Hospital there. The many
servicemen mentally traumatised by the Battle of Okinawa in
April 1945 had returned to the United States and the hospital was
closing down, but Dallas had plenty to do:

I never thought I could be so busy on a remote Pacific
"rock" as I have been here. When I arrived in November I
found absolutely nothing being done for our patients — no
athletics, no planned recreation, no occupational therapy, no
"parties". There was a central Red Cross recreation hall and
crafts shop, but since no effort was made to interest the open
ward patients in going, they were just lying around on their
beds all day. My predecessor had done some high-powered
therapy with a few selected cases, but the majority were just
left to lie around. I got some occupational therapy started,
also an athletic program, and was arranging for movies to be
shown on the wards, when the hospital was deactivated. In
another few weeks we would have been showing some

results. Not that I think that this sort of thing is therapy in a deep sense, but I am sure that it creates a sort of hopeful atmosphere in which the therapy can prosper. We have been seeing very few combat-induced cases recently, of course: instead we have been getting more and more of the feeble-minded hysterical patient with whom one can do little except send home. However, there have been a few interesting cases with whom I have been working a little more intensively than it was possible to do at Valley Forge. So it has been an interesting experience for me in spite of everything, and one which I wouldn't have missed for anything. Where I shall go next I don't know. In any case I'll be leaving Okinawa, because there is no longer a job for me here — they will only have station hospitals. I am not due to get out of the Army until May, when I shall have forty-five months. It's beginning to seem like a long time. I am wondering what I shall do after I get out — at the moment the possibility of entering the field of mental hygiene interests me very much.

These are extracts from a long letter of 26 January 1946 from Dallas, in Okinawa, to former colleagues at Valley Forge General Hospital, John and Virginia Rich.

During Dallas's months on Okinawa, he also wrote what he called his *Credo*, in which he distilled his reading and thinking of the last fifteen years. The views he expresses are humanist, liberal, tolerant, anti-racist and egalitarian. He is careful to avoid extremes. He has no belief in religion himself but appreciates the comfort it affords to others. He holds that pacifism should be preached vigorously in peacetime but, unlike John, thinks armed force must be used when a nation runs wild and threatens to wreck the equilibrium of the world. He thinks death duties should be high, since the passing of great wealth from one generation to another is beneficial neither to society nor to the recipients. At the same time, he recognises that the benefits of wealth, so long as they are neither flaunted nor disguised by false modesty, can heighten our enjoyment of our friends and of life. As for friends, wealth usually is more of a hindrance than a help. "The qualities I look for in a friend are sense of humour, intelligence, aesthetic appreciation, lack of affectation and a capacity for enthusiasm." These qualities, in his experience, are mostly to be found amongst professional people.

Such a brief account as this fails to do justice to the thought and sensitivity behind the views expressed. What stands out about this piece is, first, how far he had moved from the values of the world he was born in and, secondly, how the principles it describes are those he believed in and acted on for the whole of the rest of his life.

In a long essay written at this time on illusion and reality, Dallas summed up some of his thoughts on psychiatry:

> The therapist's duty is to reduce the patient's anxiety to the point where he can experience life with the least utilisation of defence mechanisms, the least mental conflict, the least split between unconscious drives and conscious ideals and the greatest possible spontaneity.

Dallas's time in the army ended in May 1946. He and John were re-united in New York that summer. With their wartime activities behind them, they embarked on post-war life in an extraordinarily systematic and deliberate way. Element by element, they put together a pattern of living to match their remarkable abilities and resources, sharing several homes, and each of them pursuing multiple careers. During the working week they lived in New York and, at weekends, at their farmhouse in Pennsylvania. They made long summer visits to England and Europe. During 1946 they bought themselves a New York house, a "brownstone" in the local parlance, 222 East 49th Street. It was in the area, bounded by East 48th and East 49th Street between Third and Second Avenues, that is known at Turtle Bay, though not one of the famous group of twenty houses backing onto Turtle Bay Gardens.

John resumed the business he had started in New York just before the war. Dallas later recorded:

> His shipments, now drawn from France and Holland as well as Great Britain, became a flourishing wholesale business under the name "222 Imports". He opened a shop on Madison Avenue known as "The Quaker Shop", succeeded by premises on Second Avenue; he also exhibited at antique shows. John's stock was of high quality and scrupulously authentic. More than that, his choice of objects was characterised by "flair", a somewhat mysterious, highly idio-syncratic, aesthetic, even witty quality.

Some of the furniture, as well as John's "flair", went into the decoration of the newly-bought house. Describing John's way of running his business, Dallas wrote:

> John's practice during the first post-war decade was to go to Europe in early spring and to start forming the collection which would be shipped to the States in September. Pending shipment, it had to be stored in a London warehouse, except for those pieces needing renovation. They were entrusted to an expert London antiques restorer, C. A. ("Nick") Bell-Knight.

John found Nick Bell-Knight to be the best of all the London antique restorers. His workshop was in Smith Street, Chelsea. His slogan was "Nothing too intricate" and he could turn his hand to anything, with the highest degree of ingenuity and artistry.

According to John, Nick's re-made sections were the parts that looked most genuine.

Born in 1918, Nick was five years younger than John. The two had an immediate rapport. Like John, Nick had an idealistic and religious side. In his youth he had considered becoming a missionary. He was a conscientious objector during the war and worked for the Red Cross. Through John's influence he went to Quaker meetings. At the end of the war, Nick married and started a family.

As well as running his furniture business, John continued with voluntary work, both for the New York branch of the English Speaking Union and for the American Friends Service Committee in New York and Philadelphia.

The United Nations' new building was a short walk from where John and Dallas lived. John and his fellow New York Quakers conceived the idea of providing a quiet place, on neutral ground, where they could bring together the representatives of conflicting nations and help them to arrive at peaceful conciliation. John played a leading role in the purchase, by the American Friends Service Committee, of a house for this purpose, 247 East 48th Street, backing onto the Turtle Bay gardens. Its work for international harmony continues in the twenty-first century. Now named Quaker House, it has an apartment for its resident director, several rooms for meetings, and its own section of the gardens, where world affairs can be discussed in a setting of calm and beauty. Another of the many Quaker working groups that John headed saved the early-nineteenth-century Friends School in Brooklyn from destruction.

Dallas, his war service behind him, re-established his civilian career in psychiatry. He became the psychiatric consultant of the Columbia University Medical Office. A large proportion of his patients there were students from abroad. Surprising as it may seem in today's multicultural world, many foreign students in the 1940s and 1950s suffered severe psychological disturbance from their exposure to life in America. In addition to this job at Columbia, he also lectured to medical and other students on psychiatry and, two days each week, worked as a staff psychiatrist at the National Mental Health Foundation in Philadelphia. This was conveniently close to Brandywine Farm. He spoke in public on psychiatry, took part in psychiatric conferences in England and America, and became something of a figure in the world of psychiatry. A bibliography of the articles, scientific papers and pamphlets he wrote in the 1940s and 1950s runs to more than thirty items. Most of them appeared in learned publications such as the *Bulletin of the World Federation for Mental Health* but he also wrote on psychology in a more popular way in *Opera News*, the magazine of the Metropolitan Opera House. One of his topics was mad heroines of operas, and another symbolic monsters in opera.

On 28 February 1947, Dallas's father died aged 64, after a long illness, in Palm Beach, Florida. His wife, the former Mrs Kaufman, survived him. During his last years, their main residence had been in Park Avenue, New York, but he and Dallas seldom saw each other in those years. His death is not mentioned in the journal.

Dallas spent four summer months in 1947 conducting a survey of sixteen English public mental hospitals on behalf of the American National Mental Health Foundation. This was just a year before the start of Britain's National Health Service, and his report includes a discussion of the changes this would bring. In later years, Dallas was unable to find a single copy of this "massive report", which ran to 50,000 words, but he inserted in his journal a summary of it that had appeared in the *American Journal of Psychiatry* in January 1949. His findings were also reported in newspapers in both America and England. He was quoted as saying "while England does not begin to challenge America's leadership in psychiatric research, and in the staking out of therapeutic advances, she is quick to apply new methods in a practical way". Most of the report is concerned with technical and statistical comparisons between US and UK institutions, and their different psychiatric and nursing techniques, but it also gives a vivid physical account of a typical English mental hospital of the time:

> The hospital buildings are rarely higher than two stories. The modern trend is toward construction on the villa plan. Every ward or two has an adjacent, fenced-in, open air recreation space, usually planted with grass and flowers, so that the patients (both quiet and disturbed) spend much of their time out of doors. The atmosphere in the wards is that of a "homey", old-fashioned boarding-house. The furniture is non-institutional, often grouped in the day-room around an open fireplace. The gleaming wood and brass testify to the English passion for polishing, and the omnipresent vases of flowers to their devotion to gardening. On the walls are colorful railway posters, and bright curtains decorate the windows, which are of the small-pane sash type and never screened. It is noteworthy that in all these hospitals the disturbed wards, in respect to exposed glass, furniture, pictures and flowers, are indistinguishable from the others.

Dallas notes that in England and Wales 373 per 100,000 of the population were under prolonged care for mental illness, compared to 422 in America; 54.2% of the admissions in England were voluntary, far more than in America; and that in England the female patients outnumbered the males, with the reverse in

America. His general conclusion was that England was "setting an example for America of intelligent care for the mentally ill".

Dallas taught medical students who were specialising in psychiatry and also other students with a more general interest in acquiring skills in psychotherapy and counselling. During these years his work was mostly concerned with neuroses and problems of emotional adjustment rather than with psychotic and severely disturbed patients of the kind he had often cared for at Bellevue and in the army. Whatever his audience, his style was free of jargon. The following extracts illustrate his way of addressing his students. More important, they encapsulate his views on mental and emotional development, and his approach to his patients:

> I developed the concept of the "basic emotional needs" in an article published in the journal *Psychiatry* in 1952.
>
> The *basic emotional needs* are as follows:
>
> 1. To be the object of affection; to be loved for what one is and not for what one has or does.
> 2. To protect oneself and those with whom one identifies from harm.
> 3. To assert oneself as an individual — independent in thought and action — and to be allowed to reach one's own decisions and to participate when plans are being made of which one is the object.
> 4. To love others and to have others dependent on one.
> 5. To identify with and to be like others; to be part of a group.
> 6. To match oneself intellectually and physically against the environment, and to master and comprehend it.
> 7. To live within defined limits; to seek order and structure in life.

8. To clothe reality in illusion; to create symbols, abstractions, art forms, and romance.

9. To be understood as one whose behaviour is the result of many complex environmental forces, and not to be stereotyped.

These needs vary in intensity under different conditions. They vary with age: the need to be like others, for instance, increases from birth and reaches a peak in adolescence, then slowly declines throughout life. Variations related to differences in sex, constitution, degree of mental health, culture, and other determinants also occur. But needs may still be defined as basic if, in spite of quantitative variations in expression, they are needs which seem to require some measure of satisfaction in everyone if personality growth is to take place.

In working out the role of the "basic emotional needs" and their frustrations in emotional disorders, I laid the groundwork for my psychotherapeutic work during the 1950s and early 1960s with Columbia University students, and in my private practice with a large number of foreign students.

The therapy I developed had the concept of values and value-change as its core. Values I defined as "enduring beliefs, conscious and unconscious, in the worth of particular forms of experiences". The dynamics in therapy may be outlined thus: "In the belief that a particular form of experience is valuable, the individual imagines a goal-state which incorporates the essence of the value, and then seeks to change his present state into a replica of the goal-state. The difference between present and goal-state is felt as a 'need'. The act of attempted change from present to goal-state is called 'behavior'."

I was better able to spell out my method after ten years of private therapy with students. It involved three major emphases: 1. taking full responsibility, 2. penetration in depth, and 3. actively choosing values.

I illustrated these three points as follows.

1. Whatever happens in a patient's life is his full responsibility. He cannot divorce himself from his actions or his symptoms. Looking into the past may clarify what started the symptoms and attitude, but not what perpetuates them. The purpose they serve, perhaps a physical or emotional need, is in the present, and the responsibility lies with him who is the one who chooses from moment to moment in the present.

2. The knowledge which psychotherapy is after is not quantitative but qualitative. Clarity is not likely to come from superficially raking over never-ending reminiscences from the remote past. A recent dream, a transference reaction to the therapist, if "penetrated in depth", may bring real insight.

3. Actively choosing values is illustrated in the case of a patient, A.B., a Roman Catholic with a sexual problem: he had no sexual attraction to women and feared that he might be a homosexual. Rather than concentrating on the matter of sexuality, in only six sessions it was still possible for him to review attitudes towards his father, mother, sister, a male classmate with whom he was emotionally involved, and the therapist, whom he imagined "would have a preconceived idea of the world into which he would try to fit me". At the last session, his positive feelings had expanded to include people in general.

A device I used, which I found instigated and stimulated the patient to continue the work of therapy on his own was using the end of the academic year as the end of sessions with myself — although always with the understanding that the student was welcome to return for another "course" if necessary. This seemed to facilitate "getting somewhere" by a deadline, and removed the fear of interminable therapy.

Some came back during the next academic year; others wrote to say that they were doing well and were grateful for my help; some referred friends who were emotionally upset to me, and most gratifying of all were letters which came, sometimes years later, from a few who wanted to share with me knowledge of their continued success and contentment.

Again and again in his writings at this time, he championed the cause of people he felt were misjudged or undervalued. In one paper he proposed a study of the contribution made by conscientious objectors during World War II to the care of the mentally ill. In another, he inveighed against the term "mental hygiene", which was widely used at that time, with its suggestion that the mentally ill were unclean. He was involved in a movement to arouse public opinion to the need for more humane treatment for the mentally ill. He also seems to have anticipated a number of future developments in psychiatry. In one paper he describes a condition that sounds remarkably like Gulf War Syndrome. In others he wrote of the value of looking at the emotional dynamics of a whole family rather than singling out one member as the patient and, by implication, the problem. His work was often reported in the psychiatric press, and from time to time, in the newspapers, which referred to him as "prominent American psychiatrist".

As a faculty member of Columbia University, Dallas became actively involved in the work of its library. In 1951 he became chairman of the newly formed Columbia Library Committee. In this capacity, he founded a magazine which he called *Columbia Library Columns* with himself as editor and regular contributor. In the early issues he wrote a series of pen-portraits of the many

departments of the library, such as law, medicine, maps, Far
Eastern studies and so on, focusing on the people who worked in
them. Writing these articles gave him an unusually comprehensive
knowledge of the whole institution. One of the series, "The
Editor Visits the Medical Library", November 1952, includes a
glance back at his days as a medical student at Columbia fifteen
years earlier. He adopted a self-consciously literary style for these
articles, using the editorial "we":

> Our visit the other day was made at a rather different tempo
> than visits years ago, when we used to rush in, a harassed
> medical student, chasing an elusive textbook, or intent on
> some hasty search of the literature. On this occasion we
> calmly reserved an afternoon of librarian Thomas Fleming's
> time — causing who knows what dislocation in that kindly
> man's schedule, but gratifying ourself with a luxurious sense
> of postgraduate leisure.
>
> The stairs leading up to the library still had their familiar
> aromatic but businesslike hospital odor, and the library itself
> looked much the same. In the high, vaguely Gothic reading-
> room the white-coated readers gazed at the same fat vol-
> umes. The assistant stood as before behind the counter, the
> students peered over his shoulder to see if Gray's *Anatomy* or
> Boyd's *Pathology* were on the reserve shelves. The Doctors
> Draper, father and son, still stared with bronze impassivity
> from their plaque on the east wall, noting the constantly
> accelerating influx of books, the overflowing shelves —
> wondering, perhaps where will it all end?

In 1951, after resigning from his post in Philadelphia and with
more and more to do in New York during weekends, Dallas sold
Brandywine Farm. He and John both worked with the
Committee for Student Hospitality of Friends Centre in New
York. Once a month, over a period of ten years, they gave a

Sunday evening dinner-musicale at their house for forty to fifty guests, to bring often isolated international students in contact with Americans. Ruth Draper, whose performances as a monologist were at that time celebrated all over the world, was one of the American guests who enjoyed these evenings. She happened to attend one of them two days before her death in 1956.

Each spring John crossed the Atlantic to England to start travelling round the antique dealers, accumulating stock for his business. As soon as the academic year at Columbia ended, Dallas sailed from New York to join him. Dallas enjoyed the luxurious staterooms of the great ocean liners. He particularly relished the atmosphere of the Queen Mary, with its two libraries, and its old-fashioned English tradition of grand service. On board, he kept himself to himself, writing, reading and doing his yearly accounts. Rather than eat in the First Class restaurant, he used the more exclusive grill room, where his solitary presence often aroused the curiosity of fellow passengers. He found it hardest to sustain his isolation in the train from Southampton to London, where sociable Americans from the ship finally had him cornered. Asked who he was, he tried to make himself sound as dull as he could. "I'm from New York... a doctor", was all they got from him.

The yearly round settled into a regular progress between New York, England and France. In 1952 John bought as their London base a house in Cheyne Walk which had been the painter Turner's last home, where he died in 1851. But New York was John's main place of residence and in 1954, seventeen years after moving to America, he became an American citizen. Dual nationality, British and American, might have suited him better, but that was not permitted at the time. He remained as English as he had ever been in accent and appearance. In the summer of 1954 he and

Dallas rented the Villa Caroline on Cap Ferrat, where they entertained a succession of groups of friends, mostly English and American. This was not far from Dallas's mother's Casa Estella on Cap d'Antibes, where she, now in poor health, was trying to re-create the way of life she had left in 1941.

On 21 August 1954, Dallas reached the age of forty.

Chapter Six

1954 – 1964

Forty to fifty

Once again the following summer, 1955, Dallas and John rented the Villa Caroline. At the Casa Estella on nearby Cap d'Antibes, on 25 August, four days after Dallas's forty-first birthday, his mother died.

As with his father's death, whatever Dallas may have felt at the time is not to be found in his journal. There is nothing to say whether he was with her, nothing about her funeral, indeed no reference to her at all, even though she was by far the more important to him of his two parents. It was many years before he began to talk and write about her, and to describe how in her last years, paralysed by the strokes she had suffered, she remained determined to keep up with her social life, and presided at her dinner table, beautifully dressed and coiffed by her French maid, and wearing her jewels, but unable to speak or even to feed herself.

Dallas's niece Linda, sixteen when Beatrice Cartwright died, remembers how, as a little girl, she was taken unwillingly to visit her ageing grandmother in her New York apartment, and found her grotesque and frightening. The famous tapering fingers seemed like claws. This sad old lady was the unrecognisable remnant of the "little chap" who had charmed Mark Twain in the 1890s.

After her death, the Casa Estella passed to her son Aubrey, and he continued to use it as a summer holiday home. At the same time, Dallas and John decided to buy a summer home for themselves somewhere in that region.

Even though the war had been over for ten years, France was still in the early stages of recovery. Life remained bleak for most people. Even well-to-do visitors from abroad were affected by currency restrictions, shortages of food and fuel, and disruptions of road and rail traffic. But a wonderful period was about to start, especially for the few who were perceptive enough to see the opportunities, and in a position to seize them. Dallas and John realised that the coastal strip was becoming over-developed. They also guessed that within a few years their guests would want to fly to the newly enlarged Nice airport, not come by train from Paris, so they searched for their new summer home in the hills, a few miles inland from Nice.

Their quest ended with the purchase of the Castello San Peyre, Opio, in the foothills of the Alpes Maritimes, about fifteen miles from Nice and Cannes and about five from Grasse. It was a substantial, centuries-old house, reached by a long narrow track, and set in its own fifteen acres of terraced olive groves. It looked out across a broad valley where the few local people lived, either clustered in hill-top villages or spread out on small farms, growing jasmine and lavender for the scent factories of Grasse, or olives and apricots. Everything was as it must have been for centuries. The whole valley seemed separate from its time, lost in an

Arcadian long-ago. On the country roads you were as likely to see a mule cart as a motor vehicle.

The Castello was said to have been, in its early years, the summer retreat of a bishop and a group of monks from a distant monastery. Later it was a farmhouse until, in 1921, it was bought by an American woman with an independent income, Elisabeth Starr.

Her American forebears were Quakers and she inherited from them a dedication to the relief of suffering. She also had a French grandmother, from whom came a love of France.

In France during World War I, Elisabeth Starr drove an ambulance for the Friends Relief Service. With no ties in America, she then settled at Opio, where she lived for the rest of her life. She kept up with a wide circle of friends, she was a competent amateur painter but, principally, she devoted her time and energy to caring for the local sick and needy. With a group of like-minded colleagues, she established a nursing home in the nearby village of Châteauneuf for children with bone malformation caused by rickets, the result of malnutrition during World War I. When World War II started, again working with friends, she set up and ran an organisation providing a chain of rest and recreation centres for the French troops. Later, during the German occupation, courageously, she used the Castello as a hiding place for people wanted by the Nazis. Exhausted and half-starved, she died at the Castello in 1943, still in her fifties.

In her years there, Elisabeth Starr transformed the Castello from a derelict farmhouse into an elegant, comfortable home, with a large separate studio across a cobbled courtyard. She softened the stern exteriors by adding shutters painted pale yellow, each one pierced with an opening in the shape of a seven-pointed star. Following local tradition, she planted two cypress trees, representing Peace and Prosperity, either side of the entrance. Through a doorway on one side of the courtyard she created a long garden. It occupied two terraces backed by a high wall on which grew figs, oranges and oleander. The upper lawn had a swimming pool. As a final touch, she converted the lowest floor of the main building, formerly stables, into a pair of rooms decked out in Arab style. They were reached by lifting a large trap door in the floor of the dining room and descending a rough stone staircase. Down there it was always cool.

In her will she left the estate to an English woman, Lady Caroline Duff, who had been one of a group of aristocratic and artistic English summer visitors between the wars with houses on the hillside above the Castello, earning it the name *la colline des anglais*. The war broke up this little colony and, finding she had no use for the Castello, Lady Caroline Duff put it on the market. It was bought by Dallas.

He and John felt a great rapport with Elisabeth Starr as they gradually discovered how much she had in common with themselves. They took their guests to visit her grave in the village burial ground down the hill. When Dallas and John moved in, they kept most of Elisabeth Starr's French country furniture and decorations, and even her books in the bookshelves, only adding new bathrooms, new curtains and some finds from local antique dealers. These included a pair of seventeenth-century portraits in oil of a husband and wife. John, charmed by the handsome eyes of the husband, wanted to discard the rather plain wife. Dallas balked at separating a couple who had been together for three hundred years. As with the upside-down pineapples at Brandywine Farm, Dallas's will prevailed. The couple were placed either side of the salon door.

The one major alteration to the building made by John and
Dallas was the addition of a terrace along the whole of the south
side to form an outdoor dining room, looking out over the broad
valley and across to the hill villages of Opio and Châteauneuf. It
fitted in so well, it was hard to believe it had not always been
there.

For the next four decades, Dallas spent six weeks at the
Castello each summer, reading and writing in his library early and
late, but having meals and spending the afternoon and evening
with his many guests, often half a dozen of them at a time, and
totalling about fifteen each summer. Men, women, children, work
colleagues, relatives, new friends and people whom Dallas and
John knew from their early childhoods came and went. A nearby
house, La Bastide, became the home of an old friend of Dallas and
John, by then the Chairman of Sotheby's, Peter Wilson, along
with his two sons Tom and Philip, and his long-term partner
Harry Wright. The boys' mother and her second husband sometimes came to stay with them. This harmonious, if unusual,
household was greatly missed when the surge in Sotheby's fortunes propelled them to a much larger property nearer Grasse.
Other friends, English and American, came to live in other
neighbouring houses, creating a new, post–war *colline des anglais*.

By the mid-nineteen-fifties, John's business was burgeoning.
He had owned a London house since 1951; first in Cheyne Walk
and then, from 1955, 19 Cliveden Place, the street that runs
between Sloane and Eaton Squares. There he would arrive in
May and start his buying trips. He dealt with a group of English
dealers whom he trusted to obtain furniture of the type and
quality he demanded. He deposited money with them so that
they could make purchases through the winter on his behalf.
Then, on his spring visits, he made a final choice from what they

had accumulated. If anything needed repair, it was sent to Nick Bell-Knight.

Dallas joined John in England each June, at the end of Columbia's academic year. After a week or two in London they went to the South of France for about six weeks, until early August, when John returned to work on his shipments until he and Dallas sailed to America in September.

It all ran smoothly but John could see that it would be even better to have a place where there was enough room to store the furniture and where Nick Bell-Knight, who by then worked almost exclusively for John, could have a workshop. John had found that the best sources of eighteenth-century furniture were in the West of England, so he decided to look for a large house near Bath, which was also conveniently close to the ports of Bristol and Southampton, for shipping the furniture to New York. Thanks to a family connection he found exactly what he wanted. A cousin of John's, Daisy Cunyinghame, wrote mentioning John's quest to her friends Gordon and Wylda Chesterman who lived at Freshford, a lovely stone-built village between Bath and Bradford-on-Avon. Gordon Chesterman was a solicitor, much involved in the life of the locality. Across the road from the Chestermans' house was the main gateway of Freshford Manor. The large old manor house, a neo-classical building in Bath stone, had been unoccupied for several years. It was smothered in ivy and in poor repair. A local builder had bought it and was proposing to knock it down and build eight bungalows on the site. The Chestermans were most concerned about how this would spoil the beautiful old village. Fearing that it might already be too late to stop the house being demolished, they told John about it. When he came he saw at once what an opportunity it offered. He brought the Bell-Knights to see it and suggested that they "join forces".

The timing suited the Bell-Knights, who wanted to move out of London to give their young children a country upbringing, and because Nick Bell-Knight's business premises in Chelsea were about to be requisitioned by the local council for re-development. Freshford Manor was large enough to provide the Bell-Knights with a good-sized family home in the north wing, as well as a workshop for Nick, storage space for the furniture waiting to be shipped to America, and rooms on the top floor for domestic staff: a cook-housekeeper and a butler. This left the main rooms, where John could exercise his flair for decoration, display his growing collection of English folk art, and accommodate his many guests. The developer proposing to build the bungalows was in poor health and John persuaded him to take a quick small profit and be spared the building project. The purchase was completed in August 1956.

A small local building firm was set to work on restoring the manor house but when the Bell-Knights came to move in during November 1956 it was so far from ready that Beryl and the children decamped to her mother's house in Stratford-on-Avon until early the following year. Nick endured the cold and worked on the house alongside the builders, carrying out John's decorative schemes. These were so bold and original that the solicitor Gordon Chesterman, by now acting for John, after seeing the blue-grey and crimson entrance hall, sent a note to him in New York expressing his alarm at "the atrocious combinations of colour". John replied that Nick Bell-Knight was doing exactly what had been specified. Two of Nick's most challenging jobs and, in the end, most appealing features of the house, were the stencilling of the wooden floors in the entrance hall and ground floor passageways, and the fitting, in the dining room, of wallpaper with classical landscapes, hand blocked in Paris in 1806 and exported to America soon after. John bought it from a house in New England that was being demolished. It arrived at Freshford rolled up and with paste and plaster clinging to the back. Nick restored it, painted in some missing sections, and mounted it so it could, if necessary, be removed later. Thanks to the Bell-Knights' skill and hard work (Beryl used her expertise in needlework on curtains and covers) the house was ready for John to move into in the spring of 1957. The great rapport between John and the Bell-Knights was vital to the whole enterprise. The Bell-Knight children called him "Uncle John". Both John and the Bell-Knights involved themselves in the life of the village and they had fêtes and open days in the garden for local causes.

With its superb collection of English folk art, and furnishings from many exotic cultures, Freshford Manor had some of the most striking interiors of its time. Here is Dallas on the subject of John's decorative schemes for their homes in England, France and America:

> The "flair" which John had in forming collections of antiques for sale also manifested itself in the series of interiors he designed for ourselves. Some hallmarks of John's style were the following: invariably, antique furniture, but often mixing British, French, Italian or Chinese samples; the wood, fruitwood by preference, often sun-faded, or painted; the wall colours either white, or bold peach scarlet — never cream or pastels, sometimes hung with Regency or Directoire wall paper, or covered by Coromandel screens. The drapes, in predominantly seventeenth- or eighteenth-century rooms, red or yellow silk damask; in early nineteenth-century rooms, grey or grey-blue silk, or flowered chintz. The architectural woodwork, usually

painted olive-green or greyish blue. The paintings, often naive portraits or landscapes. All these elements, to which were added a miscellany of antique glass, lamps, china, boxes and leather-bound books, arranged with John's sure eye for proportion and harmonious colour combinations, resulted in interiors which were works of art as well as extremely liveable.

So, from 1957, Dallas and John's yearly round took them from New York to London and Bath, with a six week break in the South of France, then back for another few weeks in England before returning to New York in the autumn. Dallas's life was full and fulfilling, with his patients, his students, his speeches, lectures and articles on psychiatry, as well as his work for Columbia University Library, particularly editing the *Columns*, and his map collecting. But he felt that John's business, for all its success, was not making the best use of his abilities and, at the same time, that John "was so much in demand as a committee member that I had the impression, despite his ability for highly organised concentrated work, that he was feeling the strain."

In the autumn of 1956, or was it the spring of 1957? we were driving in Massachusetts. Over the years, we had visited several American museum-restorations in country settings, Williamsburg, Winterthur, Deerfield, Old Sturbridge, and had been impressed by this innovative American cultural-historical approach. No European museums with which we were familiar had moved period rooms, appropriately furnished, and sometimes entire houses, into settings designed to illustrate the "way people lived" in particular places and times. As we drove along on that fateful day, the following ideas occurred to me:

1. If museums of this type were so popular in America, might they not be a success in Europe?

2. Furthermore, might it not be desirable to introduce an *American* museum abroad? It struck me as very odd that polyglot collections: Indian, Chinese, Japanese, and from other European countries, could be found in all the west European capitals and in many "stately homes", but as far as I knew not a single collection, much less a museum, of American cultural-historical artefacts existed outside of the United States.

3. Finally, weren't John and I uniquely in a position to found such a museum of Americana abroad, providing it could be in England?

After mulling these thoughts over for an hour or so as we drove along, I broached the idea to John. He accepted it enthusiastically, and agreed that we should undertake the project. At this stage, my desire was simply to share with the British the aesthetic charm of early American furniture and decorative arts and their historical background. John added a concern of his own: to inform the British (his countrymen prior to his becoming an American citizen in 1954) of the outstanding American achievements in these arts and crafts, a subject about which he believed them to be woefully ignorant. There is a shade of difference here, between myself as collector and prospective museum exhibitor and John as educator, and promoter of Anglo-American understanding. Both motivations merged in the outcome, a chronological sequence of historical rooms plus changing exhibitions at the American Museum, and the no less important educational program, emphasising work with schools.

The decision made, Dallas and John were in no time seeking the contents for the museum, as well as a building in England to house it, and people to work on it with them. They budgeted the project to come from their joint incomes, rather than using capital. They wanted the best of everything, but within sensible financial limits. When they encountered dealers whose prices struck them as high, they bought nothing and had no more to do with them. Sometimes they made so much of their financial limits that prices were lowered, or objects were given to them free of charge. They were also determined to retain their independence, and decided from the start to accept no government aid nor corporate sponsorship. The two of them, usually together, chose every single item that went into the museum:

> All the furniture in the series of historical rooms at the museum was selected jointly by John and myself. When European accessories were required for these rooms such as might have been there originally, these were chosen and donated by John.

When offered works of art and craft as gifts or, in some cases, long term loans, they accepted gratefully, but only if the pieces came up to their own high standards. Once the museum was established, they did seek outside support from their families and friends and from the Friends of the American Museum, which they set up. They realised that a project of this kind would always be in want of money for its maintenance and development. They felt that, having made such large contributions themselves, it was right to expect other people to pitch in too. Even so, they continued to give large sums of money for the remainder of their lives and then through their wills. Over the years, the museum has received several major benefactions, but the founders and their trustees have always kept their independence.

At the very beginning of our project we did not have a name for it. In the spring of 1957, we spent a weekend with friends in Pennsylvania, during which the present owners of Brandywine Farm, the Okie family, invited us over to see what they had done with our former house. I went up to see the northwest bedroom, which used to be mine. Half way up the old winding stairs I suddenly had an idea for the museum's name: "The American Museum in Britain"! I came down, told John Judkyn, he approved and so it was adopted. In the United Kingdom, the name is usually abbreviated to The American Museum.

Visiting the museums of Americana in the United States, Dallas and John measured, sketched, took notes and picked the brains of founders, directors and curators. As a result of one of these contacts, John persuaded Electra Havemeyer Webb to lend him a group of early American quilts from the collection she had formed at the Shelburne Museum in Vermont, for a loan exhibition, *Antique Quilts and Quilting*, which he organised at Freshford Manor in May 1958. This, a forerunner of the American Museum itself, proved to be a great draw and raised the money to re-roof the ancient parish church in Freshford village.

One aspect of 222 Imports had a significant effect on the American Museum-to-be. Since John sold only "To the Trade" his relationships with American dealers were important and carefully cultivated both by the seller and the buyers. The dealers from whom John bought were themselves cultured, sophisticated, and often, in their advertising, preferred to identify themselves as "antiquarians" rather than "antique dealers". As a result, when we decided to start acquiring Americana for the museum, an area of collecting in which neither of us had any previous experience, John sensibly insisted that we should work only with this somewhat rarefied group, whom he had found in his own dealings to be very knowledgeable, and whose insistence on quality and authenticity matched his own. We found that these dealers responded with enthusiasm to our project and, when they acquired objects which they knew we wanted for one of our period rooms, often called us by phone to alert us to their find, giving us a chance to dash off to wherever it was before they offered the items to others.

Several American dealers became deeply personally involved in the quest for exhibits for the museum. One of these was the tiny but formidable Mary Allis of Fairfield, Connecticut, a dealer so well established with her clients that it was she, not they, who decided what they would buy. When one of them said to her, of a piece of furniture, "But, Mary, I don't like it," she replied "You'll get to like it". And he did. She spent several weeks at Freshford and at the Castello, working with Dallas and John on assembling the collection. Another of the dealers providing furniture for the museum were Kenneth and Hannah Hammitt. After their divorce, in the early 1960s, Hannah Hammitt came to live at Freshford, working full time on the museum project until her retirement.

Even in the late 1950s, it was difficult to find Americana of the highest quality. Furnishing a whole museum called for thousands of pieces. Some of Dallas and John's friends feared the project was impossible, or that they would be sold duds, or have to settle for second best. All these fears proved mistaken and, as it turned out, the hard work and connoisseurship that the two of them brought to the enterprise were rewarded again and again by amazing good fortune.

> In the case of Shaker furniture, which we knew only through visits to the Shaker Museum at Old Chatham, New York, and to Fruitlands Museum at Harvard, Massachusetts, it soon became apparent that all roads led to Mrs Edward Deming Andrews and her husband, whose collection was

legendary and whose knowledge of Shaker life encyclopaedic. The Andrews started their collecting early, and, by impressing some of the aged Shakers and their Eldresses with their sincere interest, were entrusted with the finer remnants of the furniture made for the Shaker communities as, one by one, these had to be closed. The furniture the Shakers made for themselves was invariably of finer quality than that which they made to sell "to the world", and alone appealed to the exacting taste of the Andrews, who aspired always to that perfection for which, also, the Shaker master craftsman strove.

Before visiting the Andrews, John Judkyn and I carefully studied their book, *Shaker Furniture*, which was in effect an illustrated catalogue of their collection. We then went to New Haven, and in their living room, surrounded by the best furniture, told them of our hope for a Shaker Room. The Andrews were at once fired with enthusiasm at the thought of a permanent exhibition of Shaker material in the country where the founders of the sect had originated. Without beating around the bush, they asked if we had any of their things in mind. John promptly opened our copy of their book and went through it indicating the pieces which had seemed to us the outstanding ones in the collection. "Well", said Dr Andrews, "I must say you have *very* good taste!" We could hardly believe our ears when they agreed to sell us every piece we had requested, at what in retrospect seem most nominal prices. In addition, they volunteered to cull from their hoard a collection of material illustrating Shaker life and industries.

Another equally productive day's work occurred in 1959, when we spent twenty-four hours in Santa Fe. This had been prepared for by study of the subject of Spanish-Colonial material in various books, by a visit to the Museum at Colorado Springs to see its extensive collection of santos, and by an exchange of letters with Miss E. Boyd and Mr Alan Vedder, Curator and Curator of Conservation, respectively, at Santa Fe's Museum of International Folk Art. The rarity of genuine New Mexican folk art (the spurious is everywhere) made us feel that to come in search of it at an institution which was actively building its own collection might be venturing into the lion's den. But Mr Vedder (Miss Boyd was, unfortunately, away) was no lion; on the contrary his enthusiasm at the thought of exhibiting New Mexican material for the first time in England matched that of the Andrews. Then and there he agreed to make the collection for us, with the collaboration of Miss Boyd. Two years later, he came to England himself to apply the finishing touches to the "adobe" rooms which were created to house the fruits of his collection (as, indeed, did Dr and Mrs Andrews when the Shaker Rooms were nearing completion).

Another example occurred in New Orleans. Here again, considerable study of New Orleans furniture styles was followed by only one day in that city. It rained steadily, and by evening we still had not found a single American antique in that city of antique shops. Also, there was very little in the City Museum. Then we stumbled on a dealer who had some Americana, but none of New Orleans interest. However, a question to her, and mention of the early cabinet-makers Seignouret and Mallard, reminded her that a lady living in the Garden District wished to sell a suite of Mallard furniture. Telephoning recaptured the name of this lady, Miss D., and a call to the latter gained her consent to an immediate visit from us, since we were leaving early the following morning.

A taxi ride through dark streets, with rain still falling, brought us to a typical Garden District house, surrounded by dripping trees. Miss D., smiling a little nervously, opened the door. Inside, the house was an untouched Victorian set-piece. From a plantation up-river the family had come to the Garden District, but a tragic accident had removed all but Miss D. Now she was going to a small apartment, and it was necessary to dispose of some of the family treasures. We understood why when she led us upstairs to a bedroom, and we saw the suite of furniture by Prudent Mallard: a behemoth of a bed, with padded satin half-tester, an immense wardrobe, called an "armer" (armoire), two elaborately carved dressing-tables, referred to by Miss D. as the "Princesse" and "Duchesse", and a "commode" or bedside table. It took some time to adjust to the size of these dinosaurs, to their ornateness, to the thought of transporting them to Somerset, and, finally, to Miss D's idea of their value, for in each of these there was an element of exaggeration. But somehow the price was paid, a steamer induced to bring the gargantuan crates from New Orleans to Southampton, and now they invoke the atmosphere of the Antebellum South in the "New Orleans Room".

The luckiest find of all came neither in London or New York, but, of all places, in Bath. Looking about a Bath antique shop one day, John Judkyn turned up a carved whale's tooth. To his surprise, it was American scrimshaw work. On it were inscribed a representation of the ship *Susan* of Nantucket, some verses, the maker's name, Frdk. Myrick, and the date Feb. 16, 1829.

It turned out to be arguably the finest of the thirty or so surviving works of Myrick, the most highly regarded of the American scrimshankers of the 1820s. His work already fetched high prices in America at that time. They shot far higher in the 1960s when very rich Americans, such as President Kennedy, started collecting scrimshaw seriously.

While Dallas and John were forming the collection, they were also looking for premises in which to house it. The idea for the

museum came to Dallas between John's buying Freshford Manor
and moving into it. Bath seemed a good setting for the museum,
and they looked at several empty buildings in the city. During
1957:

> John, through some of his fellow Quakers in Bath, had
> heard that the Society of Friends there were considering
> moving from their Greek Revival meeting house. The idea
> of preserving an interesting building with the appearance of
> a miniature Greek temple appealed to John. However, the
> Quakers decided not to move. Next, his attention was
> caught by a building in Trim Street, which had retained its
> Queen Anne panelling in spite of the presses and ponderous
> impedimenta of a printing concern which choked every
> room. But Lydia Powel, formerly Curator of the
> Metropolitan Museum's American Wing, inspected the
> house and wisely counselled against it as too small.
>
> The city fathers had many buildings to offer. John
> inspected some of these white elephants which the City of
> Bath would have been happy to turn over to the American
> Museum on a long lease. John was disenchanted when,
> behind their elegant Georgian and Regency façades, he
> found labyrinths of Victorian rooms, an absence of all mod-
> ern amenities, and the probability of dry rot.
>
> One day the Town Clerk was struck by an idea and
> asked: "How about Claverton Manor? The Skrine family is
> letting it to the City as a residence for our school of
> domestic science, but the lease is up at the end of this year
> and they want to sell it."
>
> A Councillor present looked at the Town Clerk as if he
> had let the cat out of the bag, but John pricked up his ears
> and went to see Claverton Manor.
>
> Although the site of the Manor was incomparable, it
> seemed to have the disadvantage of being in the country,

whereas a city location had been planned for the museum. However, the scale was tipped in its favour by an English friend who cited the success of the "Stately Home" as an indication that a country museum in its own park, which could be made the goal of an "outing", might be quite as much of an attraction as a provincial city museum. So Claverton Manor was purchased in January, 1959, and the City had to find other quarters for its domestic science students.

"Incomparable" is the word Dallas chose for the building's setting, about sixty acres of steeply sloping parkland and ancient beech woods looking out over a deep valley to a perfect English landscape stretching for miles in each direction. It is a tract of land that has somehow survived, untouched by modern development, into the present time, and is now protected by stringent planning regulations. Incomparable, too, is the crisp neo-classicism of the Jeffry Wyatville exterior in pale honey-coloured Bath stone patinated with pink lichen. The best of the interior features of the house that remained after the many uses it was put to over the years are incorporated into the museum layout: the elegant entrance hall, the grand staircase, and the bow windows that now form part of the New York Greek Revival room.

To convert a Somerset manor house into a series of American period rooms, the English country house atmosphere had to be completely banished. Appropriate wall, ceiling and floor treatments went a long way to doing this. Two rooms in the museum have stencilled floors, replicas of two that Dallas saw in a house in Newtown, Massachusetts. Dallas and John found one set of panelling after another, through dealers such as Mary Allis and the Hammitts. Two customers of the Hammitts, Mr and Mrs Samuel Schwartz, great collectors of Americana, had bought not only some superb furniture from a seventeenth-century house in Massachusetts but also all of its panelling. Their plan to re-erect the house in New Jersey fell through and instead they donated it to the museum, where it lives on in several rooms, as a front door, entry and staircase here, as a ceiling there, and floorboards elsewhere.

> Although all the furniture in the series of historical rooms at the museum was selected jointly by John and myself, its arrangement in those rooms was by John.

Dallas exaggerates a little. On and off through an evening at Freshford Manor during 1960, Dallas and John talked repeatedly about two large alcoves either side of the fireplace in the museum's Deer Park Parlor. John proposed one object after another to fill them. To each suggestion, Dallas quietly but firmly replied that he pictured the alcoves filled with dried flower arrangements. That is what they contain to this day.

> Although the wood colours in most of these rooms were either original or when absent were copied from contemporary panelling, such as the cedar-graining in the Perley Parlor reproduced from a room in Old Deerfield, two rooms for which the original decoration was unknown reflect the "Judkyn style": the brilliant red wall-paper in the New Orleans Bedroom and the blue-grey colour harmonies of the Deer Park Parlor.

During the summer of 1958, as well as searching for premises for the museum, Dallas and John were also seeking a director for it. At first their quest went badly. They found only one person whom they thought was worth interviewing, an assistant curator at the Bowes Museum in County Durham. Dallas and John were not impressed by him nor he by them. He made it clear that he doubted their ability to fund such an ambitious project. Perhaps they had over-stressed their financial limits, which they had found proved helpful when they were acquiring the museum's contents. At a loss to know where to look for more suitable candidates:

> we had an idea that our friend Ian McCallum, an editor of the *Architectural Review*, might be able to help. We wrote to him asking him to suggest names, and he promptly replied, "I can think of only one, my own". It was a surprise, but a happy one and we at once accepted his proposal. He joined us in early 1959.

His arrival coincided with the completion of the purchase of Claverton Manor.

Ian, born in London in November 1919, a year after the end of World War I, was educated at Gordonstoun School in Scotland. He was unsuited to the hearty, outdoors ethos engendered by the school's founder Kurt Hahn, and did not enjoy his school days. Like many people growing up in the United Kingdom during the 1920s and 1930s, he developed an idealistic belief in pacifism, something he had in common with John Judkyn (born 1913) and Nick Bell-Knight (born 1918). In his teens, Ian joined the Peace Pledge Union.

After leaving school, Ian decided to use his flair for design in a career as an architect, but by the time he finished his training at the Architectural Association in London, World War II had started. He was called up to join the armed services but refused to go. His conscientious objection to fighting resulted in two six-month prison sentences. Although these spared him from active service, he conveyed, on the rare occasions when he spoke of them, that they were profoundly depressing times for him.

When he was released in 1943 war-time building restrictions meant there was not much work for a young architect. Instead he found a job at the *Architectural Review* under the owner-editor Hubert de Cronin Hastings, whose father had launched the magazine in 1897. From its first issue it was outstandingly advanced and stylish both in its views on buildings and in its illustrations and layout. During his fifteen years at the magazine, Ian was part of a remarkable team, all of them, oddly, bearing the title editor but all, in fact, working under the editor-in-chief, Hastings. They included John Betjeman, Hugh Casson, Osbert Lancaster, Nikolaus Pevsner and J. M. Richards, all five of whom later achieved knighthoods. Ian showed great talents both for organisation and design. He wrote little for the magazine himself though two of his articles seem, with hindsight, appropriate to his next career. One was a major feature in March 1953 on the Time-Life Building, "the most lavishly furnished building of its kind to be erected since the war". Its site was the bombed-out corner of Bond Street and Bruton Street where John Judkyn had worked as a furniture dealer before World War II. Like the museum, the Time-Life Building was a great Anglo-American collaboration. Another was an article on the decor of the state-rooms of the great Atlantic liners that were so much a part of both Dallas's and John's lives. Ian also wrote *A Pocket Guide to Modern Buildings in London*, published in 1951, and a full-size book *Architecture USA*, 1959, presenting his personal selection of the best of American architecture of the time in the form of biographies of thirty-three important American architects, with information on, and illustrations of, their work. Dallas was well-aware of Ian's great gifts:

> The historical rooms at the Museum were designed by John, but everything else there is stamped with Ian's imagination,

taste and sensibility. His high standard of excellence and demand for perfection in every detail became a byword. When Cathleen Maxwell, the Museum Herbalist, asked him how he wanted the Herb Garden to look, he replied, "As if it had just been trimmed with nail-scissors".

When problems arose in making new exhibit areas, the uglier the existing architecture, the more awkward the space, the more brilliant were Ian's solutions. From a stable filled with horse-stalls and store rooms, and pierced at random with odd doors and openings, he fashioned the many-windowed sweep of the Folk Art Gallery. A low-ceilinged, labyrinthine cellar became "belowdecks" on a ship, a tableau of mountain-men panning for gold, covered-wagons at night on the prairie, and the drama and colour of the Indian Exhibit. A narrow passage where an unpromising collection of Shaker products, tailor's materials, tools, boxes, seeds and clothes had to be exhibited, was transformed through a combination of *trompe l'oeil*, delicate woodwork, glass and lighting into a masterpiece of museum showmanship.

When Dallas and John first knew Ian he was, like them, a half of a pair, one American and one British. As the years went by, Ian's relationship ceased to be exclusive. He had, in effect, no permanent partner. Instead, a series of handsome young men would be a part of his life for a number of months or years. We, and his other gay friends, did not think of this as promiscuity. It was just one of the many ways we saw around us in which men managed the fact of being gay. Ian and his American friend always remained on good terms, and went on co-owning a London flat but, with Ian's work based in Bath and his friend's in Paris, they led mostly separate lives.

Ian had tremendous presence. To be in a room, however crowded, when he was there was to be aware of him. He kept up

with an immense number of friends from widely disparate circles.
Many of them were artists, architects and designers, some of them
still young and unknown, some with world-wide reputations. He
relished the company of the rich, the famous, the talented and the
titled. Dallas enjoyed hearing about them from Ian, though he did
not himself want to mix with them. He would smile as he listened
to Ian littering the conversation with the pet names of duchesses.
Ian's manner verged on the imperious and sometimes startled new
members of staff, but few people were able to resist his enthusiasm, his vitality and his dazzling blue eyes. Early in their working
relationship, Dallas realised that he sometimes needed to deal with
Ian diplomatically:

> It had been decided to feature "Teas on the Terrace", and
> the location of the kitchen had been settled. Ian had made
> up his mind that the visitors would be served in the present
> Country Kitchen. Rather than have them milling around in
> this room, it occurred to me that it would be much better to
> cut through the wall and serve them from a counter as they
> queued in the outside passage (to be roofed over). It was no
> easy matter to make our authoritative Director change his
> mind; the only way, I decided, was a little manoeuvring so
> that he himself would "spontaneously" hit on the right sol-
> ution. He quickly realised that it would be preferable for the
> visitors to line up in the passage rather than in the Country
> Kitchen, but how in the world would they choose their
> preferred "cookies"? He wrestled with this for a few
> minutes, then inspiration came. "I know" he exclaimed
> "break through the wall and serve them from a counter!"
> "Brilliant!" said I.

It may seem extraordinary that Dallas needed to resort to any
such subterfuge in his dealings with Ian. Dallas was, after all, the
boss. Ian, on the other hand, could be formidable. During the

years that followed, a relationship grew up between them that seemed sometimes like an echo of the earlier one between Dallas and his mother.

Some of the highly charged qualities of Ian's character may have come from unresolved conflicts within him. His idealistic pacifism assorted oddly with his worldliness. His love of grandees seemed to be in stark contrast against his enthusiasm for the austerity of modern architecture and his choice of industrial furnishings for his home and cheap work-clothes as his leisure wear. Perhaps, as both a conscientious objector and a gay man he feared being socially unacceptable and over-compensated. If this theory is valid, it could account for the way that many gay men, not just Ian, bolstered their sense of self-worth in those intolerant days by seeking acceptance in the exclusive worlds of the titled and the super-rich.

So forceful was Ian that people were inclined to give him all the credit for everything to do with the museum, ignoring all the craftsmen, builders, architects and landscape designers who had contributed. Some people even assumed that Ian was the founder and sole creator of the project. Far from minding this, Dallas and John found it suited them. They were glad to have someone other than themselves to represent the museum, enabling them to retain their privacy.

On the top floor of Claverton Manor, above the period rooms of the museum, were two spacious flats: one for the caretaker and his family, and one for the director, providing him with a suite of well-proportioned rooms looking out across the Avon valley. There he entertained his friends, his colleagues and his distinguished visitors: on one occasion Mary Martin, on another Ethel Merman, two queens of Broadway; on yet another Queen

Elizabeth the Queen Mother. One visitor, who was the queen of Hollywood in her day, gave Ian a photograph of herself signed "More than sincerely, Joan Crawford". This is now in the museum's collection.

From the moment of his appointment, Ian involved himself with tremendous energy in every aspect of the museum, but it never became his only interest, nor did he try to do everything himself. Instead he built a strong managerial and curatorial team. This enabled him to keep up with what was happening in the visual arts in Britain, America and other parts of the world. He worked on many committees, with the Georgian Group, the National Trust and the Bath Preservation Trust, of which he became chairman and where his involvement was the catalyst in Number One Royal Crescent becoming another local museum. He spent the middle of each week in London, returning to Bath at the weekends, when social life there was at its most active. In time, he was able to combine all his enthusiasms to the advantage of the museum when he invented the concept, now used by many museums, of international art and architecture tours as a way of raising funds. On these he accompanied a group visiting any-where from Florence to Kyoto, along with a tour organiser and an expert guide. The party was entertained by local art collectors and saw their treasures as well as the pick of the places open to the general public. A donation to the museum was a condition for inclusion on the tour. Over the years the money raised in this way has helped the museum substantially.

Ian was appointed in the late summer of 1958 and took up his new appointment in the spring of 1959. In July of that year, during Dallas and John's third stay at the Castello, I, Dick Chapman, had the great good fortune to be introduced to them.

Like many major events in life, it came about by the slightest chance. My American partner, Ben Duncan, was on a three-month break between jobs. He used this interlude to explore remote parts of Greece, and to learn the modern Greek language. For my two-week summer holiday, I went to the South of France. In Cannes, I encountered a friend from London, the designer and decorator David Hicks. He was staying at the Castello with Dallas and John, whose names were new to me. At his suggestion, they asked me to lunch there, and this led to our life-long friendship. David Hicks, as it happens, soon moved out of all our lives after marrying the following year, 1960, Lord Mountbatten's daughter Pamela and thus entering the outer reaches of the British royal family.

From the moment I met John, I responded to his warmth and sparkle. Dallas, much more reserved than John, took longer to know. Like Dallas, I too was often quiet and reserved in company, tending to hide behind Ben.

From my first visit to the Castello, I was greatly impressed, not only by Dallas and John, but also by the setting and the way of living that they had created for themselves. The ancient house and its surroundings seemed to me magical. Outdoors, where the complete absence of any sound was a new experience for me, the air was scented with herbs and flowers. Indoors, the domestic routine ran like a clear mountain stream. An almost unseen staff saw that refreshments and meals appeared, rooms were cleaned and tidied, beds made, towels changed, and vases filled with bright flowers from the garden near the kitchen door that also supplied fruit, vegetables and herbs for the cook.

As soon as we were all back in England, Dallas and John met Ben. From the start, the four of us found we had an endlessly

stimulating mixture of similarities and differences in our backgrounds, interests and activities that drew us ever closer. Ben was
born in 1927 in Birmingham, Alabama, was orphaned at an early
age, and grew up in children's homes. Despite this unpromising
start, he won a scholarship to Oxford to read English. There he
met me, the son of an Oxford professor of mathematics. I too was
reading English. By the time we met Dallas and John, we were
both copywriters in London advertising agencies, and living in a
flat that happened to be a few hundred yards from one of Dallas's
childhood homes, 28 Curzon Street. Like John, I had a youthful
fascination with America and, as he did, I went to work there.
During 1956 and 1957 I worked in the copy department of
Young and Rubicam on Madison Avenue. By chance, my tiny
apartment was in East 49th Street, a block east of where Dallas
and John then lived, at 222. This was two years before I first met
them, but John claimed to remember seeing me pass their door
on my walk to and from work.

In the summer of 1960, Ben and I had our first of many
weekends at Freshford. The other guests were a mixture of people
working with Dallas and John on the museum and others, like
ourselves, who were simply friends. In their enthusiasm for the
project, Dallas and John seemed to give a different account of
their purpose each time they were asked about it. John explained
it to me as an attempt to give English people an alternative to
their impressions of America derived from gangster films,
Westerns, and the millions of American servicemen in England
just before the 1944 Normandy landings. Dallas was eager for
visitors to appreciate the simplicity of seventeenth-century
American furniture. Dallas and John showed us round Claverton

Manor where the panelled rooms were still being put together in an atmosphere of hammering and sawdust.

The work had started in January 1959, as soon as the building was bought, a few months before Ian's arrival. John's family firm, based in Nuneaton, came and laid an approach road and parking areas. Local builders made structural repairs to the manor house. Nick Bell-Knight and his newly appointed assistant cabinet maker Ron Sprules started work on the period rooms. Nick Bell-Knight later recorded how shipments of "old boards, mouldings, window frames and an apparent clutter of old bits and pieces" had to be converted into panelled rooms that fitted the house. "Doors had to be changed around to suit the planned route for future visitors, windows also had to synchronise. Apart from which, broken and missing parts had to be repaired and replaced". During the thirty months to the museum's opening, Nick Bell-Knight wrote:

> "I poured every ounce of effort and skills into the enterprise. I became almost unbearable to live with, days were too short, nights were too long — I would have worked twenty-four hours, seven days a week. At times my wife would exclaim in annoyance that 'You live for that museum as if you're married to it, not to me'... she was right! I began to suffer with burning sensations in the stomach. I knew I had developed stomach ulcers. One time John found me doubled up with stomach ache. John insisted I take a vacation — I refused as I wanted to see the Museum project through to the end. Those are words I actually used and his reply was 'Nick, if you carry on like this — it will be *your* end'. The result was that he negotiated plans for me to have a three week vacation abroad. Not only did he work out the itinerary but he contacted friends on the continent who would take me around — he also

met all the cost of travel. It would not have been feasible for my wife to travel with me, our daughter was still a child of seven and someone had to be at home in any case. So it was planned that our son should accompany me. We had hotel bookings in Amsterdam where we were to meet two friends of John who were antique dealers. We would meet them each evening and on the weekend, when they would take us by car to numerous places both in Amsterdam and outlying areas. From Holland we travelled via Belgium into France. We stayed at a pension in Paris and again were met by another friend of John who also took us on many tours, including Versailles. From Paris to Avignon thence Marseilles and along the coastline to Nice and Monaco. We were met by John at Nice and he drove us to Opio. After our stay at Opio, we were taken by D.P.'s driver to catch the train from Nice. It was a nightmarish ride — the car sped along winding narrow unmade roads. We arrived at the railway terminal with minutes only to spare. Shakes of hands, 'merci-bokos' — donating some spare francs we took farewell of our 'mad' driver! We had a sleeping car to Paris. We changed trains in Paris for Calais, then the British Rail ferry to Dover. The vacation was over — it had been a beneficial experience and I felt the better for it."

In September 1960, a year and three-quarters after the work began, with the museum still looking like a lumber yard, Dallas and John returned to America. Beryl Bell-Knight said they left Freshford to catch the train to Southampton and the liner to New York "as happy as two schoolboys". Vast amounts of work had been done but there was still a lot for Ian McCallum, Nick Bell-Knight and their teams to do, not just the completion of the construction of the museum and its contents but lighting and labelling, printing leaflets and tickets and, most important of all, appointing and training staff including a small army of room guides who did an intensive course in American history, domestic life and the decorative arts so that they could talk knowledgeably to the visitors. The neglected grounds had to be tamed, and part of the old stables converted, to designs by Ian, to form a folk art gallery. The finishing touches were accomplished during the 1960/1961 winter in Dallas's absence.

In the early 1990s he wrote:

> John returned to England in February 1961, at which time there was still much to do. But when I returned on May 3, 1961, I had one of the greatest moments in my life on entering the Museum. It was virtually finished. All the plans we had made, the thousands of items we had bought, like the pieces of a gigantic jigsaw puzzle had all miraculously fitted together. Everything we had dreamed 3000 miles away had materialised in the improbable setting of an English manor on a Somerset hillside. And the ultimate sensation was this. Not only did the historical rooms look exactly like those in the American houses I had seen and stayed in over the years. You could close your eyes and the experience of being in America not only persisted, it increased, because the old panelling and beams had brought the *scent* of America with them. And after more than thirty years, it's still there.

Surprisingly, Dallas never wrote about another aspect of the museum, that its rooms represent his own ancestry. The Pratts, the Benjamins, the Rogers and so on might have lived through the seventeenth, eighteenth and nineteenth centuries in these very rooms. In the basement, the reconstruction of a whaling ship could almost be the one in which Henry Huttleston Rogers's father, Rowland Rogers, went to sea as a young man.

In his journal, Dallas recorded the museum's opening ceremony in these words:

> On 28 June 1961 Countess Alexander of Tunis, Vice President of the English Speaking Union, introduced by Dallas Pratt, opened the museum; the American Ambassador, David Bruce, introduced by John, opened the Folk Art Gallery. Trenchard Cox, Director of the Victoria and Albert Museum, said, "I can honestly say that yours is one of the most exquisitely presented museums I have ever seen." Newspapers and magazines were full of praise.

From the start, the museum attracted visitors in large numbers. School parties came in the mornings, soon amounting to more than ten thousand children a year; the general public in the afternoons, a further fifty thousand annually. During the 1960s, with England's great surge in car-ownership and leisure activities, visiting country houses became immensely popular. The American Museum conveyed a completely different ethos from that of the grand English homes, built to promote ancestral power and display wealth in the form of masterpieces of painting and sculpture. The American Museum showed the simple, the naive, the domestic, in work done by provincial craftsmen or by women working in their own homes. Few English people had ever seen Shaker furniture, hooked rugs, patchwork quilts or any folk art. One of the museum's most popular exhibits was a room filled with quilts and other textiles, displayed on racks like the pages of immense books. Placed halfway through the series of period rooms, it made a refreshing change of visual interest and became so popular that some visitors hurried through the earlier rooms to reach the quilts and then spent an hour or more studying them in detail.

Dallas and John had started collecting American quilts soon after first seeing them at the Shelburne Museum in Vermont, before they had any thought of starting the museum. They went on adding to their collection, and it continued to grow as American visitors to the museum presented ever more examples that had been treasured in their families for generations. The collection is now not only the finest outside America, but is scarcely rivalled even there.

The influence of the museum was out of all proportion to its size. One early enthusiast of it was Laura Ashley who was just starting to establish her fabric-printing business. She spent many days there studying American fabrics and wallpapers. After her death, her husband Bernard Ashley told Dallas that the museum had been one of her greatest sources of ideas and inspiration. A whole new generation of quilt-makers, all over the British Isles, most of whom saw quilts for the first time at the American Museum, revived the craft in this country, where by the end of World War II it had all but died out.

Once the museum was open, Dallas and John, far from basking in the praise or resting on their laurels, continued to throw their energies into it. They set about filling gaps in the collection, and developing the gardens to include a replica of George Washington's garden at Mount Vernon. This was done with the help of the garden designer Ian Mylles, and funded by the Colonial Dames of America, descendants of pre-Revolution settlers. John worked hard at setting up an organisation of Friends of the American Museum in Britain, with local groups in every corner of the United States. These would receive visits, and lectures on the museum, usually from Ian McCallum, and would provide financial support. All this was on top of Dallas continuing his career in psychiatry and the editing of *Columbia Library Columns*, and John keeping 222 Imports going, and maintaining his work with the Quakers and the English Speaking Union.

Dallas and John were helped by many able people. One was James Liburd, a young Jamaican who managed the New York end of 222 Imports in John's absence. Another was Mrs Helene Walker, who acted as secretary to the Friends of the Museum. Dallas and John set up the Halcyon Foundation in New York, with a board of trustees, to take care of the museum's American finances, and an English board of trustees to supervise the museum's general management, as well as a council whose members contributed to the work of the museum in many ways, financial and practical. John had a young English secretary, John Wilson, as well as administrative help from Nick Bell-Knight's son Christopher, still in his teens, who was already showing the ability that later led to his successful career in international banking. Dallas and John continued their remarkable hospitality. The visitors' book of the Castello for each of these summers lists from ten to twenty guests. Ian McCallum as director was in charge at the museum, but shared every important decision with Dallas and John.

After buying houses in New York, London, the South of France and the West of England, as well as Claverton Manor for the museum, Dallas and John might have felt they had enough property. To think that would be to underestimate them. When 228 East 49th Street came on the market following the death of its owner in September 1961, three months after the museum in England opened, they did not hesitate to buy. It was only a few yards from where they had lived since 1946 at number 222, but it was twice as large, had a spectacular main room, and backed onto the beautiful gardens of Turtle Bay. It was diagonally across the gardens from Quaker House, 247 East 48th Street, which they had helped to buy for the Society of Friends in 1953. They did not sell 222 but converted it into apartments which they leased to friends.

The former owner of 228, who had died at her other home, in Connecticut, just short of her ninetieth birthday, was Mrs Charlotte Martin, the creator of Turtle Bay Gardens. Her second husband, Dr Walton Martin, had died twelve years earlier. His patients had included President Theodore Roosevelt. In 1919, aged about fifty, and shortly before marrying Dr Martin, she had started to acquire ten mid-nineteenth-century brownstone houses in East 49th Street and ten in East 48th Street, between Third and Second Avenues. The area was run down and the houses were cheap to buy. With the help of an architect, Clarence Dean, she modernised them and redesigned their gardens with a shared strip down the middle. Each house had its own outdoor space, but with no hedges, so that the overall look was of a single large garden.

She re-sold most of the houses to friends, aiming only to recoup what she had spent. She revived an old name that had gone into disuse when she called the whole place Turtle Bay Gardens. Her own house was in fact two brownstones that she amalgamated, making a huge library in one of them that ran from front to back of the house and was three storeys high. When Dallas and John took on this house they were, as at Opio, benefiting from the work of a remarkable woman of the inter-war years. They added an elevator, reduced the size of the ground floor kitchen to make room for a garage, and decorated the house in John's characteristic style, using many of the objects Dallas had collected on his journey round the world in 1936–1937. They also used some magnificent furniture inherited from Dallas's mother including, for example, a circular Regency-style dining table and eight chairs, all painted with Prince of Wales feathers, said to have come from the Prince Regent's yacht. The third, fourth and fifth floors, where Mrs Martin had housed nine servants, became offices for the American Museum and the Halcyon Foundation, an apartment for James Liburd, who from then on added the management of the house to his work for 222 Imports, and a two-bedroom apartment for guests. The immense library provided a splendid place for entertaining, and also for meetings, lectures, concerts and film shows. Filled with folding chairs it seated two hundred people.

With James Liburd taking care of 228, and the Bell-Knights at Freshford, John and Dallas needed somebody they could trust in the same way at the Castello. This provided a welcome opportunity for two of their friends, Bengt Soderberg, a young but already successful Swedish novelist who had taken up residence in the South of France a few years earlier, and his French partner, Marc Ribes. In 1961, they, their dog and their pet monkey moved into the studio, across the courtyard from the main building.

Bengt and Marc took over the running of the estate, seeing that the house and grounds were maintained, hiring and supervising domestic staff, and enabling Dallas and John to arrive at Opio each summer knowing that all would be in order, and with no practical problems to trouble them.

Everything was in place for a new Golden Age, stretching far into the future, for Dallas, John and their many colleagues and friends. Together, the two of them had put together a perfect way of living. But reality abhors perfection, and this serene life was not to last.

The summer of 1963 at the Castello seemed much like any other. The only significant difference was that towards the end of Dallas and John's six weeks there, Aubrey was getting married. He had met his bride that April, through mutual friends, in Paris where he was working with a section of Unesco which provided assistance for museums. He was thirty-three. Eva Tempelman, twenty-five, was from Sweden and had a job in London with a Swedish organisation.

Both Dallas and John were invited to the wedding in Stockholm on 27 July 1963. Dallas accepted the invitation, but John declined, pleading responsibility for the guests at the Castello. By then, though, the summer weeks at the Castello were nearly over, and most of the guests were gone. John's refusal may have had more to do with a fear of flying. I recall him saying that summer that he did not think air travel was yet really safe. He and Dallas still crossed the Atlantic by ocean liner even though by then most people who could afford to flew. All the same, when Dallas took the flight to Stockholm, he and John must have expected to be together again a few days later. It was the last time they saw each other.

I recall the events of the hours that followed Dallas's departure with extraordinary clarity even now, forty years later. They were imprinted on my memory because of what happened the next day.

Dallas was driven to Nice airport for his flight. John and the remaining guests dined at the Castello and then, at John's sugges-tion, we all went to Valbonne where a discothèque had opened, a novelty at that time. The young men and women dancing were far younger than any of us. We were fascinated to see for the first time the kind of free dancing the 1960s had brought in. I left the Castello the next morning to drive to Paris and then fly home.

John left the Castello a little later in the day to do some errands in Grasse. He was a careful, competent driver with whom we always felt safe. But no driver could have avoided the accident that happened. On the twisting mountain road between Opio and Grasse a local farmer was driving a cart pulled by a mule. The mule, perhaps panicked by the traffic, pulled into the lane of oncoming vehicles and into the path of a truck, which stopped abruptly. John, following in his car, crashed into the truck and was killed.

The news was brought to Dallas at the wedding reception in Stockholm. Those present on that occasion report nothing of Dallas's reaction to the unexpected, sudden loss of the major figure in his life. Whatever was going on inside him, Dallas busied himself with practicalities, sending telegrams to all their closest friends not only to tell us of John's death but to reassure us that John had "died without pain", rather than leaving us to picture him injured and suffering.

However little Dallas revealed about his emotions, it was clear to his friends that this catastrophic accident had brought a sudden end not only to John's life but, in a different sense, to Dallas's life too. After twenty-four years together they could have expected to look forward to at least another twenty-four. Now in an instant, the whole elaborate, inter-twined structure of their way of living together was swept away. Nothing could possibly console Dallas for this irreplaceable loss. From this time on, the rest of his life can be seen as series of attempts, of varying degrees of success, to adjust to his bereavement and to fill the void that John had left.

Dallas's feelings about John and his early death were not to emerge for many years. When they did, in writings about him in the journal, they were not to record grief but to present John in his prime, and in the context of their finest years together.

Nick Bell-Knight, who was as close as anybody to both Dallas and John, did write about his own feelings at the time:

> "I was stunned — it couldn't be — there was some mistake — I was having a nightmare — but no, I was only too well awake! The bottom seemed to immediately fall out of the world! John, that loveable, kindly, gifted person, our dearest friend, had been taken from us. We were devastated. Tears flowed from us all, our little daughter wept uncontrollably. I hid away and let the hot tears pour forth in my solitude and anguish.
>
> "Merciful God, if such there be — Why? why? why?… A nightmarish period followed — one went about in an unreal dream-like world. John's body was brought back to England, — there, in his sealed coffin. It was devastatingly painful but I am most grateful to D.P. for that kind thought of his in suggesting I meet John. The heavy coffin was unloaded and put into the waiting hearse that was to carry him home to Nuneaton and formal burial. A great gap in one's life ensued."

John was buried in the churchyard of Upper Stowe, Northamptonshire, where many members of the Judkyn/Judkins family have their graves, including his mother Florence Judkins, his sister Olivia Armstrong and his brother Myrton Judkins. It was there that when quite young John had seen the earlier spelling of the surname carved on tombstones and adopted it for himself.

A memorial meeting was held at the Friends Meeting House in Bath, which John had attended regularly when in England, and which he had looked at five years earlier as a potential site for the museum. Internally much altered, it is still the Bath Friends Meeting House. Taking place only two weeks after John's death, the occasion had an emotional intensity more like a funeral than a memorial service. In keeping with Quaker tradition, nobody presided. Person after person rose to speak, each talking about a different one of John's tremendously varied activities, such as his work with the Quakers in England, France and America, his devotion to the English Speaking Union, and his contributions to the founding of the American Museum. Dallas sat in silence, his head bowed, his face showing grief and exhaustion.

A few days later, Dallas came to see Ben Duncan and me at our flat in London. Dallas wanted to be told every detail of what had been done and said by John in the time from Dallas's departure from the Castello until mine the following day. He was entertained to discover how the intellectual level had dropped, with the discothèque visit, once he was gone.

Our friendship with Dallas deepened during that meeting. Dallas quoted passages from the letter about John that we had written, and he talked about the parallels between them and us. All three of us shared an understanding of the type of relationship, in a still hostile world, that they had experienced and we still had. So strongly did the tragedy of John's death draw us together that, as we were discussing our plans, a silence, unusual but not uncomfortable, fell over the conversation. All three of us seemed to be considering a possible future for us as some sort of trio. It was something that could have happened, leading to very different lives from what in fact developed for the three of us and for many

179

other people. Nothing was said, and the moment passed but, from then on, we remained amongst each other's closest friends.

John bequeathed his large holding of shares in his family's granite quarrying business to the museum. He left his American estate to Dallas, who passed it on to the Halcyon Foundation, for the benefit of the museum. Dallas founded two new organisations in John's memory: the John Judkyn Memorial and the John Judkyn Music Memorial. The first of these was designed to develop the educational function that John from the start saw as an important part of the project. It was inspired by John's enthusiasm for the Artmobile, an exhibition on wheels, funded by Paul Mellon, that he and Dallas saw in Richmond, Virginia, in October 1961. The John Judkyn Memorial had its headquarters at Freshford Manor, and its own collection of Americana, which Dallas continued adding to for the rest of his life. The exhibits were to be sent for exhibition all over Great Britain, mostly in schools, where children were encouraged to handle many of the items and so experience the very feel of American life in earlier centuries.

Dallas's most noticeable response to John's death was to keep everything as much as possible as it had been before. At 228, John's room was given no new use. John's clothes remained in the cupboards. John's London house was sold, but Dallas continued the yearly round, New York, Freshford, Opio. In London he usually stayed in a club. He even encouraged James Liburd to keep 222 Imports going. Its scale became more modest, and James obtained his stock locally, rather than continuing the buying trips to England that John had made. But however much Dallas wanted to keep things as they were, tremendous changes were on the way, starting in the form of a young Englishman, David Quarrell.

Born in 1937, David Quarrell had come to the United States
from England at the start of the 1960s. Recalling the impression
David made upon people, Dallas wrote, many years later:

> David's effect on his friends was like that of a meteor, flash-
> ing across the sky in a shower of sparks. He had great charm,
> conviviality and imagination. He was highly intelligent, in
> fact had a brilliant mind and rapidly forged ahead in Wall
> Street, eventually leaving Shearson and becoming a partner
> in another firm.

When they first met, David was working for a firm of
stockbrokers in the City of London as a specialist in metals shares.
The firm had sent him to New York. He stayed with a friend of
his, Kennon Smith, who also knew Dallas and introduced them to
each other a few months before John's death. One of the New
York brokerage firms David visited offered him a job as a steel
analyst. David returned to New York and this time shared an
apartment with a South African friend, Michael Withall, and later
with an advertising designer at Lord and Taylor, Richard Nelson.
David and Richard were a striking pair, both in the early stages of
promising careers, both remarkably good looking. But the impact
of David's presence was quite out of the ordinary. Rugged,
square-jawed, yet still boyish well into his twenties, he engaged
with people he met with a blazing intensity.

> When he and Richard separated, early in 1964, David came
> to see me. I was recovering from the shock of John Judkyn's
> accidental death. He said "I wanted to give you time before
> coming to you". Although I was 22 years older than David,
> a very strong attachment developed, and after only a few
> weeks we decided to live together.

This seems not to have meant living under the same roof. David did not move into 228.

> He wanted to move out of his West 97th Street apartment and find a house in Brooklyn Heights, a very much shorter subway ride to Wall Street than the one from West 97th. We found 34 College Place, a charming house with garage at the dead-end of the quiet little street.

Dallas bought it for David. A few years later, David moved to a second house that Dallas bought for him, in nearby Hoyt Street.

During Dallas's visit to London in June 1964, he came to see Ben Duncan and me and told us about himself and David. As it happened, we had met David in London before he first went to New York. From what we had observed of him, he seemed an unlikely successor to John Judkyn. In particular, it was hard to picture him settling down with anybody, least of all with a person of about the same age as his father. We could only hope for the best.

Dallas and David spent the first week of August 1964 together at Opio. It was David's first visit there. He was on holiday from his job, and was back at work in New York when, on 21 August, Dallas reached the age of fifty. Dallas's life seemed to be starting again, in a completely new direction.

Dallas Pratt in Knickerbocker Greys uniform, 1923

Freshford Manor, exterior and dining room

Claverton Manor, exterior and Shaker room

185

Dallas Pratt with Opie the veal calf, 1992

Chapter Seven

1964–1974

Fifty to sixty

It is hard to imagine John Judkyn ever wanting to own a pet animal. For David Quarrell, on the other hand, a dog, preferably a Scotch terrier, was a necessity. A photograph of David barely three years old shows him with Mac, his family's scottie, the first of a long line that scampered through his life. When David was living with Richard Nelson in their apartment on West 97th Street, they had a scottie named Robbie. On Dallas's first visit there, Robbie was introduced to him as "a most important member of the family". Together, Richard Nelson and David imported from Scotland another scottie, Heather, who became the matriarch of a whole clan. One of Heather's daughters came to live with Dallas, the first dog he had owned since his childhood. He named her Maud, in memory of his English governess Maud Duke, who had died in 1963.

Recalling Richard Nelson, in 1991 Dallas wrote:

> After he moved out of the 97th Street apartment in late 1963, and out of David's life, I really had very little contact with him. Yet two things Richard did, inconsequential

though they may seem, have affected my life in an unexpected and wonderful way.

The first was the scotties. The second was a house at Garrison in upstate New York.

After the ten years, off and on, of weekend commuting to our Downington farm had come to an end in 1951, and its place had been taken by both Freshford manor and the Castello, I felt I had more or less "had it" as far as an American country place was concerned. But David's enthusiasm carried all before it.

It came about as follows. Richard, living at Cornwall across the Hudson river from Garrison, used to explore the countryside hereabouts. Once, driving along the Old Albany Post Road, he particularly noticed the Heuston house. After he met David Quarrell, he brought him along this road once or twice, and they began to refer to the Heuston place as their "dream house". When David and I started our search for a country house, we made several false starts, in New Jersey, and west of the Hudson near Tuxedo. Then David, remembering the "dream house", brought me to the Garrison area, and again, after one or two near misses, we were shown a house a mile south of the "dream house" on the Old Albany Post Road.

As he had done in Brooklyn, David threw himself into the restoration of the sadly abused Garrison Post Road Cottage (as it was then called) with terrific energy. He worked out the decoration of the rooms with me, made numerous excursions to antique dealers to find the furniture, stripped the panelling, and did much of the masonry around the pool and on the terrace. Although my taste generally prevailed, his was excellent. The fabulous indirect ceiling-lighting and the brown and orange colour harmonies of the garden room are authentically David Quarrell.

Some years later came

> the opportunity to buy, not the actual "dream house" of the
> Heustons but some eleven adjacent acres of their property.

The Old Albany Post Road may once have been a busy
thoroughfare. By the 1960s it was a country trail, with half a
dozen houses strung along it. The wooded acres of the property
were surrounded by several thousand acres of State forest, which
the people of New York seemed never to visit. Like the Castello
at Opio and the two houses near Bath, Freshford and Claverton
manors, it was buried deep in rural peace. It was a modest, clap-
board farmhouse, built in the eighteenth century. Dallas and
David added one large room, named the garden room, with modern lighting and furniture and a collection of paintings by Ben
Nicholson that they acquired together. This room, big and
angular, contrasted with the cottagey period rooms of the rest of
the house, and opened onto the stone terrace with its swimming
pool. During the working week, Dallas and David lived in their
separate houses, in different boroughs of New York City, but
frequently spent their evenings together. At weekends, they were
both at Garrison, usually with one or more house guests. During
the summer months, while Dallas was in England and France,
David filled the house at Garrison with friends of his own age.
Sofa-beds in the library and the garden room made it possible to
have large weekend parties, often up to ten people.

It was clear almost from the start that the link between Dallas
and David was different from the one between Dallas and John.
Apart from much else, there was the gap of a generation in their
ages. When Dallas came to visit Ben and me in London in June
1965 he wanted us to know that their relationship was not what

he had first hoped for, but that it was by no means over. David remained the central figure in his life.

Some of Dallas's friends found David difficult to come to terms with, but Dallas managed to stay close to everybody who mattered to him. He sustained his contacts with his contemporaries from as long ago as his time at the Buckley School in New York, and with several members of his family, especially his sister Cynthia. He also got to know a whole new group of young people, mostly men of about David's age. He met some of them through David, some through other people. In their company he developed a new zest at a time when he might have sunk into despair. In his relationships with them, he played a mixture of roles, parent, uncle, older brother, dependable friend. He did not dominate them. He was as eager to learn from them as they from him. Each of them had the confidence to stand up to Dallas if they disagreed with him. He observed them benignly, encouraged them, and helped them in many ways at what he saw as one of the most interesting moments in their lives, when their careers were about to take off or to start afresh in new directions.

One such was Kaffe Fassett. He came to England in 1964 as a friend of Jeremy Fry, who lived near Bath. Kaffe Fassett was twenty-seven, born in 1937, the same year as David Quarrell. He came to England, he says, for a three-week visit and then spent his life there. Through Jeremy Fry, Kaffe Fassett met Ian McCallum and saw the American Museum. Ian McCallum commissioned Kaffe Fassett, who had trained in America as an artist, to do a set of drawings of the period rooms. Anybody familiar with the bold colourful textiles that later made Kaffe Fassett famous would be surprised by the drawings: no colour at all, simply a lively and sensitive pen line. When Dallas arrived for his yearly visit he gave his approval to making a booklet of the drawings. It was funded by Hugh Chisholm, Dallas's former classmate who had introduced Dallas to John. The result, with fifteen Kaffe Fassett drawings and text by Jim Dallett, is called *New World in the Old, drawn by a Californian Artist*. By chance, when Kaffe Fassett returned briefly to America later that summer for an exhibition of his paintings in New York, he and Dallas were on the same sailing of the *Queen Elizabeth 2*. They had their meals together on the voyage and Kaffe Fassett then spent a few nights in the guest suite on the top floor of 228, until he had to make way for Ian's arrival. While there he did a drawing, in the same style as those in the little book, of Dallas sitting in his bedroom, with its four-poster bed, and walls hung with the collection of early maps. This is now on show in the American Museum, dated, rather oddly, 1960 although it was drawn in 1964. It forms the front cover of this book.

Ian McCallum spent a week or so at 228 each year before making a round of lectures to Friends and potential Friends of the Museum in cities across America. Before arriving, he usually sent Dallas a list of a dozen or so people to invite to 228 for a drink. In December 1965, Ian did his American trip accompanied by Loelia, Duchess of Westminster (the third of the four wives of the second Duke). Dallas wrote later "The Duchess was to lend glamour; how many new Friends she attracted I don't recall". Ian's list included two magazine editors, an art gallery owner, a Tiffany's window-dresser, a future Metropolitan Museum curator and, most significantly for Dallas, "a comparative unknown: Robert Wilson, at that time an architectural student at the Pratt Institute". Dallas adds "The Duchess was not to be invited to this gay gathering". This, written in 1988, is, by the way, one of only two or three uses of the word "gay" in the thirty volumes of the journal.

The word had not begun to be used in this sense when Dallas was young. This linguistic shift resembles the kind of changes he had to make in his way of living as he started to have younger friends. He had grown up in a world where, generally, any departure from the norm was regarded as so repugnant as to be unmentionable. A few people though it "sophisticated" to have an artistic bachelor uncle and perhaps one or two unmarried male friends. Their orientation would be hinted at rather than boldly stated. Nobody before the 1960s dared to be as easy-going and open about themselves as the people he now spent his time with. The discreet, even secretive, style he had followed in his years with John Judkyn had become not just habitual but ingrained. Gay men in those days were forced to conceal a great deal about themselves if only to avoid prosecution. Now, in his fifties, it was too late for him to change his ways to the extent of becoming as "out" as his younger friends. But, without ever adopting their style, he adapted to it.

Robert Wilson quickly became one of Dallas's close friends.

> He was still a student of architecture at Pratt Institute. He was about twenty-four years old. Very courteous, neatly dressed, with nothing whatever bohemian in his appearance one might have assumed he was preparing to enter a conservative New York architectural firm. However, he mentioned that the kind of architecture he was interested in was stage design, in fact, he had already designed an off-Broadway production, Jean-Claude van Itallie's *America Hurrah*. Although there were twenty-seven years difference in age between us, he was very amiable and arranged for me to meet several of his friends.
>
> After he graduated from Pratt, he rented a loft on Spring Street in New York's Soho, and in 1966 invited me to several performances there in which he danced, either alone or

with a partner. Here was a very different Robert Wilson from the proper young man I had met at the cocktail party! On one occasion, in an incense-scented room he danced under phosphorescent light encased in transparent red-dyed plastic. In another production, *Byrdwoman*, the performers represented chickens, bouncing on boards and pressing against the wire of a large chicken coop. Bob swooped about with lurching, half-spastic steps, clucking. In later productions he continued to fascinate audiences with these movements. He claimed that he hated doing them "but I can't seem to stop."

Even more significant to me than Bob Wilson's theatre work was the fact that after the 228 gathering, he spoke about the occasion to his friend David Finkbeiner, and made a point of introducing us.

Robert Wilson had described David as "an artist-sculptor who was creating works in moulded paper — and, just imagine, he makes his own paper!" Robert Wilson brought David Finkbeiner to meet Dallas at 228 not long before Dallas left New York for his summer in England and France. Dallas said he wanted them to visit Garrison in the fall and, when he returned to New York, he remembered to invite them. Soon Dallas and David became each other's closest friends, and remained so for life.

David Finkbeiner was born in Oregon in 1936. His father was a Methodist minister. When David was five, the family moved to Idaho. There he reached the age of twenty without ever meeting anybody who was black, or Jewish, or openly gay. Eager to see more of the world, he trained as an actor at the University of Colorado in Denver and then moved to Los Angeles. In 1962 he was cast as a stormtrooper in a dramatisation of John Hersey's 1960 novel *The Wall*, about the horrors of life in the Warsaw ghetto in the early 1940s. He met a fellow actor in the play, Ron

Scott, also in SS uniform, and they embarked on a lifelong relationship. Cast for their Teutonic good looks, temperamentally they could not have been less like Nazis. Ron Scott, born in 1933, had studied chemistry at Princeton but was now beginning a stage career that lasted through the 1960s. David's time as an actor was shorter. He was soon working at the Pratt Institute's Manhattan campus, first learning and then teaching print-making, and creating works of his own. Ron became a student of the anthropologist Margaret Mead, and later worked with her as a colleague. David and Ron soon became regular weekenders at Garrison. When David Quarrell was at Opio with Dallas, the big summer weekend parties at Garrison continued, with David Finkbeiner and Ron Scott as hosts.

In 1967 David Quarrell's firm sent him on a business trip to San Francisco. He returned with Major Matthews, whom he introduced to Dallas as "my new lover". This announcement may have come as a shock to Dallas but it led to no rift. Instead, he accepted the situation and accommodated himself to it. From then on, the three of them regularly spent much of their free time together, and went to Garrison together most weekends.

Major Matthews: the name may suggest a military man, white, Anglo-Saxon, Protestant. It could not be more misleading. Matt, as he was generally called, was African-American, descended from slaves. He was born in Florida in 1936, one of the nine children of a father who deserted them. Despite this, they held together as a family, they all did well at school and college, and got interesting, worthwhile jobs. Matt stayed on the best of terms with them and visited them regularly in Florida and Philadelphia where they lived. Strangely, though, they seem never to have recognised or accepted that he was gay. He was a gifted linguist and musician and had a mixture of intellectual ability and social ebullience that carried him into other worlds. After university in San Francisco, he became a social worker in the New York City education system, helping children from backgrounds much more deprived than his own. Dallas not only accepted Matt as a close friend, he was almost as fascinated by him as he was by David Quarrell. He became one of the most important figures in Dallas's life. Here was a man from a different race and upbringing who met him on equal terms. James Liburd deferred to Dallas, Matt did not. To give just one instance of this, when Matt was driving the car, at the end of a long and tiring day, Dallas started back-seat driving. Matt put up with it for a while, then stopped the car and only drove on after Dallas agreed to keep quiet.

With Matt's arrival, the group that formed the innermost circle of Dallas's friends for the remainder of his, or their, lives was complete: David Quarrell, Major Matthews, David Finkbeiner and Ron Scott. All of them were together at Garrison most weekends. All of them loved animals, especially dogs.

> David Quarrell went each summer to the Castello where he stirred things up. Not decoratively — no one could improve on the Judkyn decor — but in the way of guests. An engaging crowd of young English friends of David shuttled back and forth between the Cannes beaches, the rocks at Cap d'Antibes, night-spots, Cannes again, and the Castello's pool, dining terrace, and Salles Arabes.

Dallas did not have the sun-tolerant skin needed for the beach, nor any inclination for the local night-life. Instead, he worked long hours in his library at the Castello, or sat and read in the shade of a fig tree by the pool, or groomed the scotties, while the younger generation sunned themselves on the beach in Cannes. He enjoyed their company at breakfast, sometimes joined them for lunch at one of the beach restaurants, and the whole house-party dined together at the Castello before the youngsters took off again for the bright lights of the coast. Dallas gave every sign of enjoying his quiet hours alone in the old house. Before and after the two weeks of David's electrifying presence, Dallas continued to have his older friends and members of his family to stay. David Finkbeiner, Ron Scott and Matt were also often there.

On 25 June 1967 an unexpected pair of visitors drove into the Castello's courtyard, a Polish Jew and his wife, Mr and Mrs Kolinski. In 1943, William Kolinski, then a young boy, had been hidden there from the Nazis by Elisabeth Starr. Now twenty-four years later, he had come to see the place again and to show it to his wife. Their visit set Dallas thinking about the contrast between Elizabeth Starr's altruism and courage and his mother's selfishness in their response to World War II. Three years later, at the end of 1970, he distilled these thoughts into his last testament on his mother, "The War Upset Everybody", which appears at the end of this volume.

After his 1967 summer in France and England, as Dallas was returning on the *Queen Elizabeth 2* to New York:

> it suddenly occurred to me that one way to tackle the problem of cruelty and violence which had been preoccupying me was to try to do something, perhaps through public education and the use of the media, to counteract these abusive tendencies as they affected animals.

This was another important new beginning in the life that Dallas was rebuilding after John Judkyn's death.

His thought, as it developed, was to set up an organisation not to campaign against the mistreatment of animals but to gather and disseminate information on the subject. He believed that campaigners often let down their cause because they lacked the backing of reliable research. Consciously or not, he was fulfilling

196

his youthful ambition to found a medical research institution. When friends suggested he might better use his resources for human rather than animal welfare, he argued that the two were linked and were mutually dependent. Nor did he stop supporting what might be called human humane causes. In 1970, after reading in a newspaper article that slavery still existed in some thirty countries, he joined the London-based Anti-Slavery Society (called since 1990 Anti-Slavery International). He continued to give it an annual donation for the rest of his life. But he put the bulk of his energy and enthusiasm into animal welfare.

He named his new foundation Argus Archives. This was partly after the mythological creature with a hundred eyes (representing research), and partly after Ulysses's faithful dog that recognised him after his long wanderings when no human did (representing the love between animals and humans that underpinned the enterprise). He appointed trustees, including Kennon Smith, who had introduced Dallas and David Quarrell to each other; Anne Marie de Samarjoy, a Hungarian refugee friend; Ron Scott, who eventually became its director; and David Finkbeiner. Dallas provided funding, and office space at 228 for the director and a secretary. He used 228 also for meetings and film shows for the animals cause. The films shown ranged from wildlife documentaries to horrifying scenes of human cruelty to animals. Some of these were secretly filmed by dedicated animal-welfare supporters, including David Finkbeiner and Ron Scott, who went to small-town fiestas in Spain, where goats, for example, were tormented and killed. Dallas had reservations about the filming, fearing for his friends' safety.

In the early days of his association with the animal cause, Dallas was troubled by his instinctive revulsion against reptiles. He cured himself of this with a visit to a zoo, where he gazed into the eyes of the snakes until he felt he could identify with them and see the world as they saw it.

Argus Archives's first two studies were, first, of the possible cruelty of keeping large dogs in small New York apartments and, second, of the ritual slaughter of cattle for food, demanded by the Jewish and Muslim religions. This latter provoked a hostile response from Jewish groups. They claimed that the Nazis' persecutions had started with objections to this ritual killing. Dallas was clear in his own mind that it was possible to kill animals humanely without becoming a Nazi.

In 1967, Dallas brought his psychiatric work to an end. He cited his increased workload from the American Museum as his reason for this. The museum had been created partly as an outlet for John Judkyn's excess energy. All the responsibilities John would have shouldered, or shared with Dallas, now fell on Dallas alone. He could also have mentioned the time he was devoting to Argus Archives. Privately he admitted he realised he was getting too old for the work with students which he had by now done at Columbia University for nearly twenty years. He was well into his fifties and his patients were mostly in their teens and twenties. One of them said she enjoyed seeing him because it was like talking about her troubles to a kindly grandfather. That clinched his decision to quit.

With more time at his disposal, Dallas was able to accept an invitation from Robert Wilson to act in his first major theatre piece, *The King of Spain*.

> It was produced in New York early in 1969 at the large but decrepit Anderson Theatre, on Second Avenue and 4th Street. Bob planned to assemble a group of people, all from very different backgrounds, in a "musty Victorian drawing-room," and within the framework of certain bizarre

activities, which he would prescribe, let them "do their own thing." I was to be one of the three men, described as "elderly" or "portly", who stood, squatted or slowly circled around a games-table, played something "that wasn't chess." Pushing a number of small cubes, triangles, and spheres of glass around the table, we were supposed to be totally oblivious to the extraordinary happenings around us. But it was hard not to glance at the grand finale, when four enormous "cat's legs" appeared from the wings and, as the stage-hands above the proscenium arch frantically worked the pulleys, crossed the stage in three giant strides.

Freed from the academic calendar, Dallas was now able to travel outside the months of high summer. Intrigued by my partner Ben Duncan's accounts of travelling in Greece, Dallas decided to hire a yacht to explore the Aegean islands. He invited us to join him, bringing, if we wished, some of our friends. We suggested the publisher Charles Monteith and asked Dallas if he had any women friends who might like to come. Ben felt Greece might not be ready to welcome an all-male party. Dallas brought Anne Marie de Samarjoy, and Olive Gavert with her husband Paul. He had taken over the leading role of Grieg in the 1946 London production of *The Song of Norway*, and now lived in New York coaching singers for Broadway musicals. The *Alkyon*, modest compared with Aunt Cara's yacht *Sapphire*, was grand by our standards, with a crew of eight to care for the seven of us. Ben and Charles Monteith planned the route in consultation with the captain, though Dallas intervened to veto the southern coast of Crete. Why? Because dangerous sudden storms blew up there. How did he know? Because he remembered that that was where St Paul was shipwrecked.

Our two week tour, starting on 25 May 1969, took us to several major classical sites, as notable for their beautiful settings as for their antiquities. We had Mycenae, Epidaurus and Olympia, and many lesser sites, completely to ourselves, arriving rested and refreshed, soon after our breakfast on the yacht, and well before the hordes that normally would have included us. We did have a sudden storm. As we crossed from the coast of the mainland to the island of Zakinthos, the *Alkyon* was buffeted by furious winds and waves. The crew worked as best they could, the guests sat in a nervous group, Dallas disappeared to his cabin. After some time, I was sent down to investigate. I knocked on his door, he opened it, and acted as if nothing was out of the ordinary. Clinging to the rocking doorpost, he expressed surprise at our concern. When the storm dropped and we reached Zakinthos, the seven of us went to look at the local church. We found our entire crew there lighting candles. They told us they were giving thanks for the *Alkyon's* survival.

In December of the same year, 1969, Dallas appeared in another Robert Wilson production, *The Life and Times of Sigmund Freud*:

> The play had very little to say about Freud, but the action was so delightfully lunatic that it might well have been subtitled "Fifty characters in search of a psychoanalyst." Still, there was nothing haphazard about it; every movement, every line, was rehearsed over and over again, until, timed to the second, it satisfied our meticulous director.
>
> The action in Bob's early plays alternated between immobility and sudden bursts of speech, screams and rapid movement. The big extravaganza in *Freud* was Bob's famous Mammy Dance. Thirty of us were chosen, myself included, regardless of age, sex, or color, to take part in this caper. In "blackface", topped by bandanas and wearing red dresses enormously padded up front and down behind, it was impossible except by voice and the occasional beard to tell

the girls from the boys. When the first strains of the "Blue Danube Waltz" were heard, the stage was inundated by the mammy throng, solemn-faced, shaking their upraised hands, turning right, turning left, bowing — then up! with the bustle. "*One*, two, three; *one*, two three" intoned a voice. The audience roared, and we found ourselves the hit of the show.

Although my more sedate friends refuse to believe it, yes, I was a mammy and shuffled and swayed on the stage of the Brooklyn Academy of Music. It was fun and it was funny. Who could ask for anything more? Well, one could ask for critical recognition, but from *Freud* the critics stayed away in droves. Honorable exceptions were two who came from the *Village Voice*; they called the play "one of the major stage works of the decade" and Bob a "genius." There were only four performances: two in December 1969, and two in May 1970.

The years that followed Dallas's retirement from his psychiatric work should have been serene, and could have been but for David Quarrell becoming increasingly difficult to live with. His wilful and contrary behaviour, scenes and tantrums were sometimes like a reprise of those of Dallas's mother. Lessons learned dealing with her, together with his psychiatric skills, were often needed, as were Matt's calming qualities and his professional expertise as a social worker. Almost anyone else would have given up on David. Matt did, indeed, part from him. Dallas did not, though David often reduced him to tears of confusion and despair.

David was a diabetic, and had to take injections of insulin daily. The level of blood sugar had a decided effect on his emotions, and he was subject to outbursts of rage and excitement.

His father, Arthur Quarrell, was Professor of Metallurgy at the University of Sheffield. Arthur was an exacting

201

perfectionist, and a fierce rivalry manifested itself whenever the two were together. Worse, David carried the image of his father's achievements, which were very considerable, always in his mind. The father-son competitiveness occasionally spilled over in his relationship with me, although at the same time I undoubtedly projected for him the more benign and fostering father figure which he craved.

On March 22, 1970, David took his own life with an overdose of insulin. The psychosis which manifested itself in the final weeks was sudden and brief, so much so that I am sure that there was an organic cause, probably related to some loss of diabetic control. Also, a series of dire events must have created, as I see in retrospect, considerable anxiety. His physical appearance deteriorated, with frontal baldness, an especially vexing condition to him, and very different from the "golden boy" of four years before. Another worrying event, to a partner of a recently organised brokerage firm, was a decline in the Stock Market. The unkindest cut of all, I believe, was the accidental death of his beloved scottie Heather in the summer of 1969. Owing to my unforgivable negligence in not fencing off the parking area, the dog crept under the gardener's car to enjoy a shady siesta, and, unseen by gardener Larry, was killed when he backed out. The most traumatic event of David's childhood was when he accidentally killed his baby brother in a ghastly kitchen accident. Perhaps the original scottie Mac was acquired as a kind of substitute for the baby brother. Heather's death, which David no doubt partly attributed to his own negligence, may have conjured up some of the terrible guilt over his brother's death which tormented him for years.

As I said, his passage through our sky was meteoric, and, meteor-like, he ended in darkness. But his memory is very bright among his friends, and in whatever house I happen to be, in Opio, Freshford or in the US, I have the image of David in his "salad days" by me, photographed with his arm protectively around Heather, and in another version, smilingly offering her a biscuit. Separated they were, tragically, in life, but in memory for me they are forever united.

In memory of David, Dallas arranged for trees to be planted in Brooklyn, saplings then, now fully grown. Each summer he visited David's parents in Sheffield until Professor Quarrell's death in 1983, and continued visiting the widowed Rose Quarrell after that.

The photographs of David joined one of John Judkyn seated by the harp in the Greek Revival room at the American Museum. For the rest of Dallas's life, these three framed photographs were with him in whichever of his houses he was living, in America, England and France. David's death, less than seven years after John's, was not only a second shattering bereavement but marked the end of his focusing his life on one special person. Never again after this did he have what he called when writing about David "a very strong attachment". Instead he formed an even closer bond than before with David Finkbeiner, Ron and Matt.

Soon after David Quarrell's death, Matt moved into the house in Hoyt Street which he and David had shared and it remained his home for the rest of his life. Although they had parted, David had not altered his will, leaving the house to Matt. What had been David Quarrell's room at Garrison became Matt's room. At about the same time, David Finkbeiner and Ron Scott moved from a loft on the Lower East Side to an old house near the Manhattan Bridge in Brooklyn. Almost every weekend they were in the guest room at Garrison. From then on, these four, Dallas, David, Ron and Matt, gathered together at Garrison for weekends, Thanksgiving and Christmas, and they celebrated their birthdays together. David, Ron and Matt, together or separately, stayed with Dallas at Opio and Freshford; and each year Dallas travelled with one or more of them to different parts of the world. Dallas referred to them as "the family". David and Ron had each other; Matt had a series of lovers; Dallas, now in his late fifties, concentrated on maintaining the daily and yearly routines of his life, and on his self-imposed regime of hard work. He spent a lot of time alone, or with only the dogs for company. He crossed the Atlantic by sea, usually on his own, long after most people took to flying. He liked the quiet of the ships' libraries, where he read and wrote and did his yearly accounts.

In the Princess Grill on the *Queen Elizabeth 2* in June 1970, three months after David's death, Dallas found himself at the next table to Tennessee Williams and a much younger man. He could not help overhearing their conversation:

> Physically, T. is short, slightly dumpy but not stout, he has brown hair close cut and a small moustache. His features are good; with horn rimmed glasses on he looks like an academic type. He is fifty-five. His voice is drawly, "fruity", reminiscent of people like Louis Bromfield, Cecil Roberts, Somerset Maugham; homosexual, American expatriate café society voice. His laugh is a kind of fiendish hysterical giggle. He gives the impression of being drunk, or stoned, both at lunch and dinner: his speech is often thick. Once he burst out with "I hate the establishment, fuck the establishment!"
>
> His friend was attractive, in his twenties; was connected with the stage. T. was anxious to give him a good time in Europe, promised to introduce him to interesting people, stars, etc, in England and Italy.
>
> His money is in a custodian account at the Chase Manhattan. "I don't have to worry about money. I have to see that my sister is provided for."

He didn't sleep well last night. "I think I am apprehensive about these readings. I am afraid they will laugh at me. I didn't tell them what I am going to read I prefer to surprise them!" (He has two public readings in England, and in Rotterdam).

Speaking of death. "Death comes when a man's art dies." "I have said everything I have to say." "But aren't you interested in theatrical effects?" "Oh yes, I've always been interested in that but you have to think always of the director and actors."

Prior to the showing of the film *Hello Dolly*, they went down to smoke pot. T. said he wouldn't stay long — but Streisand is good.

Nureyev: "He's rather savage. He walked off the stage during a performance, leaving the ballerina to finish alone, when the conductor made the tempo too fast. But he's always been very loving to me."

"Are you ever afraid of going mad?" he asked his friend. "No — I'm more likely just to give up," said the latter. T. said "I'm not afraid. I've been through too many therapists — Freudian, Jungian etc.

"I took a course of injections from Dr— in New York. He gave you the first, then you gave them to yourself. I don't take those anymore. But occasionally I take hypnotics when I'm writing and want to release my unconscious."

"Too close for comfort", I thought, and sacrificing curiosity to prudence, had my table changed to a quieter spot after the second day.

Only in the early 1970s did Dallas start to fly regularly. By then the liners were turning into cruise ships, the standard of service was dropping, joggers disturbed the tranquillity of the decks and, in Dallas's view, worst of all, the linen sheets on the *Queens* were replaced with cotton. Quarantine restrictions had always ruled out taking the dogs to England. Dallas discovered that Air France,

alone amongst airlines, allowed dogs in the cabins with their owners, rather than in the luggage hold, but only in First Class. So
each year Dallas paid the fare for one of his younger friends,
usually Matt, to bring the scotties to Opio.

In February 1971, Dallas flew to Rome for a celebration at the
Keats Shelley Memorial House of the 150th anniversary of the
death of Keats. Dallas chose this sesquicentenary to present most
of his Keats collection, started in his teens, to the Keats Shelley
House. For legal and tax reasons, he did this through the Halcyon
Foundation. Some of the items were already on loan to the house,
and he changed these loans into gifts, including Benjamin Robert
Haydon's first edition of *Endymion*, with his handwritten com-
ments throughout. He also gave much else, including a reliquary
that had belonged first to Pius V (the pope who excommunicated
Queen Elizabeth) and later to Robert Browning. One side of the
reliquary contains a lock of Milton's hair owned in turn by
Addison, Dr Johnson and Leigh Hunt who showed it to Keats,
hence his *Lines on Seeing a Lock of Milton's Hair*. Years later, Leigh
Hunt divided the lock and gave part of it to Robert Browning.
He put it into one side of the reliquary and in the other side put
the lock of Elizabeth Barrett's hair that she gave him during their
courtship and which she fondly commemorates in two of her
Sonnets from the Portuguese. Dallas retained his two most treasured
pieces of Keatsiana, the manuscript of *I stood tiptoe upon a little hill*
and the life mask of the poet.

The next year, 1972, brought Dallas yet another untimely
bereavement, the third such blow he suffered in less than ten
years. His half-brother Aubrey Cartwright had caused increasing
concern for several years. In spite of having a beautiful, highly
capable and intelligent wife, Eva, two young sons, Charles and
Christopher, who were full of vitality and promise, a worthwhile

job with the International Committee of Museums, an apartment in Paris, and the magnificent Casa Estella at Antibes for family holidays, all was not well with him. He had difficulties in both his personal and professional lives, his moods swung from one extreme to the other, and his behaviour became alarmingly erratic. It particularly worried Dallas that when things went badly at work, Aubrey would try to win approval by making a lavish donation to the organisation that employed him. In Dallas's view this was a disastrous course for a rich person to follow.

Aubrey showed the first signs of serious instability in 1966. In 1972 he was put into the care of a sanatorium in Switzerland, where Dallas went from Opio to visit him in July 1972. With his professional knowledge of mental illness, Dallas saw that there was little hope of a recovery. On 6 October 1972, Aubrey, aged forty-two, committed suicide while still a patient there. Dallas was not only deeply distressed, he was severe in his judgement of the Swiss sanatorium for allowing it to happen.

Much as after the deaths of John and of David, Dallas tried to keep everything going as nearly as possible as before. Hard work, friendships and travel helped him to keep his equilibrium. In May 1973 he took a group of his friends on a second Mediterranean yacht trip, once again including Ben Duncan and myself. The destination this time was Turkey. The other guests were Matt and the Cacciatores, Vera, the Director of the Keats Shelley House in Rome, and her poet husband Eduardo. The six of us assembled in Izmir and our journey began with a few days on land. We visited the great classical site of Ephesus.

Then we had ourselves rowed across Lake Bafa, a half-hour boat ride, to look for the spot where tradition has it that the goddess Diana saw and fell in love with the beautiful shepherd boy Endymion. From the boat, we had a steep climb to a cluster

of farm buildings, where we found a group of men who took in
what we were seeking:

> a deaf-mute, his crippled, probably mentally-defective,
> friend; a child of about five who kept repeating in
> triumphant tones the word "Endymion"; a young man, per-
> haps the school teacher (our self-appointed guide), and a
> yokel, perhaps a shepherd.

They led us along a path through a wood until we came to what
they indicated was our destination: a depression in the rocky
ground with the remains of some ancient pillars, the shrine, we
took it, of Endymion. We seated ourselves in a circle and the
group of local people stood nearby.

> Vera Cacciatore read Endymion's words to his sister about
> friendship and love, and I read the invocation to Pan. To
> these words in an unknown tongue, written about this spot
> by an English poet, dead 150 years, who had never seen it,
> and celebrating their ancient legends and remote ancestors,
> this little audience gave respectful attention, as if listening to
> a reading from the Koran. Perhaps they thought we were
> conducting a religious ceremony — and so we were, invok-
> ing in turn the spirits of friendship and love, nature and
> poetry.

This was the fulfilment, near his sixtieth birthday, of the wish he
had recorded at the age of twenty-two in the passage from his
journal quoted on page 88. The next day we saw more
magnificent classical sites at Miletus and Didyma. Then we set sail
on a Turkish yacht along the coast to Antalya, spending twelve
nights on the boat in places so remote that for three days we did
not see or hear a motor vehicle or an aeroplane. The few boats we
passed were those of local fishermen.

A few weeks later, in July 1973 at Opio, Dallas received a letter from Robert Wilson, who was now recognised almost universally as a theatrical genius. The exception was England. In conversation with Ben Duncan and me, Dallas expressed resentment and anger at the failure of the British theatrical establishment to appreciate Robert Wilson's work:

> The French critics raved even more than the American. Louis Aragon, the distinguished man of letters, declared, "I have never seen anything more beautiful in the world."
>
> Bob wrote me from his house in British Columbia, saying he was working on a new play "in 7 acts and 12 hours long." It was to be called *The Life and Times of Joseph Stalin*, and would open in Copenhagen. He added, "I'm hoping that you might be able to come either as audience or performer… it would be great if you could be there for the opening."
>
> So I flew to Denmark in September. I arrived during a rehearsal in the splendid white, red, and gold setting of the Det Ny Theatre. Bob was coaching an elderly lady who turned out to be his grandmother, Alma Hamilton, aged eighty-seven. "Grandmother." "Yes, Bob." "Walk downstage right, stand facing the audience, and let out with two screams." Mrs. Hamilton produced a surprising volume of sound. Satisfied with his grandmother's ability as a screamer, he took us out to lunch. Said Mrs. Hamilton, "Who would have though I'd be acting in Copenhagen when I ought to be at home in Waco. But when Bob wants a thing he's very determined."
>
> That determination had collected over one hundred people for his play. Many were eager young Danish volunteers who had answered a newspaper appeal for help. I thankfully settled for the "talk-on" role of the telephone voice of the Russian dictator. "This is Joseph Stalin!" I

boomed. Then I joined the audience to watch, wide awake most of the time, the twelve-hour-long show.

The six of us on the Turkish yacht trip were amongst the fifteen people who stayed at Opio the following summer. There we were also joined by Dallas's scottie Maud and her daughter Scout, Matt's dog. As Dallas reached his sixtieth birthday he seemed more and more to value long-lasting friendships, both the human and canine kinds.

Chapter Eight

1974–1984

Sixty to seventy

In August 1974, when Dallas reached the age of sixty, he was working on the most ambitious project Argus Archives had undertaken. He had done his share of the research and writing for its earlier reports, *Pets in Urban Housing* (1970), *The Pre-Slaughter Handling of Livestock* (1971), and *Unwanted Pets and the Animal Shelter in New York State* (1973). The new study amounted to a full-length book and was researched and written almost entirely by Dallas, working on his own. Its subject was animals in laboratories. Dallas's medical background proved extremely useful in this context. As a doctor, he was able to gain entry to research institutes in America and England that would have refused access to someone introducing himself as an animal welfare campaigner, though he was usually open about his aims. Once inside, he understood what he saw, and could speak to the scientists in their own language. Argus Archives published the 200-page book, *Painful Experiments on Animals* in 1976.

In the Acknowledgments he writes:

I sincerely thank the many individuals who helped me during the writing of this book. In the course of visits to laboratories and organisations I was always courteously received, no matter how unacceptable my point of view may have been.

The book is distressing to read. For Dallas, what he witnessed must have been deeply disturbing. On at least one occasion he intervened:

> In 1973, Argus made an unannounced and unsupervised visit to the animal quarters at Berg Institute, New York University, at ten o'clock on a Friday evening. Floors infested with cockroaches, and several large dogs confined to cages obviously too small, made a poor impression. We noticed a female dog lying over a pool of blood in a cage with a gaping, undressed throat wound which ran from ear to ear. The dog appeared to be dying. We searched in vain for an attendant to notify. Finally, we telephoned the surgeon whose name was on the cage label at his home in the suburbs, and told him about the dog's condition. He said he had performed an experiment on the heart vessels (an anastomosis) which had been "unsuccessful", and that the dog should be "allowed to die". He had no suggestions for terminal care or euthanasia. We made our own arrangements for immediate euthenising of the animal through an outside source.

Although he does not say so in the book, what happened on this occasion was that Dallas and a colleague disguised themselves in white coats as laboratory staff, abducted the animal, and took it to a vet to be killed humanely.

As well as visiting laboratories, Dallas sought out any writings he could find that attempted to justify the use of animals in laboratories. He found surprisingly little had been written. He looked into the legislation intended to protect the animals, and found it was ancient and inadequate. He enquired about the inspection of laboratories by state and federal officials and discovered that such legislation as existed was not enforced:

> All the experiments described in this book have one thing in common: the suffering of animals. Basically, that is all we are concerned with here; we have not tried to assess the experiments in terms of their value to the human race. It is easy for a critic to make much research sound unproductive, even silly. It is equally easy for a scientist to confound a layman who has overlooked some important application of an animal experiment to human health. While this kind of debate bogs down in charges and counter-charges, the public is confused and loses sight of the fact that an animal suffers just as much in productive as in unproductive research. To repeat, therefore: the object of this book is to evaluate animal suffering, and to consider each and every case as a serious ethical and humane problem, not to be dismissed on grounds of economics, scientific freedom, statutory requirements, health benefits, or alleged divine sanction.

Dallas was shocked at the vast numbers involved, tens of millions of warm-blooded animals in America each year, including tens of thousands of non-human primates. He was appalled at what was done to the creatures. Many pages cover the acquisition of the animals, their transportation, care and disposal, but most of the text describes the actual experiments. He found a scientist in Kalamazoo who had spent years surveying "pain as a cause of aggression". This involved giving up to thirty-eight electric shocks per minute to rats and burning their feet by heating the floor of their cage, to discover how the rats responded:

Bursts of intense noise (135 decibels, sustained for more than one minute) were introduced. The effects of castration were tried; the animals were shocked wearing hoods, and, finally, one pair had their whiskers cut off and were blinded by removal of their eyes.

Ulrich looks forward to studies on humans. "Naturally the moral and practical difficulties are tremendous. Yet, as our knowledge of aggression in lower animals progresses and as more and more feasible methods of studying aggression in humans are developed, a clear picture should emerge". (Ulrich, R., 1966).

Dallas's comment on this was "Are there any volunteers?"

Many of the experiments Dallas came across seem arbitrary, even bizarre.

A series of distressful experiments on cats has been performed over a period of many years at the American Museum of Natural History, New York City, by L. Aronson and associates M. and K. Cooper. Their first report was a 1962 study on desensitisation of the glans penis of domestic cats. This caused "permanent decrements and qualitative changes in the mating pattern". In 1969 the Museum's experimenters worked with nineteen male kittens. They severed nerves in the penis tips of eight of them. The remaining eleven were each raised in isolation and "not permitted contact with any other cats". When mature, they had similar surgery.

Dallas observed that when writing about animal experiments the scientists referred not to pain but to "pain".

Whether written for the public or for other scientists (who sometimes remember the family pet), research literature bristles with euphemisms: stimulate (shock), aversive (painful), sacrificed (killed), voice modification (debarking), food deprivation (starvation), "fear" (fear), "forced" (forced) and challenge (anything from lethal irradiation to being battered to death).

Despite what he wrote in his introduction about studying the nature of the experiments rather than assessing their use, Dallas did go into the question of experiments that contribute to medical advances for humans. He considered the ethical question of the extent to which ends may justify means. This had been one of his main preoccupations when he was studying ethics and philosophy in his teens and twenties. Also, he found that a few scientists, particularly in northern Europe, were looking for other ways to obtain useful results without involving animals, such as using tissue cultures instead. In some cases it turned out that an experiment on human cell cultures gave a better indication of the effect of a particular drug on a human being than trying it out on an animal. This, he found, was true of thalidomide:

> If similar tests on human embryonic tissue had been performed at the time the drug was first developed, instead of misleading animal experiments, the tragedies which resulted from its use might have been avoided.

He describes new legislation being introduced in Denmark, Germany, Sweden and Great Britain to regulate the use of laboratory animals. He devotes his last chapter to alternatives to painful experiments on animals.

As Dallas worked on his book, Ron Scott conceived the idea of re-establishing his early links by buying a property in his native Massachusetts where he and David would spend weekends. Dallas, not wanting to lose them as regular weekend visitors to Garrison, bought an old farm that came on the market, a little way along the Old Albany Post Road from his own house, and helped them build a weekend home there. They moved in during 1975, along with their lively collection of animals which, at its peak,

amounted to twelve dogs and five cats. For five years, they and
the animals lived between their two houses, in Brooklyn and
Garrison, until, overwhelmed by the logistics, they gave up the
Brooklyn house. From then on, they lived in their house at
Garrison, having at least one meal each weekend with Dallas and
Matt. The guest suite at the top of 228 became their New York
City base.

The year 1976, when *Painful Experiments on Animals* was published, turned out to be, in some respects, one of the best years of
Dallas's life, but in other ways one of the worst. It began with a
visit in February, accompanied by David Finkbeiner and myself,
to Sri Lanka. We saw Buddhist and Hindu antiquities, we drove
through dense jungle, visited magnificent gardens, and, to end our
day, stood on the shore of the Indian ocean amongst local people
who came onto the sands each evening to watch the sun go down
in a blaze of colour. Dallas by then had an international reputation
in the world of animal welfare and, thanks to it, we were allowed
into remote corners of the great Yala game reserve. We saw
countless animals including buffaloes, crocodiles, iguanas, a family
of elephants amongst which we lingered for half an hour, several
kinds of monkey, and even a leopard. The next day a local
ornithologist took us on a walk where, with his help, we saw
more than eighty different kinds of birds. We also experienced a
frightening ride through a Muslim village that was being burnt
down. We were told that the perpetrators were militant Buddhists
(a new concept to us!), who had killed and injured some of the
villagers, and set fire to their houses. As tourists, in a car with a
local driver, we were hurried through the mayhem under police
escort.

An even more alarming moment came soon after Dallas
returned from Sri Lanka to New York. Writing about it seventeen

years later, in a letter comforting a friend diagnosed with cancer, he wrote:

> It may help you a little if I tell you my own experiences with cancer. Probably the worst moment was when it was first diagnosed, in 1976. I thought the end was not far off, and every six months after the first operation (implantation of radio diodes in the prostate), I went for a follow-up examination, with fear and trembling. The radiation was very effective.

The bicentenary of the American Revolution was celebrated in 1976. Newspapers and magazines made much of the occasion and a grand exhibition was staged in England, at Greenwich. All the publicity gave an extra boost to attendance figures at the American Museum. They had risen steadily since the museum opened and reached a peak in 1976 which has never been equalled since.

In August 1976, Dallas and I toured Scotland with Paul Davis, an old friend of John and Dallas who, in 1957, was one of their first guests at Opio. In one of the finest summers of the twentieth century, we had cloudless skies every day. We drove up the west coast of Scotland to Cape Wrath, the extreme north-western tip of the British Isles. Returning, we stayed with my friends John and Faith Raven in what Tennyson described as "the rugged halls" of their Victorian Scottish baronial castle, Ardtornish, in Argyll. Their elder son, Andrew, took us on a superbly picturesque eight-mile walk through some of the fifty-five square miles of his family's estate. Despite his operation and implant, Dallas seemed as robust as he had been in Sri Lanka. He mentioned that he had undergone some painful surgery but made little of it and seemed not to want to talk about it. Fortunately, it was far from being the immediate death sentence he had feared, but it caused him mental and physical suffering for all his remaining years.

Work for Argus Archives continued to be Dallas's main activity. He wrote a second book, basing it on the ideas raised in the last chapter of the other one: *Alternatives to Pain in Experiments on Animals*. He set out to show, first, that many of the experiments performed on animals served no useful purpose and, secondly, how the same, and often better, results came from using microorganisms, cell cultures, human material and gene splicing rather than laboratory animals. "I have tried a new approach, namely to cite individual experiments, often in the experimenters' own words, and then to match these with specific alternatives." By a scientist and about science, the book is written in Dallas's usual clear style, but is more a work of reference than one to sit down and read. In the course of it, he evaluates more than 300 research papers. He criticises experiments not only on humane grounds but because he believed they were scientifically defective. Any page, turned to at random, reveals scarcely believable examples of cruel and perverse experiments, followed by Dallas's sane and balanced response. Just one example, slightly shortened, on the blinding of cats and monkeys, will suffice:

> Experimenters sewed up one eye in a single kitten, and both eyes in five kittens, before the animals were ten days old, and "lid closure was rigorously maintained throughout the first six months of age." Various tests were made to see how the cats discriminated between light and darkness while their eyes were still sutured and then after the lids were opened. Their ability to discriminate was affected by six variables: open lids; closed lids; dilated pupils and increased retinal sensitivity in the dark; constricted pupils and decreased retinal sensitivity in the light. (Loop, M., 1977).

Sakakura and Doty at the Center for Brain Research of
the University of Rochester, New York, working with
monkeys, noted the following:

"Blinding seemed to have the effect of calming
these highly excitable wild animals. However, the
paucity of movement and lack of appetite suggest a
physiological effect. It was common to discover the
blind squirrel monkey during the day, unlike the intact
animal, curled up in its home cage in the full posture
of sleep, i.e., with its head between its knees, tail over
its shoulders."

In this experiment, electrodes had been implanted in the
brain cortex to be used later for stimulation and
electroencephalographic recording, after which the animals,
macaque and squirrel monkeys, were blinded, two by having
their eyeballs removed, and the rest through having their
sight destroyed by induced glaucoma or photocoagulation.
(Sakakura, H., 1976).

If an experiment seems to be entirely without significance, it is pointless to seek for alternatives. I do not perceive any significant questions posed by these experimenters
who are engaged in sewing up eyelids and enucleating eyeballs. The experimenters, with their monocularly and
binocularly-sutured cats, have created a highly artificial situation: if their question had had any value to the human
blind or had needed to be asked in actuality, the answer
would long ago have been found through examination of
humans. Also, since blindness is so widely distributed among
humans, and has always aroused sympathy and exceptional
financial support, there is certainly a vast amount of research
utilising the human blind, both as whole subjects and as
operative or postmortem donors of ophthalmic material. For
these reasons, there seems to be minimal justification for the

distressful, mutilating experiments on animals reviewed above.

Alternatives to Pain was published in 1980 and, as it superseded the earlier book, this was withdrawn. More than 8,000 copies of the two books were sold, mostly to libraries, academics and humane societies. More than twenty years later, as I write, cruelty to animals continues but, far from being secret, it now makes headline news in England. Two of the main stories in today's newspapers (18 January 2001) are of the passing by a vote of 384 to 174 in the House of Commons of a bill to ban fox-hunting; and, top of the page, attempts by animal rights activists to close down Britain's largest animal experiments laboratory, Huntingdon Life Sciences. The protesters have fire-bombed its employees' cars and issued death threats to its directors and staff, and even its shareholders and bankers. Dallas visited Huntingdon Life Sciences when he was researching his books, and he disapproved of what he saw there, but he would have been outraged by the behaviour of the protestors. He saw that they brought the whole animal welfare movement into disrepute. For all his love of animals, Dallas deplored the activities of the extremists.

The anti-vivisection movement has a long history and Dallas made no exaggerated claims for his contribution, but his books were the first of their kind.

> When I began to investigate the subject in the early 1970s, I was surprised to discover that not a single book devoted to vivisection in America had been published in the twentieth century, a grim testimony to the determination of the scientific establishment to keep the laboratory door firmly closed to the public. Recently, several books have appeared describing the abuse of animals in research and testing even more exhaustively than I did, and new alternatives using non-

sentient material have been developed and published. However, my attempt in *Alternatives to Pain* to match the various types of experiments with specific alternatives, e.g. cell and organ cultures, micro-organisms, molecular analysis in drug design, and pain prevention, seems to have been an original concept and has not yet been duplicated.

In recognition of my work, I received an award from the Humane Society of New York in 1981 and the Animal Welfare Institute's Albert Schweitzer Award for 1981.

In March 1982, Dallas received a letter from someone he had not heard of, Margaret Cheney, who lived in California, and had just read his book. In the course of the long letter, introducing herself, she wrote "I too am a science writer, with a new biography out, *TESLA — Man Out of Time* (Prentice-Hall), which is the first new one in forty years on the great inventor, Nikola Tesla. And I came across your work in the course of preliminary research for a new book. You have pretty well written what I had hoped to do, that is, hammer away at the alternatives to the present horrendous cruelty in animal experiments until something gets done." This was the start of a correspondence running to hundreds of pages, and the drafting of a new book, also several hundred pages long. They agreed to write alternate chapters and to call the book *Animal Politics in America*. Ten years later, in 1993, Dallas summed up their collaboration:

> I contributed three chapters: "The Apes are Talking", "Try It Out on a Scientist (pain research)", and "Through the Cancer Labyrinth". Cheney's chapters were hard-hitting exposés of animal research and abuse. We worked and corresponded for three years, our letters reflecting our attitudes and aims, and much anecdotal material on our lives during those years. We failed to find a publisher.

Living on opposite coasts of America and, in the summer months, on opposite sides of the Atlantic, Dallas and Margaret Cheney got to know each other through letters. These often provide the best picture of Dallas's life at this time. In June 1983 he described for her how he spent the weeks after crossing on the *Queen Elizabeth II* in June:

> I spent five days motoring and resting in several country house hotels in western Ireland, then to England on June 26. After a week at my place there, Freshford Manor, Bath, I head for the South of France, and there I'll stay until August 7. Back in England, I stay put at Freshford until flying home on September 20.
>
> For years I've combined this long period abroad with study and writing. I use the British Science Library in London when I'm in town; at Freshford I live very quietly and have lots of uninterrupted time. In France, where the house is usually full of guests, I get in an hour or two before breakfast, then disappear until noon, emerge for a swim, lunch and, after the obligatory siesta, am free for the afternoon and evening, for whatever the others want to do.

The variable element in this itinerary was the week in Ireland. In other years he spent a week touring in Europe, Africa or different parts of the British Isles. For example, he discovered the magnificent regional art museums in cities all over Great Britain. He visited several of them on his own, or with Ben Duncan and myself, or with other friends. Further afield, he and Matt visited Morocco in 1980 and Senegal in 1984. In 1983, Dallas toured Sicily with Matt, Ben Duncan and myself, and also, on his own, visited Savannah, Georgia.

His family, too, was a source of pride and pleasure. He regularly visited his sister Cynthia at her house at Aiken, South Carolina. She bred camellias there and in 1974 named one of them *Dallas Pratt*. In February 1982, Dallas's cousin Bob Coe celebrated his eightieth birthday with a dinner given in his honour by his Oxford college Magdalen, and Dallas flew from New York for the occasion. Bob Coe had recently funded the restoration of the college's famous tower. Later in the same year, Dallas visited an exhibition at London's National Theatre of photographs by his niece Linda.

Anybody reaching the age of sixty-five must expect to start losing his contemporaries, and to be aware that the end of his own life may not be far away. But in the early 1980s, HIV started to bring the premature deaths of much younger people. Dallas, who had already experienced more than his fair share of bereavements, now began to suffer many more, numbering some forty caused by HIV over the next few years, including some in his innermost circle. Both Ian McCallum and Matt became HIV-positive at about this time (one of them may have infected the other) though it seems neither they nor Dallas was immediately aware of it. As we all began to learn about the virus, we saw that behaviour that had seemed merely hedonistic a few years earlier was in fact lethal. Intolerant people found it all too easy to be censorious. And to make it doubly sinister, the disease could lie dormant and undetected in a person's system for years, showing no symptoms, whilst being infectious.

In September 1982, James Liburd died of a rare and extremely unpleasant condition, in which his heart and lungs petrified, nothing to do with HIV. Since 1961 he had looked after 228, a house so large that, according to Dallas, at least one light bulb needed changing each day. Dallas described him as "a kind friend who had an apartment in the house and, for twenty years, looked after the collections, security, dogs, mail-forwarding and innumerable other details, especially when I was abroad." James Liburd

223

had also kept 222 Imports going for nearly twenty years until, a few months before his death, his landlord brought it to an end with a sixfold increase in the rent of its showroom.

After James Liburd's death one of his many brothers volunteered to take his place at 228, and moved into James Liburd's apartment. But he was not a satisfactory replacement, failing to keep up with the maintenance of the house, even to replace light bulbs, and squabbling with the staff of the Halcyon Foundation whose office was in the house. Dallas put up with him rather than look for someone else.

In a letter to Margaret Cheney of 4 October 1983 he described the restricted diet imposed on him by his doctor, "no sugar, no salt, no pepper, no alcohol, no eggs, no bacon, no coffee, no cream, no breakfast".

The implanted diodes and a series of operations were keeping the cancer in check, and he continued to travel and to lead a fairly normal, active life, but he started to spend longer weekends at Garrison, from Thursday night until Tuesday morning, unless he had engagements in New York.

In 1981 came the twentieth anniversary of the opening of the American Museum. This was celebrated twice, first with a reception in July at the American ambassador's residence in London and, in November, at the British Embassy in Washington. Ian McCallum's hand is evident in the planning of these occasions, which Dallas described in his journal. First, London:

> "Their Graces the Duke and Duchess of Devonshire!", intoned the scarlet-coated announcer. The ample matron who moved along the receiving line, from Ambassador to Ambassadress to Ian to me, recalled nothing of the former Debo Mitford, whom I had met in 1937 at Castle Howard.

"Her Grace the Duchess of Argyll", "Lord Sackville". This duchess, the "beautiful Margaret Whigham" of the late 1920s who "came out" with Cynthia, rediscovers in me, as she does every two or three years when we meet, a glimmer of her youth. "Why we knew one another as children!" she informs the master of Knole, over whose heraldic, superannuated features flits a vague smile.

"Lady Diana Cooper and Viscount Norwich". A legendary lady, ninetyish, in trousers, the Viscountess, in 1911–1912 the Nun in *The Miracle* (how many remember her now as that, when, "beautiful Lady Diana Manners", she took the play goers of the Flapper Age by storm both in London and New York?). And there with her was the Nun's son, John Julius. "I just love Ian" announced Lady D., the voice enthusiastic, but the still beautiful white mask of the much-lifted face entirely expressionless under a broad-brimmed black hat. The trousered form moved on, and Lady Rosse was before us, Oliver Messel's sister, Tony Snowdon's mother, a diminutive countess swathed in brown silk, with earrings, necklace and bracelets fashioned from gold leaves. Unlike the classical life-masks of Margaret and Diana, her face, preserved by the art which conceals art, was the most successful of the three, the face of an ageless pixie peering from a thicket of gold leaves.

The British names rang out grandiloquently. "The Earl and Countess of Snowdon, her Grace, the Duchess of Newcastle…" The handful of Americans present seemed to be making their last stand against the mighty regiment of British — but to little avail. 1981 is the bi-centennial of the defeat of the British at Yorktown: The American Museum and the American Embassy celebrated it by letting the British march in with banners flying.

225

Then Washington:

> Tea with the Ripleys in their library at 2324 Massachusetts
> Avenue. Dillon not yet back from the Smithsonian, so Mary
> picks up the telephone when it rings. Talks with someone
> about a speech. No, Mary can't remember what Mrs Ford or
> Mrs Carter said; Mrs Johnson gave a "nice talk". Will get
> Dillon to call when he gets home; *he'll* remember. Hangs
> up. "That was Nancy Reagan — she wants to know what
> she should say when she presents her inaugural gown
> tomorrow to the Smithsonian." Dillon returns, and starts the
> complicated process of getting in touch with the White
> House. Asks me if I'd like to go to the lunch tomorrow for
> Mrs Reagan at the Museum of History and Technology.
> Yes? So he starts the complicated process of getting me
> OK'd by the FBI. Life at the top in Washington is full of
> complications, but the Secretary of the Smithsonian can
> sweep them all away. Soon I was "on the list".
>
> But that evening there was the dinner-dance at the
> British Embassy. Two hundred people had paid to come.
> The occasion raised a substantial sum of money for the
> American Museum. With sinking heart, I mounted the
> grand staircase with Lutyens's curvilinear iron balustrade, and
> passed down a splendid arched hall lined with columns, and
> lighted by a glittering series of crystal chandeliers. Mrs
> Warren (Claire) Cox, Sir Nicholas and Mary Henderson
> were receiving. Dick Howland fussed up "But *you* were
> supposed to be in the receiving line"; shepherded me into it.
> I caught the last hundred arrivals. "I'm so and so". "I'm
> Dallas Pratt". People have a hundred ways of saying "I'm so
> and so", but my one and only way of saying "I'm Dallas
> Pratt" soon sounded pretty flat.
>
> I sat on the Ambassadress's left. The rest of the table
> consisted of Ambassador Sir Nicholas Henderson, two for-
> mer ambassadors: Ellsworth Bunker *and* Mrs Ellsworth

Bunker; former ambassadress Evangeline Bruce (with the head of Georgiana Duchess of Devonshire), and Mr Friendly.

The orchestra blared, and finally I ventured on the floor with Lady Henderson. We talked of their house near Marlborough; buying garden things from Robin Eden; gingerbread at the museum; how she loves New York, where she once worked as a writer for Time-Life; the ambassadorial life in Washington, more hectic than it had been in France, Bonn or Warsaw. She tactfully interrupted our dance with an offer to show me around the Embassy.

At 10.45 Dillon and Mary appeared, and he delivered a short speech thanking everyone and lauding the co-founder. Then home in his official car.

November 4

Lunch with the First Lady.
We gathered at noon in the director's dining room of the Museum of History and Technology. We stood on the terrace and admired the panorama, from the Capitol to the ever-supreme Washington Monument. Then "Mrs Reagan has arrived!" We filed in, Dick Howland introduced me as "Head of the Halcyon Foundation". She was in a black and white plaid suit. Heavy pancake make-up, but very pretty with an ineffaceable smile.

Then, after lunch, through a panoply of secret service men and museum guards, we were ushered down to our reserved seats. Dillon spoke his welcome, said suitable things about previous First Ladies and their gowns, and Mrs Reagan responded (after posing for photographs with her set smile). In spite of laryngitis, she got through it nicely. Thanked Mr Galanos the designer — and the dress, on the "Cordelia-head" model (a reproduction of Pierce F. Connelly's sculpted head of King Lear's Cordelia) which had been peeking over a screen, was unveiled, or unscreened. A white, one-strap long dress sewn with many pearls and much diamanté. It was over; the crowd invited for tea and drinks pressed forward; Mrs Reagan, the Ripleys and one or two others had retreated to an inner room. I chatted on and off with Evangeline Bruce. She seemed fragile, almost sweet, a bit deaf, chic in stripes; insisted that I must call her in June at her "set" in Albany and come for a drink. I went in to look at all the other First Ladies and their gowns, all on mannequins with "Cordelia" heads. But I was the only one who bothered with them; the crowd was preoccupied with the refreshments and Mrs Reagan, who now had moved through the crush and was saying gracious things to a throng of school children. I attached myself to Dillon and Mary. "Quick we must say good-bye to her," said Dillon, "we must run." So, like the White Rabbit, we scampered after the Queen, and the Hon. Secretary was in time to bow the smiling lady out.

We made our way back to the official car; Mary and I got in. Dillon said, "I'm going to walk." "Where to?" said Mary. "To the White House," he said. By this time, this destination seemed quite unexceptionable.

In June 1982 Dallas met for the first time a neighbour who had lived in Turtle Bay Gardens much longer than he had.

I was driving into the garage at 228 when I saw Lunsford Yandell on the sidewalk. Joan, the Halcyon secretary, appeared breathlessly in the garage. "The gentleman has brought Miss Hepburn to see you!" Sure enough, there was my neighbour, glimpsed here and there through the years I've been on 49th Street, but never met. Dark blue sweater, trousers, and hair piled up in dishevelled abandon. Face with freckles, red splotched. The famous bone structure. The voice.

The voice, with a bit more of an elderly quaver in it than I expected, expressed "Kate's" delight at seeing the surprises of 228. The round table in the dining-room caught her fancy. The glass paperweight snow-scene in the green room; the peacock feathers in the hall; above all, the library. First, mocking "Oh, it's very grand, verrry grrrand!" Then, "a stage set — fantastic for a movie! It's ridiculous but wonderful, unique" and so on.

She kept talking, reminiscing mostly about the gardens. "I'm the oldest resident, since 1931. We rented the house from the Smiths. Very nice people, but they weren't well off, and I had sort of hit it rich. Then they disappeared, leaving some of their possessions. I don't know what happened to them. It was weird. Maxwell Perkins, the famous Scribner editor was next door. He was deaf, and we never spoke. There were several beautiful daughters. Mrs Perkins, she would have loved to become an actress, like me. Whenever I came back from tour she filled my house with roses in silver vases."

"Mrs Martin, she didn't like central heating." Yes, I said, I had to put a lot of it in. "My driver had the job of keeping her fireplaces going." The thought amused her, also the memory of her (Hepburn's) car parked illegally outside her house. "Influence with the police, you know!"

"Where were you born?" she suddenly asked. New York, I said. "You have a wonderful face," said she. "That *is* a compliment coming from you," I said. "They're disappearing," she said "those Saxon faces... now don't tell me you're half Italian."

She had to go — "I'm just back from an eight months' tour. Very exhausting. Masses of mail." Lunsford steered her out through the garden, "You must come and see my house." "I'd love to."

As he approached the age of seventy, Dallas thought increasingly about the distant past. A few days after Katharine Hepburn's visit he was staying at the Grand Hotel des Bains at the Lido in Venice. He told his friends he was there to do his annual accounts, making up for the week he would formerly have had alone on an Atlantic liner. It seems that his finances were not his only preoccupation. Writing in his journal a few days later at Opio he described going on the hotel launch into Venice:

> Near and far in the lagoon floated walled and cypress-shaded islands. Which of them I wondered, was the one known as the "Garden of Eden", where I had spent an afternoon half a century ago? A friend and I were taken there by my cousin Dorothy Caruso to call on its then owner, Princess Aspasia, widow of King Alexander of Greece. I took a photograph of their young daughter, Alexandra, holding her cat, a girl who later became the queen of King Peter of Jugoslavia. Dorothy was an exuberant blonde with bright blue eyes; Aspasia a classical dark-haired Grecian beauty. The vision of the three women in their island garden haunted me for a few moments then dissolved like the foam in our launch's wake.

Then he looked back to July 1948 when he and John rented a palazzo from a "Signora C".

> It was just off the Campo San Maurizio, on the Calle Dose Ponte. I could see the staircase, which Signora C was reputed sometimes to descend on all fours: "to see how it felt to be a dog." She dearly loved her two exceptionally large poodles and was never separated from them. She saved the wool from their coats and had it spun into thread and woven by nuns. She wore clothes made from this material, and when the three walked abroad she blended remarkably with her doggy friends. Russian-born, witty, one of the sights of Venice: I hope kind Signora C in the end achieved her ambition to be buried with her poodles, in the plot she had reserved for them in the cemetery of San Michele.

Finally, back at the hotel on the Lido, he spotted on the wall of the staircase landing a large, faded framed photograph:

Taken on the beach, it showed figures in the costume of the very period, the early nineteen-hundreds, of *Death in Venice*. Prominent in the foreground was a large-hatted figure, who else but a governess? gesturing to a boy in a striped shirt. Tadzio! The fit was close enough to give a thrill, if not of recognition, at least of coincidence.

This idea was exciting enough, but in a few moments it was succeeded by an even more daring thought. A beach at the Lido in early 1900s. A boy and his governess. What about that other boy, Leonello Minerbi, and his governess, living in Venice at precisely that time? Surely during the summer months the Minerbi children didn't remain cooped up in the Rezzonico. Not if I knew Dear, born in Lincolnshire near the shore of the North Sea, devoted to beaches, sun-bathing, and to something she called "ozone" with which children she looked after, whenever the sea breeze blew, were exhorted to fill their lungs. Where would they be if not on the Lido, perhaps even staying for a few weeks at the Hotel des Bains, "parked at the beach with Dear" as my sister and I used to be?

The pieces all seemed to be falling into place.

Now this old photograph — might it not have been there when Thomas Mann came to stay? I examined it more closely. The face of the "governess" was blurred. It was a thousand to one chance that the photograph had been there at the time of Mann's visit, and that he had noticed the little figure in the striped shirt, and that his seeing it had planted the seed from which the whole fantastic tale had germinated in his fertile imagination. But the one chance that the boy might have been Leonello, and that Leonello might have become Tadzio, coupled with the undoubted fact that I, through the link with Dear, was the successor to a hypo-thetical Leonello-Tadzio — that one chance is enough to fire my imagination. So I add my fantasy to Mann's, my dream to his vision.

And how strange that I, sixty-seven years old, seem to have started my visit to the Hotel des Bains as an Aschenbach and ended as a Tadzio!

Dallas would not have crossed a continent to meet a duchess, a First Lady or a film star, but in November 1983 he flew to San Francisco

to meet, by appointment, a gorilla. Indeed only by appointment is one received by Koko, now an international celebrity because of her ability to communicate through the American Sign Language (Ameslan) of the deaf. What interested us was not that apes had learned signs for a great many words, but that they were beginning to communicate ideas and even criticism to humans in a way that animals, much less the caged victims of the laboratory whose cause we are attempting to champion, have never been able to do before. To have visual evidence of this break-through in communication, with its potential for producing a revolutionary change in human attitudes towards animals, was the reason for our trip to see Koko and for my own visit to Washoe later.

These visits were the subject of one of the chapters Dallas wrote for the book he was working on with Margaret Cheney:

The chimp, Washoe, was born in Africa. Brought to this country in 1966 when about a year old, she was acquired by Allen and Beatrice Gardner, behavioral psychologists at the University of Nevada in Reno, and named by them after Washoe county, Nevada, where they lived.

Realizing how difficult it was for primates to articulate, yet how readily they used gestures, the Gardners decided to teach Washoe American Sign Language (Ameslan). In four years the ape knew 160 signs, including combinations such as *gimme sweet* and *come hug*. She signed to herself when looking through magazines: *that drink, that food*. She

invented signs, such as one for bib, the proper gesture for
which the Gardners didn't happen to know. Later they
found that she had hit on the correct Ameslan sign, made by
outlining a bib on the chest.

Dallas praises the humane and considerate treatment accorded
to the many animals he encountered. He describes watching several chimpanzees conversing, in human sign language, with their
carers and with each other, and even squabbling.

Yes, it's a family — of primates and one in which you don't
have to make fussy distinctions between the human and
non-human members.

As we stood and watched the group, Loulis proved that
he was the live wire of the family, rushing around and
around his room and executing flying slides over places
where the floor was wet. But it was Washoe, sitting quietly
up there complacently watching the antics of Loulis, whom
I gazed at with real emotion. First, there was the feeling we
all tend to have in the presence of a "celebrity". I'd seen the
two movies that had been made about her life and her
training, looked at many pictures of her in the books where
her accomplishments are described — along with those of
Lana, Sarah, Lucy, Koko and the other signing apes, and
read many articles on the subject. But there was an
impression that went deeper than the ephemeral contact
with fame: a feeling close to wonder that through the
medium of this animal, sitting up there so casually, something momentous and irrevocable had entered the history of
our time, of the human race. It was not just the knowledge
that animals can think, can reason, have ideas about themselves and about us and share many of our emotions.
Sensitive people, from saints to shepherds, have shared their
lives with animals and have always known this. Animals
themselves have been telling us in ways which, although
non-verbal, are perfectly evident to those whose minds are

receptive. But there are also those, both scientists and laymen, with closed minds, for whom this sort of knowledge has to be spelled out. And that is exactly what Washoe has done, the first non-human creature to do so since the serpent whispered into the ear of Eve, when in 1966 she succeeded in making her first sign: the sign for the word *more*.

Symbolic word! *more* now offered by the animals than they had ever been able to give to us; *more* now asked from us than we had ever been willing to give to them. Looking at Washoe, I saw her as confirmation to the doubters, and as a challenge to all of us to enter into an entirely new relationship with the animals.

Some of Dallas's friends in the animal rights movement would have objected to keeping these animals in captivity in any circumstances, and would have questioned the value of teaching them a sign language that, in the wild, they did not need. Dallas characteristically kept an open mind. Once convinced no cruelty was involved, he praised what he saw as an enlightening experiment.

During the 1980s, Dallas started to include Italy, in addition to England and France, in his annual itinerary. David Finkbeiner and Ron Scott had established a base for themselves in Tuscany. A Pratt Institute colleague of David, Luis Camitza, moved to Lucca in 1973 and started a print-making school. He invited David to teach on its summer courses. David found a derelict farmhouse eight miles from Lucca, at Valdottavo, and bought and restored it as a second home for himself and Ron.

All his life, Dallas liked to alternate time with his fellow human beings and time alone or with his dogs. On 21 August 1984, he was at one of his London clubs, the Naval and Military, better known as the In and Out Club, because of the black-painted IN and OUT on its white stone gate piers in Piccadilly. There he wrote in his journal the piece referred to in the introduction to this book:

21 August 1984

Into the Eighth Decade

What a great way to spend one's seventieth birthday! In London, alone. The day unplanned, except for a reserved ticket at the Cottesloe for a performance of *Antigone*, 7.30 curtain. Breakfast at the Club ("In and Out"). Always very pleasant, thanks to the smiling head-waitress's mothering and her serious young assistant, blond, about twenty, with the sort of profile Oscar, in his Parisian exile, would have written home about.

I had a sort of plan to give myself presents. This started off with a visit to Smythson's to have a new die made for Freshford stationery. Since the old supply has lasted about twenty years, this shows that I'm looking forward to longevity.

Then I went to the London Library in St James's Square and enrolled myself as a member. For years I have had a ticket to the British Museum's Reading Room. Collecting books oneself from the stacks, all of which are open, at the London Library, will be an agreeable contrast to waiting for hours at the British Museum for them to be delivered. At the moment, I can't think what possible use it will be to me, but the lovely musty smell of old books, and the large, peaceful, nicely shabby Reading Room, alone are worth the annual fee. Science, they admit, is not their strong point; I checked out "vivisection" and found that the collection consisted of half a dozen nineteenth-century volumes and two by Dr Beddoes Baily, dating I think from the 1940s.

And so to Harrods, which was teeming with tourists. The only English accents belonged to the clerks. Still with the idea of giving myself a present, I visited the "Map

House" in Beauchamp Place. I expected little from this, having received very cavalier treatment on a visit three years ago. This time the assistant was at least pleasant, but harassed by phone calls. A do-it-yourself search amongst a muddle of world maps produced an unexpected treasure, Waldesmüller's *Ptolemy World*, published by Johann Schott, from the original plate of the 1513 atlas, but, according to an opinion of someone in the British Museum's map department, the second (1520) edition. This map had been in their original catalogue, in fact was reproduced on the cover. They said it hadn't sold, so they'd recently had it coloured! Alas, imagine prettifying a historical piece of this importance and rarity. If they had made any effort to sell it to me three years ago, I should probably have bought it uncoloured. But then I shouldn't have had such a lovely seventieth birthday present! — and "just what I wanted".

The evening on the South Bank began with a good dinner (avocado vinaigrette, salmon trout, and chocolate "roulade") served in the hard-to-find theatre restaurant. The National Theatre is a magnificent piece of sculpture, with the usually ugly blocks of the building transformed into a cubist extravaganza by flood lighting.

Antigone was a disappointment. A chorus in fedoras was not disturbing, and the director's idea of combining modern dress with stylised "archaic" gestures might have worked if it had been consistently performed by all the characters, which it wasn't. As for the plot: Sophocles' message is that if humans fail to conform to traditional practices decreed by the gods, in this case the burial of the dead, catastrophe will follow. An expanded version of the legend which I saw many years ago with splendid actors (who were they?) powerfully brought out the subtleties of this conflict between Creon's philosophy of the end justifies the means and an instinctive human impulse springing from a woman's heart. But the play I saw last night seemed simplistic and crudely melodramatic by comparison.

On my sixty-fifth birthday I made a resolution to "experience" life, and other human beings, more directly. But I see in retrospect that the motivation was not care for others, but rather self-love. Dare I resolve on my seventieth to seek actively to help others *before* they come to me pleading for it?

I had arrived at the National Theatre at about 6pm, leaving the taxi when we reached Victoria's Embankment, and crossing the Thames from Charing Cross on foot over Hungerford Footbridge. From here, the view to the east is very disappointing, St Paul's crouching like a grey dwarf among the dark slabs of skyscrapers which now surround it. But when we came out after the play was over, what a transformation! Night had fallen. Up and down the river moved brightly lighted restaurant-ships. Blackfriars Bridge, floodlit, was a shining band across which skittered buses which, at a distance, looked like toys. Beyond, the City was dark, except for a few red beams on the tops of tall buildings. Then, at the very moment that I reached the river's edge, St Paul's was illuminated, then Somerset House opposite, and finally, beyond Westminster Bridge to the south, the Houses of Parliament.

This magical transformation-scene was the dramatic event of the evening (not that pallid performance in the Cottesloe), the surprise present of the day!

I walked slowly back over Waterloo Bridge, the different buildings moving onto centre stage and off again as my angle of vision changed. Shell-Mex House towered up, its huge clock squatting on top of a cubistic orange-lighted facade. Then down into the street, walking past the west facade of Somerset House with its profusion of allegorical statues, and into the Strand, where I caught a bus back to Piccadilly. It was after midnight, and I was already into the second day of my eighth decade.

Resolutions for the Eighth Decade

1. Do routine things *fast*. Don't dawdle.
2. Remember to avoid the following ways of boring the young:

   (1) *Complaining*, about the inability to remember names, about disabilities of the aged (e.g. arthritis), much of this is a disguised bid for sympathy.

   (2) *Comparing*, the good old times with the bad present and horrible future. Since the young have had no direct knowledge of the past you gain an unfair advantage by using it as a criterion. Unlike you, the young can't use the reputed pleasures of the past as a refuge from the present, so again it's unfair to spoil their present when they have nothing else to fall back on. As to the future, it's the young, not you old ones, who will have to suffer its horrors. Rubbing the noses of the young in those horrors gives the impression that you're jealous of their determination to enjoy and live only in the present.

   (3) *Criticising*, Children criticise (aping some adults, per-haps), but most young adults, filled with the optimism and *joie de vivre* of their salad days, don't. So instead of criticising emulate this admirable trait and see if it doesn't have a rejuvenating effect on yourself.

Chapter Nine

1984 – 1994

Seventy to seventy-nine

I strove with none, for none was worth my strife:
　Nature I loved, and, next to nature, Art:
I warm'd both hands before the fire of Life;
　It sinks; but I am not ready to depart.

Dallas altered the last line of Walter Savage Landor's 1849 poem, adding the word *not*, and put it at the front of volume twenty-one of his journal. As he entered his seventies, after painful operations for prostate cancer and with other common ailments of the elderly, such as arthritis, far from showing any sign of sinking or departing, he speeded up. With a late surge of vitality, he was writing more, collecting more, travelling more, continuing the activities that had occupied him for years, and starting new ones.

In the autumn of 1984 he was planning a reception for 160 people in the library at 228 to launch the American Friends of the Anti-Slavery Society. As mentioned in Chapter Seven, he had joined the society in 1970 after reading a newspaper article about the extent of the survival of slavery into modern times. Following the Civil War and the emancipation of the slaves in the mid-nineteenth century, concern over slavery had largely lapsed in America. In England, thanks to the Anti-Slavery Society, the work of Clarkson and Wilberforce continued. Dallas hoped that a new generation of Americans would "join the fight against the slavery of bonded labour, of Moslem women mutilated by circumcision, and of indigenous peoples paralysed by economic and political exploitation" and that "some day a marker may be placed in the library to commemorate the events of 13 December 1984." After hosting the reception, and helping to start the American group, Dallas did not continue to play an active part in the society, pleading his many other commitments, but he went on making a yearly contribution to its funds for the rest of his life.

At about the same time, in late 1984, Dallas moved most of Argus Archives's activities from New York to Garrison. He retained only the archives themselves at 228 in the care of a part-time librarian. This gave students and people writing on animal concerns convenient access to the material that had been accumulated over the years. Argus Archives also had its twenty-fourth film presentation in the library at 228 that autumn. In David and Ron's house at Garrison, Ron and a colleague worked part-time as director and assistant. Both of them used computers in their other occupations. These were the early days of the IBM PC and there were many frustrating teething troubles. Ron was spending the rest of his time on a doctoral thesis on the use of aerial photography in archaeology, combining two strands of his previous work. Dallas was disappointed that Ron failed to complete it, if only because Dallas would have liked to see two doctors on the Argus Archives letterhead.

On Christmas Day 1984 it was Dallas's turn to cook at Garrison. For years, Dallas, Matt and David had taken turns producing the main meal each weekend and, on the same basis, they rotated the preparation of celebratory meals for Thanksgiving and Christmas. Some years, when it fell to David, he produced a vegetarian Christmas turkey, a dish of vegetables and nuts pressed into a turkey-shaped mould. He was a strict vegetarian, but pre-pared to cook meat for others. Despite their love of animals, both Ron and Matt were meat eaters. Dallas was never exclusively vegetarian, saying that he did not want to put the many people who entertained him to extra trouble, and that he believed farm animals, with no anticipation of death, well cared for and then humanely killed, led pleasant lives that the animal rights extremists would deny them. Writing on 9 January 1985 to Margaret Cheney about progress on the book *Animal Politics in America* that they were working on, Dallas said:

> A reply to your last letter is long overdue. Blame Santa and his entertaining but extremely time-consuming activities. Our snowy retreat in the mountains up-river always per-suades us that we must have a traditional Christmas, to the point that I found myself this year personally cooking and stuffing an 18 lb turkey. It would have been just retribution had I slipped a disc trying to get the big one in and out of the oven.

An 18 lb turkey? As well as the immediate "family", many guests shared these occasions. David Finkbeiner would invite up to ten of his Pratt Institute students, many of them foreign. David was impressed by how well Dallas got on with them, always quickly finding shared enthusiasms, a side of Dallas developed years earlier when he and John Judkyn regularly entertained students from abroad at 222.

Dallas reported to Margaret Cheney:

I am writing that chapter. My trouble is having too much material. It fell on me like an avalanche, but I've been tunnelling slowly out of it. You'll probably agree that the first pages are the hardest, but ten of those are done and the rest will come more easily.

I've been swamped with American Museum, Argus and personal problems. I calculate that about one letter a day is received from England, clamouring for immediate attention. France only writes about once a week. Just keeping all my pots boiling here and abroad has been a job. A rain of gifts is pouring in for the American Museum and its affiliate the John Judkyn Memorial: objects in kind, all of which I have to decide whether to accept or reject, and, if accept, then go on with infinite details of thanking the donors, arranging appraisals, accessioning and determining how and where they'll fit into the collections. The latest is an avalanche of dresses, or rather elaborate ball-gowns, of the period 1920–1950, complete with shoes, gloves, evening bags and costume jewellery, some of them belonging to my mother, which my sister, unbeknownst to the family, had been hoarding with the idea that some day her daughter or granddaughter might be interested. Vain hope! it's hardly Greenwich Village wear; but very interesting for an exhibit we are assembling in England called "New Yorkers in their City — 1915–1940, 1960–1985."

Cynthia was gravely ill at the time but summoned up the strength to sort out and send these items for the exhibition.

Most of the letters from England were about another, larger project at the American Museum. Dallas and Ian McCallum were planning a new gallery, the first major addition to the museum's buildings since it opened more than twenty years earlier. The museum needed more space, for storage, for a conservation department, a library and reading room, and a book shop, as well as extra gallery space for both temporary and permanent exhibits. Ian McCallum had for a long time wanted an opportunity to extend the museum's collection of American decorative arts to the present day, with room settings of some of the great twentieth-century designers, such as Frank Lloyd Wright, and Charles and Ray Eames. The new building might have made this possible but Dallas had a different idea for the use of any extra exhibition space. By this time his collection of early maps was probably the finest still in private ownership, and included several from before the first printed books as well as an example of every world map printed before 1500. The earliest maps in his collection date from long before Europe's "discovery" of America; later examples show the New World with increasing accuracy and detail. Dallas saw them as an appropriate introduction to the history of domestic life in America that the museum embodied. He decided to donate the whole of his map collection to the museum. Ian could see that it was an acquisition that any museum director would be proud of.

The diverse functions of the new gallery set an architectural challenge. Even more so did the setting, in the beautiful Avon Valley, and within a few yards of Jeffry Wyatville's Claverton Manor. Here at last was an opportunity for Ian to make use of the architectural qualifications he had gained more than forty years earlier. As he had never worked in an architectural practice, he employed a local architectural firm to give him technical support. His design succeeded magnificently in combining classical and modern elements in its Bath stone exterior. He gave it the look of an elegant American public building, perhaps the US embassy in a small foreign country. Dallas was eager to have a hand in every detail of the map room. He looked at displays of maps in museums and libraries wherever he went, sketching suitable cabinets, lighting systems and, in particular, ceilings.

Such a building was bound to be immensely costly. By the 1980s a project of this size could no longer be funded from surplus income, even an income as large as Dallas's. He made a substantial contribution himself, but other money was needed too. In November 1984 he reported to Margaret Cheney:

> I had to do some work on the museum's campaign to raise money for a new gallery, culminating in a trip to Washington to see a well-spoken-of fundraiser. Yes he would be willing to help us; no he didn't think we had better than a fifteen to one chance of getting a challenge grant from the US Endowment for the Arts; no he wouldn't actively ask people for money but would advise us how to do it; yes he would accept so much a day for sixty days over the next ten months. In a daze, I first thought "why that's not so bad." Then I realised after saying good-bye that I'd dropped a zero and he was talking about an enormous sum, ten times what I had thought. Back to square one.

Many of the museum's trustees, council members and Friends contributed and took part in fundraising. An American-born member of the museum's council, married to an Englishman, Mrs Evelyn de Rothschild (later Lady de Rothschild) chaired the fundraising committee. Two major benefactors were Dallas's sister Cynthia, and their cousin Bob Coe. Since the early days of the museum, Cynthia had been one of its most devoted supporters. She had travelled many times on Ian McCallum's fundraising art and architecture tours, seeing private collections, and only stopped when, as she put it, she could not face yet again putting on white gloves for cocktails with a contessa. Now, though terminally ill with cancer, she once more came to the aid of her younger brother's project.

Neither she nor Bob Coe lived to see even the foundation stone of the new gallery laid. His large contribution, amounting to more than a quarter of the cost of the building, came in the form of a legacy. He died on 26 May 1985 at his home in Cannes. Aged eighty-three, he was one of the last surviving grandchildren of Henry Huttleston Rogers (Dallas and Cynthia were, of course, great grandchildren). Educated at St Paul's school, Harvard, and Magadalen College, Oxford, he had been a career diplomat, finishing with his appointment by President Eisenhower as US ambassador to Denmark. His spectacular home looking out to sea over Cannes was a stylish modern building, cantilevered over a steeply sloping garden designed by Lanning Roper. Like Dallas, Bob Coe never married. They were on friendly, if not especially close, terms. Visits were sometimes exchanged, with their respective house guests, during the summer in France. Soon after Bob Coe's death, his house in Cannes was bought by his neighbour further up the hill, the Sultan of Brunei, who demolished it to improve his view of the sea.

On 13 July 1985, less than two months after the death of Bob Coe, Dallas's sister Cynthia died. Dallas returned from Opio for the funeral at Southampton, Long Island, and filled many pages of his journal with photographs and reminiscences of the sister, three years older than himself, who had shared with him the ups and downs of their childhood. His memory jogged by pictures, letters and other mementoes of her, he went on to write more and more about his early years. Much of the early part of this book is based on what he wrote after Cynthia's death, most of it ordered chronologically here for the sake of clarity. But his words about the last part of his sister's life do belong here, where even the references to their childhood seem appropriate. Dallas's own advancing cancer at the time adds to their relevance:

Cynthia lived on hope for more than two years with cancer of the lung. In my contacts with her doctors I asked them not to deprive her of hope, and I think they succeeded. Even in the last fortnight when, for the first time, she began to have severe pain, she hoped it was only arthritis and treated it with aspirin. In this way she kept despair at bay and inspired her friends with her courage.

She never mentioned the word "death" to me, although she clearly thought about it. This showed itself in her eagerness to give me things for the John Judkyn Memorial. I was happy to take objects like Mamma's evening dresses of the 1930–1950 period which Cynthia had squirreled away in cupboards for decades, but with the exception of two paintings of Charleston flower-sellers I wouldn't let her take things off the walls. I said it was too depressing to see gaps appearing. Perhaps I inhibited her from speaking more directly about death, but it's just not the Pratt way to dwell on unpleasant matters.

When she died, after only a few days of acute pain and distress, I was surprised at the relief I felt. But I recognise this as the natural sequel to my two years of anxiety over her sufferings. The persistent cough and the loss of appetite and weight. The incontinence, increasing feebleness and the social embarrassment provoked by all this, the last being especially trying to the reserved Pratts, although of course infinitely worse for her than for the onlooker.

The twenty-four hours I spent in the States at Southampton, under Linda's unobtrusive but meticulous management, were like being at an elegant house party. In the evening, there was Ginnie Wanamaker's dinner. At the cemetery, only the bronze urn on the gravestone wrung the heart — "Cynthia in *there*?" Otherwise it was decorous and touching; some tears were shed by Linda (Cynthia's daughter) and Melinda (Linda's daughter), but no sobbing or having-to-be-supported occurred; the minister read a few prayers and expressed hopes about Cynthia's resurrection in which nobody, considering who we were, believed; the bouquet which Melinda had gathered from Cynthia's garden looked charming in the sunshine and that was that. Dear's grave was there in a little enclave of the plot, and Billy's (Cynthia's son) stone was ready for him (Cynthia, in a typical fit of economy, had had her own, Bill's (Cynthia's husband) and Billy's stones made at the same time — probably in the early 1960s). Dear's ashes were the first to be planted there, in 1963, and had to wait patiently for the first Laughlin, Bill, to join her, 16 years later. This was nothing new, during her forty active years as governess to Cynthia, Linda, Billy and myself, she was always waiting for one or another of us while we "titivated" (her word). Patient, unassuming, loving Maud Duke — "Dear" to Cynthia and me. Her nickname says it all, both in life and as a one-word epitaph on her grave.

The luncheon that followed the funeral, 150 friends and relatives at tables on the lawn, surrounded by the splendid trees which Cynthia had planted there thirty or forty years ago, and by her garden, was the sort of party which perfectly fitted the surroundings. "Mummy should have had parties like this" said Linda ruefully, but Mummy never had nor would have had the courage to give them. As the guests began to leave, the herbaceous borders, glowing with magnificent day lilies, came into focus, a sight I had never seen before (because never there in high summer), and, I suddenly realised, would never see again.

I walked around the empty house, soon to be sold and its contents dispersed. I realised that I was saying good-bye to an association of four decades, and to a host of objects which came from even earlier periods of my life. In the dining-room were the giant pair of ceramic Fu dogs, with eyeballs which you could move in and out with your fingers. Only Cynthia and I knew that: we had discovered it as children when they had stood in our grandparents' house at Ardsley-on-Hudson. Our stepfather Carty's collection of hunting paintings were on the walls, including the naive little Sartoriuses on the stairs where Cynthia could see them as she came down in her electric chair — this and its track now the most forlorn-looking things in the house.

If I were to have anything I wondered what I would choose. Although grandpa Benjamin valued them highly, I turned down the *cloisonné* ducks because of their silly faces. The Ming figures of horsemen were very fine. The pair of small horse paintings by Herring: "The Approaching Storm" and "Peace and Plenty", would fit into any decor, as would the Wedgwood bowl decorated with figures of Apollo and the Muses. (Cynthia told me on my last visit that it came from Millicent Rogers' collection). Another favourite of Grandpa B's was the small oil, in the guest room, of a young woman tapping on a door: he said it looked exactly like Grandma at the time of their marriage. The timid maiden in the painting reminded me not at all of the Grandma I knew, an imperious figure under a parasol being driven sedately through London in the back of her "motor". "That old Tartar", as Dear called her. But Mamma loved her dearly.

I kept my last good-byes for Cynthia's bedroom. Her walk-in closet with scores of shoes was poignant. On the rack were numerous brightly flowered dresses, the colours growing ever brighter as Cynthia had aged. I had never given her bedroom more than a casual glance when Cynthia, still in bed, had called me in to say "Good morning" and to give the "drill" for the day. Everything was always planned ahead to make one's stay as interesting as possible. Now I saw the room very differently. It was a reflection in miniature of Cynthia's happiest associations: a photo of Bill as a handsome undergraduate, 1920's and '30s miniatures of Mamma (with bandeau), Cynthia, Aubrey and myself; a picture of Ilex her beloved labrador; Daddy, very upright in World War I uniform; a little cut-out figure of Carty, nattily dressed for a point-to-point; pictures of her children and granddaughter at all ages; and, everywhere, mementoes of the travels which had so enhanced her last decades.

But the most touching object of all, not only in this room but in the whole house, placed on the chaise-longue facing Cynthia's bed so that it might have been the very last thing her dimming eyes rested on, was an old doll. She was very elegantly dressed in a striped silk taffeta gown, and a mauve silk coat trimmed with fur. White hair and a smart bonnet completed the Mme la Marquise look. Although I had never noticed her here before, I remembered her perfectly. She had come as a present from Cynthia's godmother, Evelyn Wetherbee, when we were living at 1140 Park Avenue. Cynthia would have been about eight, and I no more than four. Every year Mrs Wetherbee sent Cynthia a doll, always beautifully dressed and outfitted. As she grew older, Cynthia became bored and finally indignant over these child's gifts. Yet this was the lone survivor, the only being (if you can call it such), beside myself, who had accompanied Cynthia from childhood to grave. For the first time that day I saw Cynthia not as a decrepit woman whose life had ended but as one with a long history all summed up in that room, and guarded by a faithful doll which reflected the child still present in poor C's failing body.

It was time to leave for the airport. The doll and I exchanged a last look. Then I closed the door on my sister's little world and its sole inhabitant. Both of us would now have to manage as best we could in a world without Cynthia.

As well as writing about Cynthia, Dallas wrote more and more about himself and his early memories. He found quantities of old correspondence, photographs and scrapbooks amongst Cynthia's possessions. She had kept more than a hundred of their mother's letters, as well as letters their mother had received from other people, starting soon after World War I, including those quoted at the beginning of this book. It was during this period that Dallas compiled the two introductory volumes of his journal, "Volume Zero" and "Juvenilia", and placed them before the original volume one, started when he was seventeen. At the latter end of the journal he added eight "Appendix" volumes. Twenty of the thirty-odd volumes of the journal date from after Dallas reached the age of seventy.

After Cynthia's funeral, Dallas returned to Opio and then to Freshford. He was at the American Museum on 8 August 1985 to greet its two-millionth visitor, a Mrs Howarth who had travelled from Derbyshire bringing a party of thirty-nine people recovering from strokes on an outing to the museum. Dallas presented her with a basket of goodies from the museum shop.

Back at 228 in September 1985, Dallas set about refilling the wall space vacated by his maps when they were shipped to England. For more than twenty years the maps had been displayed on the cork-lined walls of his bedroom. The 1964 drawing on the cover of this book shows them already filling most of the wall space. By the 1980s, they covered every inch, even the underside of the canopy of his four-poster bed, where he could lie on his back and look up at them. Now their place was to be taken by a collection of twentieth-century American prints which he was forming with the expert help of David Finkbeiner. The theme of the collection was the benign relationship of animals and humankind, such as pets with their owners, horses and their riders, livestock with farmers, and so on. Dallas named this collection *The Compassionate Eye*. It soon outgrew the bedroom wall space,

just as the maps had done. More recently, it has followed the maps
to England and joined the American Museum's holdings, together
with yet another of his collections, miniature American prints,
none more than two inches square, also chosen jointly with David
Finkbeiner.

Now, twenty years after he first met Robert Wilson in
December 1965, they spent some time together again:

> Since the early 1970s, Bob's extraordinary success abroad
> (operas at la Scala, ballet in Paris, productions in Iran, Japan,
> and throughout Europe) have kept him continually on the
> move. Old New York friends have seen very little of him.
> But recently our mutual interest in finding a home in the
> Rare Book and Manuscript Library at Columbia for his
> immense archive at the Byrd Hoffman Foundation and for
> my own small collection of Wilsoniana, brought us together
> for a few days. The passage of two decades had changed him
> remarkably little in appearance. Nor had fame, and the term
> "genius" which reverberates after each new production,
> altered his gentle, almost diffident manner, nor quelled his
> still-boyish enthusiasms. He talked about his recent work,
> the D'Annunzio-Debussy *Le Martyre de Saint-Sebastien*,
> which was being performed by the corps de ballet of the
> Paris Opera, and of the appreciation in Hamburg for his
> *Parzival*, and especially for his protégé and collaborator
> Christopher Knowles's interpretation of the title role.
>
> "And what do you have in mind for the future?" I asked.
>
> Bob took a couple of pieces of blank paper from my desk
> and gazed reflectively at them. "*King Lear*," he said. "I read
> and re-read it. And I'd look for a great comedian to play that
> role. Why? Because only the finest actors excel in comedy
> — tragedy is easier. And Lear should handle the body of
> Cordelia as if it were so very light — as light as paper."
>
> And suddenly the two sheets of paper were floating, pro-
> tected for a moment by an old man's fumbling hands, then

slipping away, down, down, becoming a white body, Cordelia...

In May 1986 Dallas was about to go on the spring journey that was now part of his yearly round. He had toured Spain and Portugal with Matt the previous April. Now the plan was to go to Moscow and St Petersburg (then still Leningrad) with Matt and Ron. News of the nuclear meltdown at Chernobyl came as they were about to go. Quickly changing their plans, they toured in Germany and Italy instead.

The year 1986 was the twenty-fifth anniversary of the founding of the American Museum. This was celebrated on 11 July with a lunch for 120 people, including most of the major contributors to the new gallery fund. Victoria de Rothschild's efforts had surpassed all expectations. Like Dallas, she had turned for support first to her own family. There were several Rothschilds at the lunch. It was followed by the laying of the new gallery's corner stone by the Prince of Wales.

He had lingered at his earlier engagements in Bath and arrived half an hour late. Ian McCallum greeted him at the door. Dallas described the occasion in his journal the following day:

> Charles entered. Brown hair with small curls at the edges, a blue shirt, suit with neat grey pattern, tanned face, pleasant smile. Ian said "Ambassador and Mrs Price" whom, of course, he knew; then "Dr Pratt, Co-founder of the museum". This dialogue followed:
> HRH: "I congratulate you on your achievement. Do you live in England?"
> DP: "Only in the summer months, Sir."
> HRH: "Oh, I see."
> DP: "I have the best of it."
> HRH: "Yes, the best!"
> After this brief exchange, the Prince signed the guest-book.

Ian and Dallas then showed the Prince round the museum.

> The Prince wanted to know how we acquired the furniture.
> "By gift?" Ian: "Well, mostly from Dr Pratt." We then went
> through the Shaker, Pennsylvania Dutch (where the Prince
> admired the brightly painted Toleware), glass exhibit, New
> Orleans Bedroom, Greek Revival Room and Country
> Store. The Prince looked carefully at the things Ian men-
> tioned, made appreciative murmurs, but at once started an
> animated conversation with the tea-room servers who were
> lined up behind their counter. I suspect he prefers to initiate
> a conversation rather than be lectured, especially about
> antiques. He plied them with questions such as, "I suppose
> you work awfully hard? Making huge mounds of sandwiches
> every day?" etc. They were obviously thrilled.
>
> We walked across the courtyard to where the 120
> luncheon guests were sitting in a stand waiting for us. As we
> passed by he noticed Baronesse Elie de Rothschild. "And
> what are *you* doing here?" Then, when he saw Evelyn and
> Victoria de Rothschild on the dais, said, "Why, the place is
> full of Rothschilds!"
>
> I spoke first, for about eight minutes, without notes (this
> seemed to impress people, judging by all the comments I
> received about it next day). I didn't feel a bit nervous, in
> fact, it was quite exhilarating. Then Charles rose. He made a
> graceful apology for being late, then added humorously, "I
> hope Mrs de Rothschild used the time to get some more
> contributions!" He said he had been asked a number of
> times to come to the museum and was very pleased that at
> last he had a chance to see it. He complimented me for
> having founded it and for my generosity (!) He was aware of
> "the good taste of Americans" from his frequent visits to the
> US. He commented on the many British monuments which
> had been restored through American interest — "and dol-
> lars"! Since European culture had flowed to the US, it was

253

good to see it coming the other way — as at the American Museum. He hoped to come again when the building was up. Then he laid the corner stone of the New Gallery.

Leaving the dais, he walked and chatted his way through the ninety-odd staff and guides of the museum. Then he walked across the lawn with Ian and admired the Mount Vernon Garden, and on the way back looked at the bandboxes in The Milliner's Shop. When asked if he would return and bring his sons, he said "Yes, but we'd have to lock them in the tipi." He said they quite wore him out.

As we were moving towards the gate by which he would leave, Margaret Argyll appeared on the arm of a young man. She's rather blind — and was plaintively crying "Where is Dallas Pratt — I must see him — he's my oldest friend!" She wanted her escort to see the Indian Room, but I could only show them the nearby Milliner's Shop. "Now why didn't Ian show me this?" she complained. I said I couldn't go into the museum with them because I had to say goodbye to the Prince. I was amused at myself so grandly rejecting the duchess in favour of the prince. Ian said later there were four duchesses on the premises. His collection is growing.

Finally, the Prince appeared and said goodbye to the Prices, Ian and myself, remarking to me, "I'm coming back to see your maps!"

In the spring of 1987, Matt took early retirement from his job in the social services department of the Brooklyn public schools. Cost-cutting and policy changes had made his last working years unfulfilling and stressful. He now started to devote his time to language-learning and music. His French already fluent, he studied Spanish, and, already accomplished on the clarinet, he learned to play the acoustic guitar and took singing lessons. He was also free to travel more. In April 1987 Dallas and Matt toured the Pacific West Coast together, and visited a German friend of theirs, Dieter Engel, a long-time regular visitor to Garrison and Opio, and, like Matt, born in 1936. Dieter Engel was HIV-positive and beginning to suffer opportunistic infections.

In June 1987, Matt travelled with Dallas yet again when, for a third time, Dallas rented a yacht and took a group of his friends, once more including Ben and me, sailing in the Aegean. As well as seeing several classical sites, we visited the grave of Rupert Brooke on Skyros.

In July, Dallas was at Opio. Dieter Engel and Ian McCallum, both looking unwell in the holiday snapshots, were among the twenty or so guests. Ian volunteered no information to Dallas about his health, nor about any thought of retiring. He was sixty-seven. Dallas felt he must question him directly: did he have AIDS? Ian confirmed Dallas's worst fears, but was determined to continue at the museum as long as he could. He led his last tour, a cruise along the Yugoslav coast, in early October 1987. On the 29th of that month, in his flat above the museum, he died.

Dallas flew from New York a few days later for a memorial gathering at the museum. Speaking of Ian, he said:

> This morning, on what would have been his sixty-eighth birthday, his family and a few friends saw his ashes scattered in the stream flowing through the American Arboretum which he so lovingly created. As we watched the water flowing down towards the Avon and beyond to the Atlantic, a friend said, "Ian still travels."
>
> To have Ian as a friend, was to have a passport with visas to half the countries of the world, and potential introductions to some of the most interesting inhabitants. He was passionate about history, but it was not that of the textbooks. A very visual person, he wanted to see, touch and photograph history — in the stately homes of England, the palaces of Leningrad or Udaipur, the restorations of colonial

America. He was fascinated by — and fascinating to — people who were the living embodiment of history: royalty, First Ladies, bearers of historic names, legendary millionaires. This resulted in a symbiosis from which everyone benefited, not least the American Museum. His anecdotes about these friends were inexhaustible.

The New Gallery was nearly complete, but not yet in use.

Only a few days before his death, some friends he had been entertaining in his flat went to look at it with him, and he said how pleased he was at the way the façade had turned out. This was his last act at the Museum and I like to think he gave his blessing to the new building.

Dallas was astonished by how large it was. He had examined the plans many times but never taken in the scale.

Finding a director to succeed Ian McCallum took more than a year. This was because Dallas and his fellow trustees began by choosing someone who was, to put it simply, the wrong person for the job, as was soon apparent to everybody, including the new director himself. The process weighed heavily on Dallas at a time in his life when he wanted less worry, not more. The appointment in 1989 of the museum's third director, an American, William McNaught, came as a great relief to everyone involved with the museum, most of all to Dallas. A generation younger than Ian McCallum, he brought youthful vigour to continuing all that Ian had started, including the art and architecture tours, now renamed Insiders' Tours and still a valuable source of funds. He put on a series of crowd-pulling exhibitions in the New Gallery. These were particularly welcome when, for the first time since World War II, visits to country houses and museums started to decline. In 1961, when the American Museum first opened, it had two other local museums to compete with. By the 1990s there were twenty-two. But shows, such as a series featuring Kaffe Fassett's textiles, helped to keep visitor numbers up. William McNaught's enthusiastic approach, modernising the running of the museum, whilst preserving all its best features, won Dallas's confidence to the extent that he appointed him as his executor, in collaboration with the New York law firm that Dallas had long-since employed.

In January 1988 Dallas flew to California for a last visit to Dieter Engel, both of them "realising that his time was really up". At Dieter's request, Dallas drove them, with Dieter dozing in the back of the car, to Desert Hot Springs and to visit the Southwest Museum. They spent five days together. Dieter died in March 1988, and Dallas filled twenty pages of his journal with memories of him.

In 1989, besides his usual times in 228, Garrison, Freshford and Opio, Dallas toured, in April, Canada, Los Angeles and Santa Fe with Matt; the Berry region of France on his own in June, producing forty journal pages that could serve as a guide book; and, in August, Tuscany with David Finkbeiner. The following March, Dallas and Matt, after visiting friends in Morocco, joined Ben Duncan and me for a week in Madeira. Dallas and another old friend, Jonathan Wordsworth, toured the Lake District; and, on his own again, Dallas explored the museums of Boston at the beginning of 1991.

In January 1991 Dallas made one of his rare individual inter-ventions for animal welfare. To support a refuge for farm animals in upstate New York, he "adopted" a veal calf that had been sent to a stockyard the day he was born and, taken ill, was to be left there to die. Dallas named him Opie, for Opio. The refuge's owner reported a few months later "Today, Opie is healthy and happy and enjoys his new status of being our youngest veal calf 'ambassador'. Everyone who meets Opie is deeply touched by his story, from the local repair man who stated he will never eat veal, to the shelter volunteer who decided to give up all dairy products. Opie reaches thousands of Refuge visitors in a way that only a calf could, and it's no wonder that his message is so effective." A photograph of Dallas with Opie appears on page 186.

At Opio that summer, Dallas met some newcomers to the area. The Villa Romarin, formerly the home of Dallas and John's American decorator friend, Margretta Jamieson, the widow of an English merchant banker, was bought after her death by Prince Albert of Belgium. He was soon to become King Albert II. Friends and followers of the Belgian royals bought other houses close by, turning the *colline des anglais* into the *colline des belges*. In June 1991 Dallas and his house guests exchanged neighbourly visits with the Prince and Princess. On one of these the Princess

> manoeuvred me off to see the garden away from the others. "Now Dr Pratt, I hope you don't mind my bringing this up, but I hear that they have reduced the permitted size of a building lot here from 5000 square meters to 1500." (I had already been told this, with the result that, theoretically, forty-two houses could be built on the Castello property.) "I don't know what provisions you are making for your property, but would you not be willing to join with others in the community to prevent building developments?"
>
> I had to tell HRH that the Castello estate was left to the Halcyon Foundation for the benefit of the American Museum, and it was too late to make other arrangements. She was crestfallen, but rallied, and we joined the others making a tour of the house. I admired the old tiles on the floors, replacing, so she said, "Lady Jamieson's hideous ones" (poor Margretta!).

In a similar way, Dallas declined to join his Turtle Bay Gardens neighbours in an effort to preserve their properties from any future development. He told them he had left 228 for the benefit of animal welfare and was not willing to risk reducing its potential value.

Plans for a picnic with the Belgian royals a few days later were cut short when Dallas was taken ill at Opio and flew back to New York for another operation. He was soon back in England, and made nothing of his illness when, in early September 1991, he joined Ben Duncan and me for a tour in Wales and Scotland. In October he visited friends and distant relatives in Indianapolis.

Later that month the New York State Humane Association presented Dallas and Ron Scott with awards for "outstanding services on behalf of animals". Dallas recorded in his journal at this time that he had read that Ruskin believed that vivisection was a blasphemy:

> When Oxford university built a laboratory where it would be practised, Ruskin revoked his decision to leave his library and some of his finest Turners to Oxford and, in 1855, resigned his professorship: "I cannot lecture in the next room to a shrieking cat." He never went to Oxford again.

By the spring of 1992 Dallas was visibly in poor health, often in pain, but he kept up his usual round. By then he had to carry out distressing and time-consuming routines in place of the scarcely-noticed bodily functions of the young. In the late spring he joined Ben Duncan and me for a trip to Derbyshire. He wrote at length in his journal about Kedleston and Calke Abbey. By chance, as we drove through Derbyshire, we found ourselves in Repton, where John Judkyn went to school. None of us had been there, and all three of us were curious. We stopped to look around. Luckily for us a retired teacher saw us and volunteered to take us on a tour. Though from long after John's days, he evoked vividly for us an earlier era and the atmosphere of an English public school in the 1930s.

In December 1992, Margaret Cheney wrote suggesting that she and Dallas might work on a new enterprise, bringing their unpublished *Animal Politics in America* up to date. Dallas replied, writing late at night as he often did. It was New Year's Eve:

> As I write, 1992 has turned into 1993. The old-fashioned way we celebrate Christmas — presents under the Christmas tree to one another; these to be wrapped; then the dogs' presents to the neighbours' dogs and cats, which we have to wrap; house decorated, home-manufactured cards prepared, etc — all this has prevented me from answering your letter.
>
> But I mustn't keep you in suspense over the surprising and indeed flattering offer to once again be co-author with you in the new venture. Because, sadly, it cannot be. Too many negatives have accumulated as I approach my eightieth year. Although I *feel* fine most of the time, certain parts of the anatomy have let me down, necessitating two operations this year in the plumbing area, and consequences which involve the wearing of bags, tubes etc which are very demanding time-wise. The old head is in pretty good shape, except that recent memory is often conspicuous by its absence.
>
> As it is, I am dedicating my remaining wits and energy to:
>
> 1. a written recapitulation of the founding of the American Museum and the forming of the collection;
> 2. indexing and adding appendices to my journal (a commonplace book, not a diary), which I've kept since I was seventeen;

3. participating in a drive to raise an endowment fund for the Museum;
4. keeping all my real estate in the US, France and England in good shape against the time when they will pass to the foundations for the museum and the animals, or to my companions.

However, your letter made me dig out the manuscripts and correspondence of *Animal Politics*. I was amazed to discover that it all happened ten years ago, or at least began then. I rarely keep letters, but I'm so glad ours are saved, chiefly because of the engaging Cheney style and point of view, but also for the record of my own thoughts, travels, etc during the years 1983–86, which I shall now add *en bloc* as appendices to my journal for those years, all of which will be added to the personal papers that I will be leaving to the museum. Our comments, plus the manuscripts, form a commentary on the animal rights movement and alternatives to research in those years.

In January 1993, medical examination revealed that Dallas's cancer had spread to his right lung and hip. Severe pain was successfully controlled with cobalt radiation, but he became lame. Yet he was at Freshford again in June. Nick Bell-Knight seemed to be in good enough health, but when Dallas was in Opio in July a letter came from Nick revealing that he too had cancer. In the course of a long and sympathetic letter, Dallas wrote:

We're not only friends of "long standing", we're very close friends — and I may add that my "very close friends" can be numbered on the fingers of two hands. I could add a eulogy here; suffice it to say that in addition to the friendship, you particularly have made possible some major aspects of my life: namely, the creation of the museum and my life at Freshford since John's death.

It may help you a little if I tell you my own experiences
with cancer. Probably the worst moment was when it was
first diagnosed, in 1976. I thought the end was not far off.

Dallas recounts his symptoms and treatments and then continues:

After the problems earlier in the year, there was some doubt
whether I could get to France. When I finally got here, I felt
more joy being in the old Castello and its beautiful garden
than I have for many years.

Life at the Castello had changed a lot since Dallas and John's
early days there. Photographs from the 1950s show hosts and
guests neatly dressed and, by Riviera standards, stiff and formal;
cosmopolitan but all representatives of a social and intellectual
elite. Increasingly, from the 1970s on, bright young black friends
of Matt's, gay actors and dancers from London, or a lesbian Jewish
couple would be there. By the 1990s guests like these were mix-
ing happily not only with some of Dallas's oldest friends but also,
unthinkable in the 1950s, with the staff. The people who cooked
and served the meals were different too, not lifelong servants but
artists and students enjoying a summer job. In the evening they
joined Dallas, the guests and the dogs in the Arab rooms where
Matt would play his guitar and sing, and anybody else with a gift
for performing would entertain the rest.

The surroundings of the Castello had changed drastically from
the rustic nowhere of Dallas and John's early years there. Opio
now had busy roads, countless holiday homes, a municipal park, a
supermarket, even a golf course, but the Castello remained
secluded in its acres of olive groves. Even its wildlife survived.
Every evening a male-voice choir of tiny frogs with huge voices
serenaded Dallas and his house guests. They lived in an ancient
stone cistern far below the salon windows. They were said to be
repeating "Get Pratt! Get Pratt!" I (Dick Chapman) tried many

times over the years to see them but could never find one. In July 1993, Dallas wrote:

> *Cousins*
> Slowly descend difficult steps
> Cautiously open cistern door
> Find green thumbnail–sized froglet
> Resting after loud nightly croaking
> Precariously perched
> Again this year.
>
> Carefully close door,
> Slowly ascend difficult steps
> Panting.
> Froglet and I
> Cling precariously to our perches —
> Cousins.

In August, Dallas left the Castello, probably realising it was for the last time. He went to stay with David Finkbeiner in Tuscany and they toured the region together, Dallas writing it all up in his journal in his usual way.

Back in London, on 16 September 1993, Dallas invited Bill McNaught, Ben Duncan and me to lunch at the In and Out club. Bill had to leave us straight after lunch for an afternoon appointment. Dallas, Ben and I visited some Bond Street galleries together. When the time came for us to part, I noticed a taxi approaching that could take him back to his club. I turned to hail it for him, but he reached for my arm and stopped me. During the past thirty-five years, we had become accustomed to the simple farewells of people who would soon be exchanging letters, and seeing each other gain. Now Dallas stood on the pavement and made a touching goodbye speech, uncharacteristically elaborate and emotional. We were puzzled and rather awkward. Only after he had gone did we realise he was bidding us goodbye for the last time. We were completely unprepared for this. He had concealed how ill he was so successfully that we still thought of him as a permanent part of our lives. During the days that followed we struggled to take in the terrible reality that was facing us, that Dallas, whose wonderful company and brilliant letters we had counted on for more than thirty years, was mortal. His health was failing. His life was under threat. We might never see him again. We felt a need to be with him as soon as we possibly could. A week or two later, when he was back in New York, we telephoned saying we would like to come and see him there. He asked us not to come because he might be too ill to see us.

The last entry in Dallas's journal is dated 16 December 1993. As so often in the past, it records a meeting with someone out of the ordinary, in this case Peter Moores, heir to the Littlewoods football pools and retailing fortune amassed by his father John Moores, who had died aged ninety-seven in September 1993. Dallas noted in his journal that the *Sunday Times* said the Moores family fortune was the third largest in Britain, surpassed only by the Queen and the Duke of Westminster. Peter Moores was converting a country mansion near Stratford-on-Avon, Compton Verney, into an arts centre, and had recently bought for it the Andras Kalman collection of English folk art for a spectacular sum of money. An idea had been floated that John Judkyn's parallel collection at Freshford Manor might be added to it, the two combined making a pre-eminent display. Dallas, it seems, hoped to be made a large offer for the collection, to benefit the American Museum's endowment fund. Peter Moores may have hoped that Dallas might wish to keep the collection intact by presenting it to Compton Verney. "He duly appeared at 228 and we chatted for an hour or so". Dallas showed him illustrations of several of the items in the collection:

> He said he looked forward to visiting Freshford Manor and seeing what we had. Nothing was said about a possible sale, but he made a special point of saying that he was short of income, partly because he owned so many residences, and partly because much capital was tied up in the company and the Foundation. With the publicity about his immense wealth, no doubt he has to protect himself in this way from those who are after it for their pet causes. He was pleasant and informal, and when he heard about the Castello, said "Oh, I'd like to visit you there."

In the event, nothing came of their meeting.

A few weeks later, in January 1994, Dallas had a fall at 228 and hit his head on a marble fireplace. David took him by taxi to a doctor, not one they knew, who bandaged him. The doctor was shocked by Dallas's condition. "Your friend has no muscle tone," he said to David, who explained that Dallas had advanced cancer.

That night, eight inches of snow fell on New York City. Dallas's appointments for the following day were a meeting at Columbia University Library, and entertaining three old lady friends for dinner at the Union Club. David urged him to cancel but, as David put it, "Dallas was so fucking stubborn." He went by taxi to 115th Street, then had another fall, outside the Butler Library. A student found him, face-down in the snow. He picked him up and helped him to the meeting which, because of the weather, was attended by only three of the ten committee members. Then on to the Union Club, where only one of Dallas's three guests appeared.

Halfway through the month, the sad news came from England that Nick Bell-Knight had died.

During February, Dallas spent his time quietly in New York and Garrison. In New York, David took him to exhibitions and concerts. Thursday 3 March was Dallas's last night at 228. He postponed his usual Thursday departure to Garrison because Friday was the first day of the big annual international prints exhibition at the 68th Street Armory. David took Dallas round the show in a wheelchair. Dallas bought ten prints.

From then on he was at Garrison. At the beginning of April, he was taken ill and rushed to hospital. There, a nurse said to David "Your friend should be spanked!" He had failed to remove and clean his catheter. That he, a doctor, meticulous in his ways, could fall so short in an elementary matter of hygiene, suggests that his powers were failing badly.

After a week in hospital, he returned to Garrison. A hospital bed was set up for him in the library off the living room, with twenty-four hour hospice care. For the rest of April, Dallas "held court", as David put it, in his hospital bed in the library, receiving visits from friends and family, including his old classmate Augie Heckscher with his French wife Claude, and Dallas's niece Linda with her husband Russell Munson.

To everybody's surprise, and in complete contrast to Dallas's other friends, Matt kept apart from him. He continued to spend the middle of the week in Brooklyn and weekends in Garrison but, even when he was there, he stayed mostly in his own room alone. Perhaps he found the sight of Dallas so ill more than he could bear. Or perhaps he was in a turmoil caused by becoming aware of his own HIV infection. He also avoided the company of David and Ron, who were at their house nearby, together with Ron's sister Janet, who had come to live with them. The only people Matt seemed on easy terms with were the nurses looking after Dallas. He talked with some of them for hours. Then, in late

April, he fainted in the street outside his house in Brooklyn. A friendly neighbour summoned an ambulance and he was taken to hospital.

On 5 May, David had to return to Italy to teach on a print-making course. He and Dallas had a tearful, loving goodbye.

Dallas stopped eating and became weaker each day. His friends remembered later that he had said, years before, that ceasing to ' take any nourishment was the best way to end your life. It seems that now he *was* ready to depart, and had made his own decision about dying, as he always had about living.

Ron and his sister Janet took it in turns to sit with him. On the morning of 20 May, Ron came to see Dallas, bringing with him an old friend Jim Mason, lawyer, author and leading animal welfare activist who, some years later, became the director of Dallas's animals charity. Dallas was extremely frail. He wrote a note and handed it to Ron, who folded it and put it in his pocket to read later. It turned out to be an indecipherable scrawl.

Later in the morning, Janet came to Dallas's bedside to intro-duce a new nurse, and then stayed and sat with him, holding his hand. After a while he turned to her, said "Goodbye", and closed his eyes. With this courteous last word his life ended.

He was cremated a few days later. He had asked for there to be no funeral or memorial service, nothing religious. He had suggested instead a gathering of his friends. Discussing it with David a few weeks before he died, he said that if the occasion started to go flat the scotties should be brought in to liven it up.

The course David was teaching in Italy ended three weeks after Dallas died. As soon as he was free, David flew back to New York, which was enduring record-setting heat and humidity. He remembers his feet sinking into the asphalt. It was the sort of New York heatwave that Dallas had managed to avoid almost every year of his life. David moved into 228, using Dallas's bedroom, the only one in the house with air-conditioning. He sent out 175 invitations for the memorial get-together. He also set to work photocopying the journal, making a set for Dallas's niece Linda and another for himself. All Dallas's personal papers, including the journal, were soon to be shipped to England for safekeeping in the archives of the American Museum.

At the same time, Ron Scott was moving the remaining papers of Argus Archives from 228 to Garrison. Dallas had arranged for the charity to change both its nature and its name after his death. It was to cease its research and educational work and instead became a grant-giving foundation, supporting other animal charities. It was to be called The Two Mauds, in honour of Dallas's governess Maud Duke, and of his first scottie. This sometimes led to confusion later. Ron or David would answer the telephone and be asked "Which Maud am I speaking to?" But it has proved distinctive and memorable.

Also at 228, William McNaught, the museum's director, and Louis Trapp, Dallas's New York lawyer, in their capacity as executors, were at work with Dallas's secretary and the staff of the Halcyon Foundation, starting the complex job of settling Dallas's estate. Apart from personal bequests to his family, his "family", and a few close friends, and legacies to various charities, such as the animal sanctuary where Opie the veal calf, now fourteen years old, lives on to this day (2004), Dallas left most of his estate, both his capital and his houses and their contents, to his two foundations: 228 and its contents for the animal charity; the Castello and its contents for the museum. Freshford Manor and its contents were also sold for the benefit of the museum. The life mask of Keats, perhaps Dallas's most loved possession, went to the Wordsworth Trust's Dove Cottage Museum at Grasmere.

Yet another team at work in 228 during June 1994 were staff from Sotheby's, cataloguing the contents of the house for auction. At Dallas's suggestion, they worked with David Finkbeiner, who knew more than anybody about the collection. The house was to be cleared on 30 June, so David planned the memorial get-together for the last day 228 would be its old self, 29 June. By then, everything in the house bore a tag with a Sotheby's reference number.

David knew that the short notice and the time of year would limit the number of acceptances. Yet eighty people came. William McNaught addressed them, speaking about Dallas and his achievements, and then called on David. He talked about the diversity of Dallas's talents and interests, and the correspondingly wide range of his friendships, observing that this would be the one and only time so many people who knew Dallas would ever have the chance of meeting one another. There were nods and murmurs of agreement. He invited others to speak and a few did. Then Ron, who had been delayed by traffic, arrived from Garrison, bringing the scotties. They were let loose and mingled with the crowd. It was just as Dallas had planned.

Matt was not there for this occasion but still in the hospital, extremely ill. Whenever David and Ron visited him, they were glad to find his brothers and sisters with him. Nothing was ever said about what his illness was. Ron waited until he and Matt were alone and then asked directly, "What *is* it?" Matt told him it was AIDS, but he wanted it kept from his family. In 1994 an AIDS diagnosis was even worse news than it would be a few years later. Palliative care was about all that could be provided. David and Ron were more than half expecting it but they were still profoundly shocked to hear what amounted to a death sentence for a man still in his fifties, and as close to them as Matt was.

Their distress was increased, almost to anger, by the realisation that Matt, who had lived with them at Garrison for more than twenty-five years, had felt unable to confide in them. It seemed to them that Matt had never really trusted them. Matt did not come out of the hospital. He died there during the first week of August.

Dallas's eightieth birthday, had he lived to see it, would have been Sunday 21 August 1994. Ben Duncan and I suggested this day for a memorial gathering of Dallas's English friends at the American Museum. William McNaught responded with enthusiasm and organised the occasion.

The last of the day's museum visitors were leaving as the fifty or so guests were greeted, with American champagne or cranberry juice, on the terrace. It was a warm and sunny evening. The Avon valley and the Jeffry Wyatville manor were looking their most magnificent. Above the house, on its two flag-poles, flew the Stars and Stripes and the Union Jack, not at half-mast as they had been on 20 May.

Welcoming the guests, William McNaught explained that this was definitely not a funeral or memorial service, as Dallas had specifically asked for there to be neither. It was to be a thanksgiving for Dallas's life.

In the old picture gallery of the house, entered from the terrace, some of the museum's finest quilts were displayed on the walls. At each corner of the room stood a huge and dazzling arrangement of flowers from the museum's gardens. Chairs were set in gently curving rows. The City of Bath Soloists played the last movement of Dvorak's *American Quartet*.

Several old friends and colleagues of Dallas spoke about different aspects of his life, with the emphasis not on sadness but on good cheer and laughter. Two of the speakers were attractive young women of great character: Vicki Moore, an animal welfare activist, who had trained as an actress, gave a brilliant reading of some of Dallas's early memories of animals from his journal; Judith Elsdon, the museum's curator, read two of Dallas's poems.

Out on the terrace again, in the evening sunlight, a group as diverse as the gathering at 228 eight weeks earlier, met one another for the first and last time: here an elderly dealer, John Teed, who in the 1950s had supplied John Judkyn with English furniture for 222 Imports; there a young woman, Rachel Quarrell, who had been a baby when her uncle David died. She told us that David had been her godfather as well as uncle and that, after his death, Dallas took over both these roles in her life. Keith Carmichael, Director of the Redress Trust, which works for victims of torture, told us that Dallas had given financial support for this charity. They had met through Peter Davies who, before his death in 1993, had chaired both the Redress Trust and Anti-Slavery International.

The person who had known Dallas the longest was an elderly woman, Mrs Susan Beauchamp. The sister of the thirteenth Baron North, and born soon after World War I into a milieu of fox-hunting and horse-racing, she had a clear early memory from the mid-1920s of Charles Cartwright, a friend of her parents, turning up with his extraordinary American bride and her two children from a previous marriage: a girl with her hair frizzed out at the sides, and a little boy, quiet, with brown eyes, taking every-thing in.

The War Upset Everybody

Reproduced from *Columbia Library Columns*, 1971

Columbia Library Columns was edited by Dallas Pratt for thirty years, from its first issue in 1951 until 1981. Almost every issue included something written by himself. In this article he seems to sum up a lifetime's thinking about his mother: one of the "personalities of the Cote d'Azur" sketched in the article, and the owner of one of the two houses it describes. In an introductory note he mentions her connections with Columbia University Library, as the granddaughter of the bibliophile Park Benjamin. Books from her grand-father's and her father's libraries form two of the holdings of Columbia University Library: the Park Benjamin Collection and the Beatrice Benjamin Cartwright Memorial Collection: Books about New York.

"The War Upset Everybody"

DALLAS PRATT

THIS is the wartime story of two houses in the south of France. One of them, "Casa Estella," is a white-painted, pine-shadowed villa, with many terraces leading steeply down to the blanched rocks of Cap d'Antibes and the sea. Before the discovery of the Riviera's "summer season," beginning in the late nineteen-twenties, the house belonged to Lloyd Osbourne, stepson and collaborator of Robert Louis Stevenson. It had a literary atmosphere, with Osbourne at work in his studio under the eaves, and George Bernard Shaw sometimes to be seen, afloat, beard and all, off the rocks. Then came the sun-seekers, English and American, tired of the rain and formality of the Channel resorts—among them my mother, Beatrice Benjamin Cartwright. She bought the villa in 1932. With the arrival of the summer people, the *literati* abandoned the coast (with one or two exceptions: Somerset Maugham at Cap Ferrat; Paul Gallico at Antibes) and sought the seclusion of the mountainous back-country or less fashionable refuges elsewhere in the Mediterranean.

The other house is very different. A small, ancient, rustic "château," with vineyard and several hundred olive trees, ten miles inland from Casa Estella, it is on a 1200-foot ridge, with a tremendous view commanding the valley of Opio-San Peyre and sweeping around the semicircle of the Maritime Alps above Grasse. This property was bought about 1921 by Elizabeth Starr,

Casa Estella in the 1930's.

an artist from Philadelphia. She restored it with great care, and renamed it, rather romantically, "Castello San Peyre."

When I acquired the Castello in 1955 from Miss Starr's heir, Lady Caroline Duff, a daughter of the Marquess of Anglesey, I found that the life there of Miss Starr and her neighbors had been described in a series of books published from 1935 to 1949. Lady Fortescue, widow of the well-known historian of the British Army, had lived next door, and, in volumes with titles such as *Perfume from Provence*, *Sunset House*, and *Midsummer Madness*, had reeled off many hundred of pages about herself, her neighbors, their "dear peasants," their *bonnes*, their houses and, of course, their dogs. In these sentimental but endearing memoirs, for many years best-sellers in England, Elizabeth Starr figures largely. She is called, simply, "Mademoiselle;" the Castello is the "Château," and its adjoining dependency, the "Studio." Their adventures at the outbreak of World War II are breathlessly recounted in *Trampled Lilies*, published in 1941.

Castello San Peyre in winter.

The opening scene of the book is a description of columns of weary recruits, the harvest of general mobilization, plodding along the valley road below the Castello. Soon that house, and its three neighbors—Lady Fortescue's, Miss Cotton's and Lord Anglesey's —were sheltering scores of *poilus*. Officers had taken over all the bedrooms; Elizabeth Starr had opened a first-aid station in the Studio; a barber was at work in the stable. A quotation gives a vignette of life at the Castello in Lady Fortescue's winsome style:

"I shall never forget the picture of the Studio that night. A little fire crackling cosily in a corner, its flame flickering over *Mademoiselle's* pictures on the walls; the green-painted medicine-chest; *Mademoiselle* herself sitting on a three-legged stool, her small dark head bent over a spirit-lamp as she sterilized something or other; a big man, with a queer heart and threatened bronchitis, lying peacefully in a real bed with real sheets, his head, recently tended by his *copain*, the *coiffeur*, resting on a soft pillow, watching the long fingers of his friend stroking waves into my hair; turning at intervals dogs' eyes, which filled up slowly with tears, in the direction of his adored *Mademoiselle* from whom in so few days he must be parted."[1]

There was a different atmosphere in many villas on the coast. Instead of rolling up their sleeves and "mucking in" with the old timers, members of international "café society" on Cap Ferrat and Cap d'Antibes, at Cannes and Monte Carlo, took one look at the approaching tempest and fled.

But even the old hands had to go in the end. Thirteen hundred British subjects, including my mother's friend, Somerset Maugham, and a motley crowd of retired Army officers, teachers, governesses, as well as several *grandes dames* attended by butlers, maids and chauffeurs, all shepherded by the British Vice-Consul, were crammed into two coal ships, and made a nightmare passage to England. This was in the summer of 1940: southern France, still unoccupied by the Germans, was ruled by the Petain regime from Vichy.

A coal ship, even with Willie Maugham, would never have done for my mother, who had no intention of abandoning, even for a world war, her customary panoply of travel. Furthermore, she had recently remarried, and she and her new husband, Freddy McEvoy, were content to linger on. In August she wrote: "The British are sadly missed here. Cannes looks depressed as compared with other years. None of the women look very smart, pajamas and shorts are forbidden in public. We are always hoping that there might be an armistice in September; the War and its complications have upset everybody. The weather is divine. . . ."

But in the fall, the sound of anti-aircraft guns installed nearby warned them that the honeymoon was over.[2] Their travel plans

---

[1] *Trampled Lilies* (William Blackwood & Sons, Edinburgh), p. 32.

[2] This was literally true. After several unhappy years, my mother obtained a divorce and resumed the name of her third husband, Charles Aubrey Cartwright.

were complicated by the necessity of taking my mother's personal maid and fast friend, Jeanne Lemaire, as well as the inevitable mountain of wardrobe trunks, Vuitton suitcases and the ponderously heavy jewelry case which Jeanne, during her devoted

Beatrice Cartwright at Casa Estella, circa 1935.

service of thirty-two years, carried through hell and high water. Only a train could accommodate such an entourage, and by train they went, westward, one of the lavatories commandeered for the luggage over the protests of the other passengers. A friend encountered on the way—a destitute French duchess—was rescued and added to the party. They all arrived safely in Lisbon, and, eventually, secured transportation on an American Export ship to New York.

As soon as the family left, Casa Estella was emptied of its furnishings. Even this might not have protected it from occupation if Anthime, our *maître d'hôtel*, a master of the French art of "unscrambling," had not had the wit to strip all the bathrooms of their plumbing. A sign was placed at the entrance stating that the villa was "under the protection of the Finnish Minister," fortunately a family friend. The furni-

277

ture and fixtures were carted away to the mountains and hidden in a barn.

In Opio, meanwhile, the troops had left for the north and the houses had been returned to those owners who were still there. On our hill, only Elizabeth Starr remained. Some years before, she had taken French citizenship, and was determined to stand by her adopted country. I pieced together the brave story of her hard, wartime years at the Castello from various sources. The mayor of Opio told me of his surreptitious visits to hear the B.B.C. broadcasts, *"Ici Londres,"* on her secret radio. These night sessions always ended with a toast, drunk in wine from the Castello's vineyard: *"à la Victoire!"* Miss Starr's companion, a daughter of the actor Lou Tellegen, described their efforts to live off the 15-acre estate, which yielded olives, grapes, figs, vegetables, and supported chickens, rabbits, a cow (named "London Pride") and several pigs. But slowly the house filled with refuges, some of them in hiding, and there was barely enough to go around.

In February, 1944, during the lean final period of the war, Elizabeth Starr died of heart disease aggravated by skin infection and near starvation.

It was not until 1947 that my mother was able to return to Antibes. Seven years, a world war, a German occupation and an Allied invasion had passed over the Riviera. Houses had been gutted, gardens had been ruined by trenches and land-mine explosions, owners had died, staffs had been decimated by war and some of those who had remained on the properties had lost their lives fighting for or against the Resistance. But Casa Estella, that white, terraced villa by the sea, had lain undisturbed through it all. Entering it in 1947 was like walking into the palace of the Sleeping Beauty. Anthime, a little more grey around the temples, appeared beaming at the front door. Then, like a magician, he threw open the door of the *salon*.

Nothing had changed. Here, and in the entire house, nothing was missing. Furniture, curtains, the small but precious collection of *blanc de Chine*, all were there. Someone opened a cigarette box: it was filled with pre-war cigarettes. . . .

Obviously, some god, more powerful than the Finnish Minister,

Interior, Casa Estella. The "white on white" style was originally introduced in the 'twenties by Syrie (Mrs. Somerset) Maugham.

had had the house under his protection. Perhaps it was the tutelary deity of *maître d'hôtel*, who, in tribute to Anthime's surpassing devotion, gave him the unique satisfaction of conducting us into a house which had been through the cataclysm of a world war but which was still, as he said, "in perfect order, Madame!"[3]

The epilogue to the more sombre wartime history of Castello San Peyre was not told until 1967. A couple drove into the courtyard and asked to see the owner. They were a Mr. and Mrs. Wil-

[3] Beatrice Cartwright died in 1956, at Casa Estella. Her son, Aubrey Cartwright, the author's half-brother, now owns the property.

liam Kolinski: Mr. Kolinski said he had waited twenty-four years for the opportunity to return to the house where, as a boy, he had found sanctuary in 1943. He was a Polish Jew whose parents had died in a concentration camp. Elizabeth Starr had hidden him, along with many others, from the Germans, who had occupied southern France in November, 1942. With great emotion he showed us the attic room where he had lived. He asked to see another room which he had never been allowed to enter, but where he knew a refugee lived in secret, even cooking there. A primitive stove, built into the fireplace, is still in place. He recalled the fellow-inmate who, one day, rashly answered a knock at the back door and found himself confronting the Gestapo: he was taken away and shot. He told us about the woman in the village who was willing to sell those in hiding for one litre of olive oil apiece.

Elizabeth Starr was an American heroine of the Resistance. Unhappily, she died before the moment of liberation, when another column of soldiers, Americans this time, appeared on the valley road, to the joyous relief of the village. Some stopped for a moment at the Castello; they soaked their hot feet, boots and all, in the pool, smoked a quick cigarette, downed some *vin du Castello*, and were on their way.

"*Vives les Américains*"! To the inhabitants of Opio—San Peyre, those of us who still live in their midst are not unwelcome guests.

The Pratt Family

Thomas Pratt d 1539

Andrew Pratt

William Pratt 1562–1629

William Pratt 1622–1678

John Pratt 1644–1726

John Pratt 1671–1744

John Pratt 1703–1756

Asa Pratt 1734–1811

John Pratt 1763–1827

Linus Pratt 1792–1877

Horace Logan Edgar Pratt 1823–1897

Dallas Bache Pratt b 1849

Alexander Dallas Bache Pratt 1883–1947
m1 1909 Beatrice Mai Benjamin 1889–1956
(see Benjamin and Rogers family trees)
m2 1919 Mrs Katherine Barrymore
m3 1942 Mrs Daisy Kaufman

Cynthia Pratt 1910–1985
(see Rogers family tree)

Dallas Bache Pratt 1914–1994

The Benjamin Family

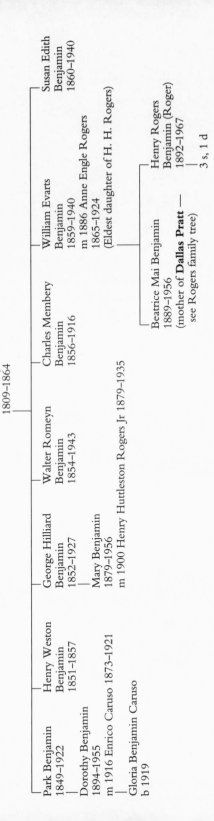

John Benjamin
1580?–1645

Joseph Benjamin
1633–1704

John Benjamin
1682–1716

John Benjamin
1714–1791

David Benjamin
1743–1785

Park Benjamin
1769–1824

Park Benjamin
1809–1864

Susan Edith
Benjamin
1860–1940

William Evarts
Benjamin
1859–1940
m 1886 Anne Engle Rogers
1865–1924
(Eldest daughter of H. H. Rogers)

Charles Membery
Benjamin
1856–1916

Walter Romeyn
Benjamin
1854–1943

George Hilliard
Benjamin
1852–1927

Mary Benjamin
1879–1956
m 1900 Henry Huttleston Rogers Jr 1879–1935

Henry Weston
Benjamin
1851–1857

Park Benjamin
1849–1922

Dorothy Benjamin
1894–1955
m 1916 Enrico Caruso 1873–1921

Gloria Benjamin Caruso
b 1919

Beatrice Mai Benjamin
1889–1956
(mother of **Dallas Pratt** —
see Rogers family tree)

Henry Rogers
Benjamin (Roger)
1892–1967

3 s, 1 d

The Rogers Family

Rowland Rogers. b.1809
m 1833 Mary Eldredge Huttleston

Rufus Allen Rogers, 1843–1919

Henry Huttleston Rogers, 1840–1909
m1 1862 Abbie Palmer Gifford, 1841–94
m2 1896 Mrs Emilie Augusta Hart, d.1912

Eliza Rogers, 1834–49

Cara Leland Rogers (Lady Fairhaven), 1867–1939
m1 1890 Bradford H. Duff, d.1893
m2 1895 Urban Hanlon Broughton, 1857–1929

Urban Huttleston Rogers Broughton,
(1st Lord Fairhaven)

Henry Rogers Broughton,
(2nd Lord Fairhaven), 1900–73

1s (3rd Lord Fairhaven), b. 1936

4s, 2d

Anne Engle Rogers, 1865–1924
m 1886 William Evarts Benjamin, 1859–1940

Henry Rogers
Benjamin (Roger)
1892–1967 (3s, 1d)

Beatrice Mai Benjamin, 1889–1956
m1 1909 Alexander Dallas Bache Pratt 1883–1947
m2 1917 Preston Gibson
m3 1922 Charles Aubrey Cartwright (Carry) 1883–1940

Aubrey Cartwright, 1930–72
(m 1963 Eva Tempelman, b.1938, 2s)
m4 1940 Freddy McEvoy, 1908–1951

Dallas Bache Pratt, 1914–94

Cynthia Pratt, 1910–85
m 1932 William Laughlin (Bill)

Linda Laughlin, b.1939
1d

William Pratt Laughlin (Billy), b.1934

Millicent Gifford Rogers
1873–1890

Henry Huttleston Rogers Jr (Harry) 1879–1935
m1 1900 Mary Benjamin 1879–1956
(see Benjamin family tree)
m2 1929 Mrs Margeurite von Braum Miles
m3 1933 Mrs Pauline van de Voort Dresser

Millicent Rogers
1902–1953
m3 times, 3 s

Henry Huttleston Rogers III
1905–1948

Mary Huttleston Rogers (Mai) 1874–1924
m1 1893 Joseph C Mott
m2 1900 William R. Coe

son
b & d 1870

Natalie Mai Coe
1910–1987
m 1934 Count Vitetti

Henry Huttleston
Rogers Coe
b 1907

Robert Douglas Coe
1902–1985

William Rogers Coe
b 1901